The purpose of this study guide is to provide supplemental educational material. It is not intended as a substitute for or replacement of the original source text.

Published by SuperSummary, www.supersummary.com

ISBN - 9798832630885

For more information or to learn about our complete library of study guides, please visit http://www.supersummary.com.

Please submit comments or questions to:
http://www.supersummary.com/support/

Table of Contents

Overview

These Truths (2018) by historian Jill Lepore is a one-volume chronicle of American history that attempts to tell the United States' story from beginning to end, something that, as the author notes in the introduction, has not been attempted in a long time. A comparable attempt was made by the British historian and journalist Paul Johnson, who published *A History of the American People* in 1997. Lepore's title was inspired by a line from the Declaration of Independence. Lepore, borrowing from one of the nation's first historians, George Bancroft, sets the nation's beginning at Christopher Columbus's accidental "discovery" of what became North America. Lepore describes her work as a political history with the hope that it will be useful to readers "as an old-fashioned civics book" (xviii).

Lepore, the daughter of public school teachers, is the David Woods Kemper '41 Professor of American History at Harvard University. She is also an instructor at Harvard Law School. Since 2005, Lepore has been a staff writer for the *New Yorker*, writing mostly about American history. *These Truths* is the winner of the Council on Foreign Relations' 2020 Arthur Ross Book Award. Lepore's other books include *The Name of War: King Philip's War and the Origins of American Identity* (1998), winner of the Bancroft Prize; *Book of Ages: The Life and Opinions of Jane Franklin* (2013), a finalist for the 2013 National Book Award for Nonfiction; and her national bestseller, *The Secret History of Wonder Woman* (2014), which won the American History Book Prize.

This guide uses the electronic book version of the text.

Summary

The organization of *These Truths* is chronological. Lepore decidedly marks the United States' origins within the Age of Discovery—particularly, Genoan explorer Christopher Columbus's adventures on the island that the native Taíno called "Haiti," and what Columbus called "Hispaniola," or "little Spain." Unlike many previous histories of the United States, Lepore frequently reminds the reader of the nation's roots in dispossession, enslavement, colonialism, and the act of claiming both territory and authority through writing.

The book is divided into four major parts, each chronicling the nation's genesis. The main text is bookended by an introduction and an epilogue that examine the feasibility of forming a nation out of three political ideas rooted in Enlightenment-era thought: political equality, natural rights, and the people's sovereignty. Lepore explores how those ideas have been revisited over the centuries, particularly as the nation faced upheavals over slavery, the Civil War, industrialism, Progressivist reforms, two world wars, the Cold War, periods of economic crises and prosperity, and the election of the first African American president. Lepore also assesses the success so far of the political experiment that is the United States.

The first part, "The Idea (1492-1799)," carries the reader through the era of early settlement to colonial America, when the nation's foundational principles took root and Americans fought their first battles over territory and political sovereignty.

The second part, "The People (1800-1865)," deals with the rise of Jacksonian Democracy and industrialism, as well as the nation's moral struggles over the maintenance of slavery, culminating in the Civil War, and its displacement of indigenous peoples as the nation's border stretched to the end of the continent.

The third part, "The State (1866-1945)," covers Reconstruction, the rise of Jim Crow at the end of the 19th century, the Progressive Era, and the two world wars, which centralized the United States as a global power and influence.

The fourth part, "The Machine (1946-2016)," chronicles the Cold War's beginning and end, the consumerism of the 1950s, the civil rights movement, and the rise of the Silent Majority and its creation of a fervent conservative movement whose influence reverberates to date. Lepore also describes the outcome of the 2016 election, which was the result of both decades of political discord and the nefarious influences of both enemies abroad and a tendency within to eschew facts and careful political engagement.

In the Epilogue, Lepore summarizes all of the major historical themes that she details in the book. She returns to the atmosphere of the Constitutional Convention of 1787 and describes how much has changed since, for better and worse. She reminds the reader that the results of the American experiment are still inconclusive, and that it will be up to a new generation to steer the course outlined by their ancestors.

Chapter Summaries & Analyses

Introduction

Introduction Summary and Analysis: "The Question Stated"

On October 30, 1787, the *New-York Packet* printed a copy of the Constitution of the United States—a 4,400-word document that attempted to describe the functions of the new republic's branches of government and the separation of their powers. After decades of historical unpredictability, the document tried to make history predictable, in addition to forming a government that would be determined by reason and choice. The delegates to the constitutional convention in Philadelphia had argued and toiled in secrecy all summer. By mid-September, they had "drafted a proposal written on four pages of parchment" (xi). Some who read the document feared that the new system gave the federal government too much power.

The second page of the *New-York Packet* featured an essay entitled "The Federalist No. 1," which had been written anonymously by the 30-year-old lawyer Alexander Hamilton. Hamilton noted that the United States was "an experiment in the science of politics" (xiii). The results of the experiment, according to Hamilton, would answer an important question: Are people capable of establishing good government based on choice or will they allow chance to determine their political outcomes, which could lead them down the paths of corruption and demagoguery? This question rests at the center of this text, which deals with the "origins, course, and consequences of the American experiment over more than four centuries" (xiv).

The American experiment, according to Lepore, is based on three key political ideas: political equality, natural rights, and the people's sovereignty. Thomas Jefferson initially described these political ideas as "sacred and undeniable" truths, leading Benjamin Franklin to cross out his words and suggest that they were instead "self-evident" (xv). Self-evident truths, after all, are based on empirical knowledge. The founders of the United States were lifelong students of history who looked toward historical events for their ideas about truth. They also looked toward ideas about morality, often rooted in Christian faith.

In writing this book, Lepore notes, she has tried to tell a story, though not the whole story. No one, she writes, could tell the whole story. She has sought neither to avoid criticism of the United States nor to make criticism a focal point.

In the introduction, Lepore focuses on the nation's birth during the constitutional convention in Philadelphia. She sets the mood, particularly by illustrating to the reader the centrality of the printing press, a relatively new technology, in helping the public understand what would become its foundational document. It was important, too, for delegates to keep their deliberations secret until the Constitution was finalized—a decision that both deterred gossip and prevented the spread of misinformation, which might have destroyed plans to form the early republic.

Lepore also illuminates the early founders' sense of the importance of creating an ordered government after living during the colonial period within a federation of states that acted autonomously. The importance of establishing a union was likely partly rooted in the American colonies' need to provide themselves with protections against potentially hostile foreign powers. Meanwhile, there were also concerns over the vulnerability of the new citizenry and its capacity to establish a government based on reason, rather than being swayed by fads, sentiments, and nefarious interests.

The Founding Fathers sought examples for government in history, but the idea of the United States was unprecedented, despite having ideological roots in ancient Greece, the Roman Republic, and the writings of Enlightenment thinkers. It was to be a secular society rooted in Christian values. In later years, the latter influence would sometimes take precedence over the former, leading to political, social, and judicial battles.

In her conclusion to this section, Lepore does not claim authority over the national narrative and subtly negates assertions that some historians, journalists, and pundits have made over the years in this direction. The book is not a critical analysis of the United States, nor does it attempt to give a singularly objective look at the nation's history. While history is largely a matter of fact—that is, a record of dates, names, and events—it is also an attempt to understand a people, in both their domestic and global contexts, through historical records. This latter effort is always subjective and fraught with debate.

Part 1: The Idea (1492-1799)

Part 1, Chapter 1 Summary and Analysis: "The Nature of the Past"

In October 1492, Christopher Columbus supposedly wrote in his diary that he and his crew had seen naked people on the island they called Haiti—"land of mountains." Columbus called the island Hispaniola—"the little Spanish island"—because he believed that the island on which he had landed had no name. Columbus noticed that the people who lived there had no weapons and no tools. He figured they also lacked a faith and exercised no guile. He wrote to King Ferdinand and Queen Isabella of Spain, telling them that he would take six of them back to Spain so that they could learn to speak, for neither he nor his crew understood a word that they spoke.

Two months after his journey to Haiti, Columbus intended to go back to Spain, but his three-masted ship sank. His crew "salvaged the timbers to build a fort" (4). The sunken ship has never been found. Columbus thought about the people he had met, whom he called "Indians" because he believed he had sailed to the East Indies.

When Columbus arrived in Barcelona, he hired Ramón Pané, a priest and scholar, to accompany him on his next voyage. He figured that Pané could come to understand the indigenous people in Haiti and how they worshipped. Pané sailed to Haiti with Columbus in 1493. There, the priest met a man named Guatícabanú, who spoke all of the island's languages and who then learned Castilian—Pané's native tongue. Pané lived among the natives of Haiti, the Taíno, for four years. He provided Columbus with a report on them— *An Account of the Antiquities of the Indians*. Soon after Pané wrote the text, it disappeared, but while writing a biography of his father, Ferdinand Columbus copied Pané's account. This was then copied by other scholars, including the Dominican friar Bartolomé de Las Casas.

The Taíno had no writing, but they did have a faith. Their god was named Yúcahu. They also had origin stories for the heavens and the sea, and a belief in the afterlife. In addition, they had a form of government, whose laws were preserved in ancient songs, according to Pané. Around 3 million people lived on Haiti at the time that Columbus landed. Half a century later, there were only 500 native people there. The rest had died, largely from diseases the Spanish had introduced.

In 1492, 75 million people lived in what are now North and South America. Some had created amazing settlements. The Cahokia, for example, had constructed "the biggest city in North America, on the Mississippi floodplains" (7). There were "giant plazas and earthen mounds, some bigger than the Egyptian pyramids" (7-8). Before the natives abandoned the settlement, around 1000 BCE, over 10,000 people lived there.

However, most indigenous peoples lived in smaller settlements. They were hunters, fishermen, and gatherers. Many farmed squash, corn, and beans. They raised pigs and chickens, but no bigger livestock. They also "spoke hundreds of languages and practiced many different faiths," despite having no written language (8). They were polytheistic and believed that all living creatures and the earth itself were divine. The Taíno lived in small villages, composed of one to 2,000 people led by a *cacique* —the Taíno word for a king or prince. They also fought with their neighbors and adorned their bodies.

In 1492, around 60 million people lived in all of Europe—15 million fewer than lived in North and South America. Europeans lived in diverse arrangements—"in villages and towns, in cities and states, in kingdoms and empires," some of which had castles and universities, cathedrals and mosques, and numerous universities (8). Most farmed. They raised crops, cattle, sheep, and goats. Before Columbus's voyage, Europe faced famine and a paucity of resources. After 1492, Europe became flush with the wealth extracted from the Americas by enslaved Africans' forced labor. This new wealth led to the emergence of nation-states, which led to new origin stories. Everyone in the new English nation, for example, was said to have the same ancestors; though, this was not true. The United States, when it formed in 1776, also created an origin story. Having just fought England for its independence, its populace did not wish to celebrate its English origins. To solve this problem, the new nation's earliest historians tied their origin story to Columbus's 1492 voyage. The United States was not merely "an offshoot of England," but a nation rooted in Greco-Roman traditions, politically tied to France, and religiously connected to Palestine (10).

Western Europeans, however, were not the only group who knew enough to cross an ocean. The Maya people "knew enough astronomy to navigate across the ocean as early as AD 300" (10). The ancient Greeks were skilled cartographers and astronomers, but much of their knowledge was lost during the Middle Ages when medieval Christians dismissed them as pagan. The Chinese invented the compass in the 11th century and had sailing capabilities. However, by the late 15th century, the Chinese had become inward-looking, convinced that little of interest existed beyond their borders. West Africans, too, navigated their coastline and rivers, leading to the construction of an extensive trade network.

In the mid-15th century, Prince Henry of Portugal sent ships to West Africa and began trading enslaved people with African merchants. They also set up forts and colonies on islands off the coast. By 1482, Columbus was a sailor on Portuguese slave-trading ships. Two years later, he proposed to the king of Portugal a plan to take a westward route to Asia. After consulting with a group of scholars, the king rejected the proposition. Columbus next went to King Ferdinand and Queen Isabella, who initially rejected the plan. They were preoccupied with their wars of religion and with expelling Jews and Muslims from their realm. By 1492, however, they agreed that Columbus should sail west to trade and spread Christianity. They also asked him to keep a diary, in which he would chronicle his experiences.

Writing is part of the reason why the historical record is so unfair, as Lepore reminds us. Most people who have lived either did not have writing as part of their culture or, if they did write, left nothing behind. In October 1492, Columbus declared that he would take possession of Haiti, the island on which he stood, for the king and queen of Spain. He then wrote down this declaration. Columbus took no record of the beliefs and customs of the people he met; instead, he decided that they had none. He also determined that they had no civil government, which meant that they could not own anything. He did not, however, consider the island a new world. It was Amerigo Vespucci, an explorer from Florence, Italy, who had crossed the Atlantic in 1503, who made this declaration about the new lands he visited. In his *Mundus Novus*, Vespucci remarked on the abundance of land and people in this strange place. Martin Waldseemüller, a

German cartographer, drew a map of the world onto 12 woodblocks. In recognition of Vespucci, Waldseemüller invented a new word for the fourth part of the world: America.

Between 1500 and 1800, around 2.5 million Europeans immigrated to the Americas. They carried 12 million Africans, whom they had enslaved, with them. As a result of their immigration, up to 50 million indigenous peoples died, mainly of disease, during these years. The seizure of American lands helped to propel Europe's economic growth and led to the end of famine. This development of wealth fostered the rise of capitalism. Between 1500 and 1600, Europeans carried around 200 tons of gold and 16,000 tons of silver from the Americas back to Europe. Adam Smith listed the discovery of America and the southern route to the East Indies through the Cape of Good Hope among "the two greatest and most important events recorded in the history of mankind" (17).

Columbus was a veteran of the slave trade, which had been practiced throughout the world for many centuries, usually as a result of conquering nations taking prisoners of war. He told Ferdinand and Isabella that it would be simple to enslave the Indigenous Taíno. Thus, the Spanish worked to death those whom they had enslaved in gold and sugar mines. Those who didn't die from overwork and starvation died from disease, leading the Spaniards to turn to the enslaved Africans routinely traded by the Portuguese.

In 1493, Columbus made a second trans-Atlantic voyage. This time he led a 17-ship fleet that carried 1,200 men, as well as seeds for various crops, including wheat and sugar cane, and various livestock, male and female, two by two. Inadvertently, they also brought seeds from plants that Europeans regarded as

13

weeds, such as bluegrass, ferns, daisies, and dandelions. Those weeds grew in soil that had been disturbed due to forest razing, as well as the hooves of horses and cattle. The cattle, pigs, goats, sheep, horses, and chickens that Europeans brought to the Americas had no known natural predators, but they had plenty of food, leading them to reproduce more prolifically than they had in Europe. Meanwhile, indigenous peoples in the Americas died exponentially. Having been isolated "for hundreds of millions of years," they had no immunity against diseases such as smallpox, measles, influenza, chicken pox, and bubonic plague (19). Spanish conquistadors arrived in the North American mainland in 1513. Within decades, they had conquered what became Mexico and over half of the future continental United States in what they called New Spain.

Six years later, Hernán Cortés, mayor of Santiago, Cuba, led 600 Spaniards and over 1,000 indigenous allies into Mexico, where he captured Tenochtitlán, "a city said to have been grander than Paris or Rome, and destroyed it without pity or mercy" (22). This destruction included the Aztec libraries. In 1540, Francisco Vásquez de Coronado took an army of Spaniards to what is now New Mexico, looking for a rumored city of gold. There, the Zuni people confronted them. The tribe was, ultimately, overcome by the Spanish, who had the advantage of firearms.

The Spanish, unlike future English colonizers, did not travel to the Americas with families. When the all-male armies arrived, they took indigenous women. In some instances, they raped them. In others, they loved and married them, raising families together. Their offspring resulted in "an intricate caste system marked by gradations of skin color," caused by the mixtures of European, Indigenous, and African ancestors (23). The English, on the other hand, would only acknowledge people as "black" or "white."

However, the priest and historian Bartolomé de Las Casas and Spain's royal historian, Juan Ginés de Sepúlveda, who had never been to the Americas, would debate the justness of the conquest. Sepúlveda had argued that the difference between the Spanish and the natives "was as great as that 'between apes and men'" (24).

While the French and Spanish had settlements throughout the Americas in the 16th and 17th centuries, the English did not send the Italian explorer John Cabot (Giovanni Caboto) across the ocean until 1497. Cabot disappeared during his return voyage, and the English did not bother to send anyone else. The English were interested in colonization, but their focus, until 1584, was on the East. In that fateful year, Queen Elizabeth asked one of her ministers, Richard Hakluyt, whether she ought to found colonies in the Americas. He believed, as many other English did, that they were nobler than the Spanish. Thus, their presence could liberate the natives from the Spaniards' cruelties. Elizabeth, the Protestant queen, had resolved to fight Spain in every arena she could.

Still, while she liked the idea of the English having a presence in the Americas, she did not want to pay the costs of conquest. She issued a royal patent to Walter Raleigh, one of her favorite courtiers, allowing him to seize land south of Newfoundland. Raleigh, a writer and adventurer, sent out a fleet of seven ships and 600 sailors in 1584. Raleigh's men landed on what are now the Outer Banks of North Carolina. One hundred and four men stayed behind, intending to remain through winter while they awaited a supply ship and planned their search for gold. They built a fort against potential Spanish invaders. They wrote home, reporting about "a land of ravishing beauty and staggering plenty" (28). However, the supply ship was delayed, leading the colonists to starve. In June, Sir Frances Drake commanded a fleet to Carolina, carrying 300 chained Africans. Drake offered to leave the colonists with food and a ship, or they could go home. Every colonist chose to leave. They replaced the Africans, whom Drake may have simply dumped into the ocean.

A 1587 expedition to Roanoke failed due to England's preoccupation with defeating the Spanish Armada in 1588. England won the fateful naval war, but John White, the colonizer who hoped to establish a permanent colony at Roanoke, was unable to secure more ships to sail there. When he finally made it back in 1590, he found no colonists.

Lepore starts the chapter by recounting the nebulous and complex history of Columbus's explorations of what became North America. Columbus's "discovery" and its aftermath read as a mixture of luck, naïveté, and avarice. His vision of Haiti was that of a Garden of Eden. His saw the beauty of its natural landscape and sensed, wrongly, that its inhabitants, due to different customs, were guileless. His view was a paternalistic one—similar to that which would later be usurped by the English, though Columbus and the Spanish were more ostensibly focused on conquering land and seizing mineral wealth, while the English developed the pretense of wanting to civilize. Both nations had the false, Eurocentric sense that only Christian faiths and European languages were valid. Their internal rivalry was rooted both in desires for colonial dominance and in the religious wars that had engulfed Western Europe.

The accuracy of Columbus's history, and that of Pané's interactions with the Taíno, are dependent on the veracity of the transcriptions and the transcribers' commitments to veracity. We have only pieces of Columbus's diary and no way of knowing the intentions of those who took care to maintain records. In this regard, our understanding of history is dependent on our agreement to trust the recordkeepers, in addition to drawing conclusions based on fragments of information.

Lepore, to give the reader a sense of the grandiosity of some early Indigenous civilizations, compares some of their early wonders to the Egyptian pyramids, noting that some edifices were even bigger. Unlike Westerners, many tribes were likely not beholden to their settlements and creations but were migratory—a distinction that early explorers probably would not have understood. Lepore also contrasts the indigenous peoples' lack of writing with the West's emphasis on it, as exemplified by the recording of Columbus's and Pané's respective accounts. Finally, she points out how some indigenous peoples had the capacity and knowledge to explore foreign lands, thus ruling out the view that, unlike Europeans, other peoples and cultures lacked the capability or curiosity. With these details, Lepore contrasts Columbus's ignorance with the facts we have about who indigenous tribes were—peoples with hundreds of languages and diverse polytheistic faiths. Unlike the Europeans, many of them seemed to have a respect for nature and other living beings.

Lepore explains in this chapter how European exploration and the subsequent establishment of trade routes, which included the pillaging of mineral resources, early enslavement, and human trafficking, were integral to the continent's modernization during the Renaissance. The project of constructing America, both geographically and ideologically, was one that involved multiple Western European nations. The land Europeans imagined also comprised more territory and future nations than the US alone. This may explain why some Europeans still think of both North and South America when mention is made of "America."

Conquest was about the dominance of both peoples and land. The latter occurred through the introductions of new plant species and animals. Like Noah, Columbus sent pairs of animals—one male, one female—to populate what is now North America.

The English and Spanish had disparate notions about conquest and early concepts of race. The Spanish were sexually indiscriminate and intermarried, while the English either avoided what their American descendants later termed "miscegenation," or denied that they engaged in it. The English took on a paternalist view of themselves as a superior and more benevolent people, though the actions of Sir Francis Drake directly contradict this notion. Like the Spanish settlers, they went to North America and saw a land of plenty, then availed themselves of its resources.

The English defeat of the Spanish Armada displaced Spain as a world power. It also contributed to the rise of England as a naval and colonial power. England's use of its entire naval fleet to battle the Armada may have been integral to its catastrophic failure to colonize Roanoke. The disappearance of Roanoke colony reveals the limitations of England's capacities during this period, compared to that of Mediterranean countries. The island nation's resources were eclipsed by its colonial ambitions, which later became boundless.

Part 1, Chapter 2 Summary and Analysis: "Two Rulers and the Ruled"

The English called the Indigenous ruler Wahunsunacock, Powhatan, or "king," for diplomacy. James I, Elizabeth's successor, regarded himself as king of Virginia, thereby making Powhatan his subject. James believed that he had been divinely appointed, making him more determined than Elizabeth to create a colony in the Americas. In 1606, he issued a charter allowing men to settle in Virginia. This emphasis on settlement encouraged trade with Powhatan instead of war. Still, the settlers dug for minerals. James also granted land to two corporations: the Virginia Company and the Plymouth Company. Virginia, then extended "from what is now South Carolina to Canada" (33). England's colonies would be commercial and comprised of "free men, not vassals" (33). The English, who were also Protestants, would teach converts to read Scripture and set up churches.

Throughout the 17th and 18th centuries, the English set up over two dozen colonies, comprising Eastern coastal settlements and rice fields in Georgia and the Caribbean. To settle Virginia, the Virginia Company gathered both soldiers from England's religious wars and men who were eager to make fortunes. John Smith, who was later elected the colony's governor, was among these former fighters in religious wars. While there, he crowned Powhatan "king" and draped over the chief's shoulders the scarlet robe that James I had sent. Meanwhile, the English colonists starved and sent Smith back to England, complaining that, under his rule, Virginia had become a hell. In the winter of 1609-10, 500 colonists were reduced to 60 as a result of starvation. Soon they resorted to cannibalism. England received word of these conditions. In 1622, the indigenous people rose up against the English and killed hundreds. The colony recovered with the help of a cash crop—tobacco, a plant then found only in the Americas and "long cultivated by the natives" (37).

In July 1619, "two men from each of eleven parts of the colony" met in the House of Burgesses, "the first self-governing body in the colonies" (37). A month later, 20 Africans arrived in Virginia—the first enslaved people in British America. They came from what is now Angola and were seized by the English from a Portuguese ship.

In the summer of 1620, the *Mayflower* "lay anchored in the harbor of the English town of Plymouth" (38). There were around 60 passengers on the ship—41 of them were men who had clashed with the Church of England. They brought their wives, children, and servants. William Bradford was the chronicler of these people whom he called "pilgrims." He also became the governor of the colony, in addition to its primary historian. The pilgrims, Bradford explained, had left England for Holland a decade earlier. They settled in Leiden, a university town known for its religious tolerance. Then, after 10 years in exile, they decided to start anew elsewhere. They thought "of those vast and unpeopled countries of America [...] devoid of all civil inhabitants," Bradford wrote (38). They sailed for 66 days and ended up on the coast of Cape Cod, due to drifting off course. They had intended to sail to Virginia. Unwilling to risk the choppy seas again, they rowed to the nearest shore. On the day they arrived, they signed the Mayflower Compact—a pledge to form a civic body.

Unlike the men who settled in Virginia, those who set up New England had no charter from the king. They were fleeing from the king. In England, members of Parliament also questioned James's "divine right" to rule. The battle that ensued between the king and his government would send tens of thousands more exiles to North America. Those who immigrated to the colonies would have within them "a deep and abiding spirit of rebellion against arbitrary rule" (39).

John Winthrop, one of another band of church dissenters known as Puritans, joined an expedition to found a colony in Massachusetts Bay. In 1630, Winthrop became the first governor of Massachusetts. In his address "A Model of Christian Charity," he described the union between his people as one held together "by the ligaments of love" (43). Roger Williams, who had once been Edward Coke's stenographer, arrived with the Massachusetts Bay mission. For his commitment to religious tolerance, he was banished. The following year, he founded Rhode Island. Colonies that were not founded on religious principles were still created by dissenters of some sort.

English migrants arrived as families and, sometimes, as entire towns, "hoping to found a Christian commonwealth, a religious community bound to the common wealth of all" (44). Their understanding of the world was hierarchical. Their family units were also small commonwealths, in which the father was the head. They built towns around land owned in common. They also believed that everything happened for a reason—all events were ordained by God, particularly the accretion of wealth.

In 1636, Puritans in New England founded Harvard College with the intention of educating both Indigenous and English youth. The following year, in Connecticut, colonists and the Pequots began warring with each other. After the colonists won, they sold captured Pequots as slaves to English settlers in the Caribbean. In 1638, the first enslaved Africans arrived in Salem, Massachusetts on board a ship called *Desire*. They had been traded for the Pequots. The ship also carried cotton and tobacco. About half of colonial New Englanders' wealth would come from profits derived from the sugar grown by those enslaved in the Caribbean.

Though the English came late to slave-trading, once they entered the trade, they quickly dominated it. Between 1600 and 1800, 1 million Europeans migrated to the British colonies, while 2.5 million Africans were forcibly transported there. Though they died faster than the European settlers, they still outnumbered their free counterparts by "two and a half to one" (45). While the English had previously told stories of the cruelty of the Spanish and condemned the Portuguese for trading Africans, they abandoned these judgments by the 1640s. By then, English settlers in the Barbados had started to plant sugar. The planters purchased Africans from the Spanish and Dutch and, later, from the English. In 1663, the English founded the Company of Royal Adventurers of England Trading with Africa. In the final quarter of that century, English ships, piloted and crewed by English captains and sailors, carried over 250 million men, women, and children across the Atlantic in shackles. Most of the Africans were Bantu speakers, while others were Akan and some Igbo.

Having found no clear guidelines from antiquity or modern Western civilization on how to determine who would be enslaved and who would be free, the English settlers created new practices and laws in which they established the division between "blacks" and "whites." They used a Roman law, which declared that one's position in society was determined by whatever one's mother was, to ensure that no children begat by white men and Black women would be free.

While English colonists sought to justify the enslavement of Africans, the English king's subjects struggled over his "divine right" to rule. As a result of this battle, the notion of divine right was replaced by another idea: the people's sovereignty. English American colonists rewrote laws to determine the relationship between governors and the governed. Indigenous tribes, meanwhile, revolted again and again in the final quarter of the 17th century. New England Algonquians, led by Metacom, tried to oust the colonists by attacking a series of towns. As a result of their efforts, over half of all English towns were either abandoned or destroyed. Metacom was later captured, shot, and beheaded. His severed head was set on a pike. The colonists then sold his nine-year-old son to the Caribbean, while a slave uprising broke out in Barbados. The Barbadian legislature passed a law banning the purchase of indigenous peoples from New England, believing their presence would help stoke rebellion. Native peoples also attacked English towns in Maryland and Virginia.

William Berkeley, governor of Virginia, refused to retaliate against warring tribes, causing a colonist named Nathaniel Bacon to lead 500 men to Jamestown in revolt. Bacon and his men, in what came to be called Bacon's Rebellion, burned the town to the ground. Before Bacon's Rebellion, poor white men in the region had little political power. Most were "debtors or convicts or indentured servants"—neither enslaved nor quite free (56). After the rebellion, such men were granted the right to vote. The rebellion also helped to solidify race as a marker between who was enslaved and who was free—"to be black was to be a slave" (56).

Meanwhile, in 1692, 19 men and women were convicted of witchcraft in Salem, Massachusetts. Those declared witches were likely coping with the trauma of being attacked by indigenous tribes. They repeatedly described the devil as a tawny or brown man. Some described the devil as "a black man." Both descriptions led Boston minister Cotton Mather to think that Black people and native peoples were evil.

Uprisings of enslaved Africans broke out throughout North America. In Jamaica, which had a majority Black population, a Black man named Cudjoe built towns in the mountains that the English called "maroon" towns. The First Maroon War ended in 1739 with a treaty in which the British agreed to acknowledge the five maroon towns and freed both Cudjoe and his followers. The formerly enslaved men were granted over 1,500 acres of land. Rumors of rebellion in the Caribbean reached the Carolinas and Georgia within weeks. Slaves, like colonists, traded gossip with those who arrived on ships. In 1739, during the Stono Rebellion, over 100 Black men killed 20 white people in South Carolina—"a colony where blacks outnumbered whites by two to one" (58). The rebels hoped to go to Spanish Florida, where the Spanish had promised fugitive slaves freedom. They were led by a man from Angola named Jemmy who spoke his native Kikongo, English, and Portuguese. He could also read and write.

In response to the Stono Rebellion, the South Carolina legislature passed "An Act for the Better Ordering and Governing Negroes." The law restricted the movement of enslaved Black people, developed standards for their treatment, created punishments for their crimes, and explained procedures for their prosecution and set the rules for presenting evidence at their trials. The law also made it illegal for anyone to teach a slave how to read or write. Meanwhile, literacy was growing among white colonists, who had started to print pamphlets and books, as well as their own newspapers. The first printing press in the New World developed in Boston in 1639. The colonies' first newspaper, *Publick Occurrences*, appeared in Boston in 1690. At first, the news comprised developments from Europe. Increasingly, the newspapers reported more about what occurred in colonies. They began to question authority and insisted on their liberties, particularly the liberty of the press. Benjamin Franklin was one of the fiercest advocates of freedom of the press.

A major battle over the freedom of the press occurred in New York, where German immigrant John Peter Zenger published the *New-York Weekly Journal*, founded in 1733. The newspaper frequently criticized the governor of New York, William Cosby, who had been appointed by the king. Thin-skinned and imperious, Cosby ordered that all copies of the paper be burned and had Zenger arrested for seditious libel. Zenger was tried before New York's Supreme Court and was represented by Andrew Hamilton, an attorney from Philadelphia. Hamilton argued that everything Zenger had printed about the governor's misbehavior was true, leading the jury to find Zenger not guilty. Cosby died the following year. While white New Yorkers believed that if a governor misbehaved they had the right to remove him from office, they also worried that enslaved Black people in New York would similarly depose them from power. They were especially concerned because many of those enslaved in New York had come from the Caribbean, particularly from islands known for slave uprisings. Their fear led them to arrest and imprison over 150 Black men in the city. Some were hanged, while others were burned at the stake.

By 1750, the colonies had regionally distinct characteristics. New England settlers had the greatest longevity, while those in the South had a high mortality rate and were outnumbered by enslaved Africans. The middle colonies had a mixed population of European immigrants and a population healthier than those in the South and the Caribbean, but not as healthy as those in New England. However, there were few differences in the manners and characters of the people. A religious revival, led by the English evangelical George Whitefield, was partly responsible for making them more alike. Whitefield told his followers that they could be reborn in the body of Christ. He also "emphasized the divinity of ordinary people" and targeted farmers, artisans, and servants when proselytizing (68).

In this chapter, Lepore illustrates how the settlement of North America depended, too, on the ambitions of new monarchs. Commercial interests were often tied to missionary ones—that is, James I sought to spread Protestantism, perhaps to counteract the increasing influence of Catholicism in French, Portuguese, and Spanish colonies. The settlement of Plymouth County was, unlike Columbus's landing in Haiti, a matter largely of happenstance and good fortune. The Pilgrims and Puritans who arrived had a different purpose—freedom from religious tyranny. The precedent they set contrasted sharply from the avaricious interests of previous settlers though their vision was somewhat aligned to the idea of America as an Eden: an untouched land in which they could begin anew and live in relative peace. In this vision, they had discounted those who already lived in the Americas, as well as their will to preserve their own autonomy and ways of life.

By pointing out the involvement of the Northern colonies in the slave trade, Lepore debunks the myth that the North had little to do with slavery. Not only did these colonies and, later, states engage in the slave trade and slaveholding until the early 19th century, they continued to depend on the profits of cash crops, harvested by slave labor. Later, they would be particularly dependent on the labor that harvested the cotton supplying the textile mills in Lowell, Massachusetts.

Lepore's chronicles of the slave rebellions throughout the Americas also debunks the myth of Black docility—the belief that reinforces white supremacy by claiming that a lack of resistance among enslaved Africans fostered the institution of slavery. Lepore enumerates and describes rebellions in the Caribbean, particularly, but also in the US, from the 1739 Stono Rebellion to Gabriel Prosser's attempted revolt in 1800 to Nat Turner's massive uprising in 1831 to John Brown's failed attempt to seize Harper's Ferry on the eve of the Civil War.

Lepore juxtaposes these uprisings which, for many years later were not contextualized as freedom struggles, with Bacon's Rebellion, which helped lead to the use of race as a marker of one's citizenship status.

In the 1690s, both racial and gender lines were solidified. Women who behaved outside of the realm of respectability could be severely and mortally punished. "Black" Africans and "brown" Indigenous peoples became agents of evil in the white imagination, partly to demonize those whom white people struggled against for power and dominance. That control came to include restrictions on Black people's access to information, which would later evolve into vociferous limitations on free speech in the South. Southern states, such as South Carolina, which had a large population of enslaved Black people—so large that it outnumbered the white population—were most dependent on slave labor and, therefore, strongly opposed to any instigations against slavery both internally and externally. Even in New York, a city with a relatively small Black population, the fear of Black dominance was palpable. This suggests that, since the Colonial Era, American political and social structures were built on the notion of hierarchy—the dominant seeking to maintain control over the dominated while living in constant fear of being toppled.

Part 1, Chapter 3 Summary and Analysis: "Of Wars and Revolutions"

In 1757, Britain and France were attacking each other's ships, continuing a war that had broken out three years earlier. The fighting had begun in Pennsylvania, as the British had wanted "land that the French had claimed in the Ohio Valley" (76). A skirmish broke out in May 1754, when a small group of Virginia militiamen and their indigenous allies, led by 21-year-old Lieutenant Colonel George Washington, "ambushed a French camp" (76). Washington, however, was inexperienced in battle and the attack proved disastrous for the colonists.

Several weeks later, colonial delegates met in Albany to consider Franklin's proposal that they set up a common defense. Ultimately, the assemblies rejected the idea. The French and Indian War broke out soon thereafter. William Pitt, Britain's new secretary of state, was "determined to win the war and settle Britain's claims in North America" (77). Pitt had also promised the colonies that the Crown would pay for the war. However, Britain broke that promise and, instead, levied taxes on the colonists. This decision would lead the colonists to seek independence.

In 1759, weeks after the British and American forces defeated the French in Quebec, George III was crowned king of Great Britain. The new king, out of fear of more Indigenous uprisings, "issued a proclamation that no colonists could settle west of the

Appalachian Mountains," though many colonists already resided there (80).

In 1764, to help pay for the debts from the Seven Years' War and to "fund the defense of the colonies," Parliament passed the American Revenue Act, also called the Sugar Act (80). The colonists argued that because they had no representatives in Parliament the legislative body "had no right to levy taxes on them" (81). Samuel Adams, a Massachusetts assemblyman, suggested that the levying of taxes without legal representation reduced the colonists from subjects to slaves.

The following year, Parliament passed the Stamp Act, which "required placing government-issued paper stamps on all manner of printed paper" (81). Those who opposed the act called themselves the Sons of Liberty, modeled on the Sons of Liberty in 1750s Ireland. They also believed that they were rebelling against slavery. John Adams invoked this sentiment when he declared that the colonists would not be the "negroes" of British creditors. The tax most severely penalized those who printed newspapers. Printers throughout the colonies complained that "Parliament was trying to reduce the colonists to a state of slavery by destroying the freedom of the press" (82).

One month before the Stamp Act was set to take effect, 27 delegates from nine colonies met in New York's city hall. They called themselves the Stamp Act Congress. The congress declared that the colonists were to consent to taxes or have them levied by their own representatives. In 1766, Benjamin Franklin appeared before the House of Commons to explain why colonists would not pay the tax. He told the members that the colonists' respect for Parliament had lessened considerably, and that their understanding of common rights, under the Magna

Carta, had influenced their aversion to Parliament's exercise of this authority.

Meanwhile, colonists in the West Indies hardly complained about the Stamp Act. They were too worried about slave insurrections. In the British Caribbean, Black people outnumbered white people eight to one. A quarter of all British troops stationed in British North America were in the West Indies. In exchange for this protection, the Caribbean planters were very willing to pay a tax on stamps. The planters also blamed the colonists on the mainland for stirring a desire for liberty among those enslaved. The American colonists, on the other hand, regarded the West Indian planters as slavish and timid in response to the Crown. Their response was a boycott on Caribbean goods.

Parliament repealed the Stamp Act in 1766. A week after the news reached Boston, the town voted to abolish slavery. Pamphleteers advocated for the abolition of slavery throughout Massachusetts Colony. In 1767, Parliament passed the Townshend Acts, which levied "taxes on lead, paper, paint, glass, and tea" (87). This, too, caused rioting and boycotts among colonists.

In March 1770, British troops fired into a crowd in Boston, killing five men in what came to be called the Boston Massacre. The Sons of Liberty demanded relief from an occupying army, while the colonists in the West Indies asked for a larger military presence to protect them from Black people.

In 1766, the Massachusetts Assembly considered an antislavery bill. However, some in Massachusetts worried that a move toward abolition would divide the Northern colonies from those in the South. John Adams, particularly, worried about the bill's impact on colonial union. The following year, the British court took up the case of *Somerset v. Stewart* in which an African man, James Somerset, successfully sued for his freedom from a Boston-based British customs officer, Charles Stewart. The case taught the enslaved two lessons: First, that they could possibly seek their freedom through the courts; and, secondly, that they were likelier able to secure freedom in Britain than in the American colonies.

In May 1773, Parliament passed the Tea Act—an attempt to save the nearly bankrupt East India Company by, once again, placing a tax burden on the American colonies. In the fall, when three ships carrying tea arrived in Boston, "dozens of colonists disguised as Mohawks—warring Indians—boarded the boats and dumped chests of tea into the harbor" in what came to be known as "the Boston Tea Party" (88). In response, Parliament passed the Coercive Acts, which closed Boston Harbor and "annulled the Massachusetts charter" (88).

In September, 56 delegates from 12 of the 13 colonies met in Philadelphia as the First Continental Congress. George Washington was the delegate from Virginia. While the Stamp Act concerned all of the colonies, the Coercive Acts seemed to be only Massachusetts's problem. Worse, delegates from Massachusetts seemed fanatical in their desire to declare independence from Britain. Washington spoke to the Massachusetts delegates and, by the following month, was certain that it was now no one's wish to seek independence.

Another Virginia delegate, Patrick Henry, suggested that the delegates should "cast a number of votes proportionate to their colonies' number of white inhabitants" (90). However, without any accurate population figures, the colonists decided to give each colony one vote. Henry was pleased that there would no longer be any distinction between colonists. They were all, simply, Americans.

The new Continental Congress urged colonists to stockpile weapons and form militias. It also decided "to boycott all British imports and to ban all trade with the West Indies" (91). Lord North, the prime minister, commissioned the essayist Samuel Johnson to write a response to the Continental Congress's complaints against Britain. In his book *Taxation No Tyranny* (1775), Johnson wondered how it was that the loudest cries for liberty came from those who were slave drivers. Johnson was notably antislavery: His companion, collaborator, and heir, Francis Barber, was a Black man from Jamaica.

On April 19, 1775, 70 armed militiamen met General Thomas Gage and his troops in Lexington and Concord, Massachusetts. The British killed ten of the soldiers—or, minutemen—farmers who had pledged to be ready for battle at a moment's notice. The rebels then moved into Boston, which had been occupied by the British army. Four-fifths of the city's inhabitants attempted to escape. They were the first refugees of the Revolutionary War. Those who hoped to reconcile with Britain now had to respond to the stories of those from Massachusetts, who were even more radicalized. In June, Congress voted to set up the Continental Army. John Adams nominated George Washington to be its commander. Washington went to Massachusetts to take command of the forces. At the time, most colonists remained loyal to the Crown. If they supported any resistance, it was in the interest of securing their rights as Englishmen, not as Americans. Meanwhile, Lord Dunmore, the royal governor of Virginia, offered freedom to slaves who agreed to join the British army. Edward Rutledge, a Continental Congress delegate from South Carolina, believed that Lord Dunmore's declaration created an "eternal separation between Great Britain and the Colonies" (94).

Still, about one-third of colonists were patriots, while another third remained Loyalists. The final third was undecided. At the Continental Congress in June, Pennsylvania delegate John Dickinson drafted the Articles of Confederation. In the document, Dickinson used the phrase "the united states" for the first time, which he may have found in a book of treaties from the mid-17th century. The first draft of the Articles of Confederation called for each state to contribute to the defense and the government according to their respective populations, which therefore required a census to be taken every three years. The final Articles of Confederation were more akin to a peace treaty, "establishing a defensive alliance among sovereign states" and a system of government (97).

Congress then appointed a Committee of Five to draft what became the Declaration of Independence: Benjamin Franklin, Thomas Jefferson, John Adams, Robert R. Livingston, and Roger Sherman. Jefferson prepared the first draft. The Declaration explained why the colonists were fighting. The cause of the revolution, they argued, was that the king had placed his subjects "under arbitrary power, reducing them to a state of slavery" (98). To write the Declaration, Jefferson borrowed heavily from George Mason's Virginia Declaration of Rights. It included a list of grievances and charges against the king, particularly unfair taxation, the dissolution of colonial assemblies, and his maintenance of a standing army in the colonies. In the statement's longest draft, Jefferson blamed George III for imposing slavery on the colonialists and now inciting them to rise up against their owners. Congress later struck this passage from the Declaration.

In July, messengers read the Declaration of Independence aloud to cheering crowds who pulled down statues of the king and melted them for bullets. Several weeks later, another slave rebellion broke out in Jamaica, and the planters blamed the Americans for inciting it. During the Revolutionary War, one in five American slaves left their owners to be freed by the British. Most were caught, recaptured, and punished. Still, it seemed a good bet in a climate in which most expected the British to win the war. The British started with 32,000 soldiers, far better disciplined and experienced than their American opponents, who numbered only 19,000. William Howe, commander in chief of the British forces, focused on New York and Philadelphia, but his victories in those cities brought little benefit. Unlike in Europe, no city in the new nation was established enough to encourage a surrender.

For the British, the American Revolution was "one front in a much larger war, a war for empire, a world war" (100). Like the French and Indian War, it impacted other parts of North America, but also impacted West Africa, the Caribbean, South Asia, and the Mediterranean. In 1778, France entered the war as an ally to the Americans. Spain joined the French-American alliance the following year. Germany supplied paid soldiers, and the Dutch provided Americans with arms and ammunition, leading the British to declare war on the Netherlands in 1780. Meanwhile, the cessation of trade between the British West Indies and mainland North America led to a famine in the former region that most severely impacted enslaved Africans.

In 1778, the Crown sought compliance from the colonists by repealing all of the acts Parliament had imposed since 1763. The British refused, however, to recognize American independence. Henry Clinton, Howe's successor, held on to New York City and pushed west. Much of the war had moved to the South, however, where British ministers sought to hold on to the southern colonies in an effort to restore the West Indies' food supply.

In May 1779, Congress proposed enlisting 3,000 enslaved people from Georgia and South Carolina and freeing them in exchange for their service. John Adams believed that the measure would incur the wrath of South Carolina, and he was right. The state rejected the measure, and Henry Clinton captured Charleston in May 1780. The following year, with the hope of seizing the Chesapeake, British general Lord Cornwallis made Yorktown, Virginia, his naval base. American and French forces soon besieged the troops stationed there. Marquis de Lafayette led the French.

In 1782, the British fought in the Battle of the Saintes. Though they succeeded in defeating a French and Spanish invasion of Jamaica, the battle had shifted Britain's priorities away from the American colonies. Around this time, about 75,000 loyalists left the country with the British. Between 15,000 to 20,000 of those who joined the exodus were formerly enslaved people, who left in what was "the largest emancipation in American history before Abraham Lincoln signed the Emancipation Proclamation" (104). Armed slave patrols pursued the escaped slaves, capturing hundreds of men who had become Cornwallis's soldiers, as well as their families. Among those captured were "two people owned by Washington and five owned by Jefferson" (104). Washington had asked colonists to keep what he called the "Book of Negroes" so that the owners of escaped slaves could later demand compensation from the British for lost property.

In defiance of the slave patrols, pregnant Black women ran toward British lines, in the hopes that their newborns would get freedom papers. Others leapt off docks and swam toward the longboats sailing toward British warships. British soldiers tried to hack off the fingers of swimmers who refused to let go of the already crowded boats. In January 1783, the Marquis de Lafayette wrote to Washington, suggesting that they free enslaved Black people, believing that the move could also lead to the end of slavery in the Caribbean. Washington wrote back, expressing a wish to discuss the plan.

In September 1783, the Treaty of Paris was signed, thereby ending the Revolutionary War. In the aftermath of the war, slave owners in the South, particularly South Carolina, gained political power while those in the West Indies lost it due to Britain's decision to outlaw trade between the islands and the United States. The decision led to riots. Meanwhile, many freed slaves left the United States for the Caribbean. In Jamaica, the formerly enslaved began to demand the right to vote. After the treaty restored peace, George Washington rode to New York. The last British troops had departed from the city, though the last British ship remained.

In this chapter, Lepore describes the early skirmishes, debates, and battles for territory that led to the outbreak of the Revolutionary War. While American colonists struggled against some indigenous tribes and other colonists for territory, they also struggled against the Crown's authority. Unjust taxes and a lack of autonomy were the colonists' primary grievances, but their image of themselves in relation to the Crown was ironic. John Adams's comparison of the colonists' condition to that of Black Americans was startlingly oblivious, particularly in light of Adams's antislavery sentiments. The colonists' use of Mohawk headdresses during the Boston Tea Party was also ironic, considering that the Mohawk struggled against being encroached upon by white colonists. In sum, American colonists recognized the oppression of these groups, but failed both to take responsibility for that oppression and to empathize with it.

Relationships with the British government depended largely on both demographics and one's position in the respective British colonies. While the American colonies struggled against Parliament, white settlers in the West Indies sought greater support from the British government, due to their fear of the Black population that overwhelmed them. Disparate political interests led to a severance of the American colonists' relationship with colonists in the Caribbean. Enslaved Black people in the American colonies, on the other hand, found that British courts were more amenable to their desires for liberty than American courts. Another great irony was the American colonialists' general belief that, while they deserved independence from British tyranny and were willing to enlist support from African Americans who served as soldiers, they had no obligation to examine their own relationship to slaveholding. Worse, their shifting of responsibility onto the British amounted to poor reasoning: If they were able to expand white male suffrage and reduce indentured servitude, two practices that were also legacies of British rule, they also had the ability to abolish slavery. Slaveholders, which included some Founding Fathers, were disinclined to go without the immense profits they reaped from slaveholding. Moreover, indentured servitude came with the obligation that, after a man's time of indenture expired, he became entitled to his own parcel of land— a deal that would have led to increased competition in agriculture, as well as the inability of large planters to monopolize the market in cash crops.

The Revolutionary War also became an effort to temper the expansion of British powers, as other nations strategically aligned with the patriots. In the aftermath of the war, the Crown, in retaliation, severed trade relations between the US and the British West Indies. This decision likely helped distinguish the regions culturally, while also hurting the British Caribbean economically. The severance of trade relations also made the slave trade within the US a more provincial affair, leading to the rise of South Carolina as a political and economic powerhouse, due to its abilities to supply key cash crops and slaves.

Part 1, Chapter 4 Summary and Analysis: "The Constitution of a Nation"

Thirty-six-year-old James Madison arrived in Philadelphia on May 3, 1787, 11 days before the constitutional convention was set to start. He reviewed his notes on the organization of republics. George Washington arrived 10 days later and was greeted by crowds, the ringing of church bells, and a 13-gun salute. The following morning, Madison and Washington walked to the Pennsylvania State House together to attend the convention. Few of the delegates had arrived. Madison attended every day of the convention, which met from May 14 to September 17. He spent the summer taking notes of the congressional deliberations for Thomas Jefferson, who had left the country in 1784. More importantly, Madison was taking a record of how the constitution had been written.

Eleven of 13 states wrote constitutions in 1776 or 1777. Most state constitutions were drafted by their respective legislatures, while others were drafted by men "elected as delegates to special conventions" (111). New Hampshire was the first state to submit a constitution to its people for ratification. Numerous state constitutions, including those of Pennsylvania and Virginia, had a Declaration of Rights. Pennsylvania's, written in September 1776, echoed the preamble to the Declaration of Independence. Massachusetts's constitution validated the people's right to revolt. In some states, legislatures lowered property qualifications for prospective voters. Most of them had arranged a government with three branches—a governor as the executive power, a superior court as judicial power, and both a Senate and House of Representatives as legislative powers. Pennsylvania's constitution declared that every proposed legislation "had to be printed and distributed to the people" who would have up to a year to consider it (112). Vermont's 1777 constitution contained a Declaration of Rights that banned slavery and placed an age limit on indentured servitude. This would have made Vermont the first state to abolish slavery, but it was an independent republic at the time. It would not become a state until 1791.

The delegates debated over how to apportion the tax burden—a matter that remained unresolved. They wondered, too, if slaves, for the purposes of taxation, should count as people or property. Madison, for a while, put the matter to rest by proposing that slaves would be rated as five to three. This came to be known as the Three-Fifths Compromise—a formula that would determine the outcomes of American elections for the next seven decades. Then there was the matter of the value of land. Acreage was an unsatisfactory measure because a field was clearly worth more than a bog.

By 1786, the continental government was nearly bankrupt and unable to pay back its creditors, particularly France and Holland. The states struggled, too. Though they had the power to levy taxes, they could not always collect them. In Massachusetts, farmers who failed to pay their taxes could lose their property.

Many of those farmers had fought in the Revolutionary War. In August 1786, they decided to fight in protest against seizures of their property in what came to be known as Shay's Rebellion. The armed farmers from western Massachusetts, led by veteran Daniel Shays, "blockad[ed] courthouses and seiz[ed] a federal armory" (116). In January 1787, the governor of Massachusetts sent a 3,000-man militia across the state in an effort to suppress the rebellion. The state, which had received no authority to act from the federal government, instituted martial law.

By May 1787, only about 30 delegates were usually on hand. On May 14, the day the convention was set to begin, hardly any delegates arrived. Benjamin Franklin and James Madison were in attendance. Additionally, four members of the Pennsylvania and Virginia delegations, respectively, were in town, including George Washington. Instead of revising the Articles of Confederation, the six men agreed to create a national government. The next day, Madison began writing what became known as the Virginia Plan.

On May 25, 1787, 29 delegates arrived at the convention and unanimously elected George Washington as president. They began deliberations in earnest on May 29 and agreed to keep them secret. Their most pressing problem was debt and an absence of revenue. Franklin argued that there should be no property requirement to vote. The new constitution also required that congressional representatives be paid. This way, the office would not be limited to the wealthy. Additionally, only a short residency would be required of immigrants before they, too, could run for office. They then wondered how to fairly apportion representation in Congress. The problem, Madison understood, was not only the size of the states but the nature of their respective populations. After the end of the American Revolution, the United States "had witnessed the largest importation of African slaves to the Americas in history—a million people over a single decade" (122). The slave population soared from half a million in 1776 to 700,000 by 1787. The banning of American merchants from West Indian ports encouraged a slave trade within the United States. As slave populations rose in Southern states, their populations fell in the North. By 1787, it had been abolished in New England and was becoming increasingly unpopular in New York and Pennsylvania. In Georgia and South Carolina, slavery was central to the states' economies.

Slaves were critical in two calculations: the wealth they represented as chattel and their population as individuals. States with large numbers of slaves wanted them to count as people "for purposes of representation but not for purposes of taxation," while non-slaveholding states wanted the opposite (124). A compromise was reached over slavery with the caveat that Congress would be prohibited from interfering with the trade for two decades. Madison would have preferred no mention of slavery in the Constitution at all. To some, the mention of slavery was incongruous with their mission: The delegates were present to build a republic, while there was "nothing more aristocratic than slavery" (126). Ultimately, the words "slave" and "slavery" appear nowhere in the final document, which amounts to an attempt to conceal the formation of a free government powered by slave labor.

The day after the constitutional convention adjourned, the document that had been kept secret from the public was printed in newspapers and on broadsheets. In *The Federalist Papers*, 85 essays published under the pen name Publius between October 1787 and May 1788, argued for the ratification of the Constitution. The debate around ratification spurred the development of the two-party system that persists to date. Those who supported ratification, the Federalists, stood opposed to the Anti-Federalists, who opposed ratification. It was all or nothing.

Anti-Federalists insisted that a republic had to be "small and homogeneous," but the new nation was too big to support this form of government (129). They also believed that the Constitution was too difficult to read, making it inaccessible to the common man. Nevertheless, ratification moved forward. By January 1788, Connecticut, Delaware, Georgia, New Jersey, and Pennsylvania had ratified the document. Massachusetts voted in favor in February after Federalists promised to "propose a bill of rights at the first session of the new Congress" (130). Next were Maryland in April, South Carolina in May, and New Hampshire in June. Three weeks later, New York joined the coterie and ratified by the narrowest of margins.

The First Congress convened in New York's city hall on March 4, 1789. It had been renamed Federal Hall to fit its new purpose. It was redesigned by French-American engineer and architect Pierre Charles L'Enfant, who would later design the nation's capital. The new hall also ushered in a new architectural style: Federal.

The new president was inaugurated on April 30, though no one new how Washington, who ran unopposed, was going to assume office. A congressional committee decided that he should take an oath of office on a Bible. At midday, before a crowd, Washington took the first oath of office. After he was sworn in, he entered Federal Hall and read a speech written by Alexander Hamilton, in which he declared that the preservation of the republic rested in the hands of the American people.

The Constitution says little about the president's duties. Article II, Section 2 establishes the president as commander in chief of the army and navy, but the document does not require a cabinet. Nevertheless, Congress established numerous departments and Washington appointed secretaries to each. The Department of State was headed by Thomas Jefferson, who became secretary of state; Alexander Hamilton led the Department of Treasury; and Henry Knox headed the Department of War.

The new government's most pressing order was the drafting of a bill of rights. Madison presented the House of Representatives with 12 amendments on June 8. Article III, Section 1 set up the judicial power and the Supreme Court. Washington signed the Judiciary Act on September 24, 1789, which set the number of justices at six, defined the court's authority, and created the office of attorney general. The Supreme Court did not meet in Federal Hall, but in a room on the second floor of the Merchants' Exchange. On the first day in court, only three justices showed up, leading the court to adjourn. The day after Washington signed the Judiciary Act, Congress sent Madison's prospective bill of rights to the states for ratification.

Meanwhile, Congress once again took up the question of slavery. On February 11, 1790, a group of Quakers urged Congress to stop the importation of slaves and to slowly emancipate those already held in bondage. After a few hours of debate, Congress sent the petitions to a committee, though Southern delegates delayed it. William Loughton Smith of South Carolina expounded for two hours, arguing that emancipation would result in intermarriage and the extinction of the white race.

In West Africa, the new colony of Sierra Leone was being settled. The first expedition sailed from London in May 1787.

They founded a capital and elected the Philadelphian Richard Weaver, a Revolutionary War veteran and runaway slave, as their governor. Five months later, 122 of the settlers died from famine and disease. Others were kidnapped and sold back into slavery.

Back in New York, the congressional committee charged with responding to the antislavery petitions "forbade Congress from outlawing the slave trade until 1808" (136). It also assumed the power to tax the slave trade heavily enough to discourage it and, ultimately, to end it. Finally, the report declared that Congress had no authority to interfere with the emancipation of slaves or their treatment. The resolution passed along sectional lines. The issue of slavery was not to be revisited until 1808.

On December 15, 1971, 10 of the 12 amendments that Madison had drafted were approved by the necessary three-quarters of states. The ratified amendments became the Bill of Rights, which is a list of powers that Congress does not have.

During Washington's first term, Alexander Hamilton proposed that the federal government assume responsibility both for its own debts and for those incurred by the states by establishing a national bank. Congress passed a bill in February 1790 establishing a national bank for 10 years. Jefferson believed that the plan violated the 10th Amendment. Since the Constitution does not explicitly grant Congress the power to establish a federal bank, and the 10th Amendment says that all powers not granted to Congress are held either by the states or the people, Congress, Jefferson concluded, could not create a national bank. Washington signed the bill anyway, thereby setting a precedent for interpreting the Constitution broadly. States such as Virginia and Maryland that had already paid off their war debts resented bearing a tax burden incurred by states like Massachusetts and South Carolina, which had not paid their debts.

The next question concerned where the government should permanently meet. Hamilton supported a plan to place the nation's capital in the South, in exchange for Madison's support for his federal plan for the federal government to take on states' war debts. In July 1790, states voted to establish the capital "on a ten-mile square stretch of riverland along the Potomac River" (139). It would be called Washington.

Part of Hamilton's economic plan included raising tariffs—taxes on imported goods. Jefferson worried that Hamilton's plan would encourage speculation, and it did. Hamilton believed speculation was necessary for economic growth. In 1792, speculation led to the nation's first financial panic. One of the effects of the Panic of 1792 led Hamilton to decide that "the United States should have unshakable credit" (141). Debtors' prison was replaced by bankruptcy protection, spurring investments and other risk-taking. The panic also "led New York brokers to sign an agreement banning private bidding on stocks," a decision that founded the New York Stock Exchange (141).

Haiti, then called Saint-Domingue, was both the Caribbean's largest and richest colony. It was also France's most important colony, due to it being the leading producer of sugar and coffee. Haiti exported almost as much sugar as Cuba, Brazil, and Jamaica combined. Haiti was home to 452,000 enslaved people, 28,000 free people of color, and 40,000 white people. The nation contained half the slave population of the West Indies. Ironically, the revolutionary events that unfolded in Haiti mirrored those that had occurred in France in 1789. During the Reign of Terror that ensued in the summer of 1794, over 1,300 people were executed. While the French Revolution seemed never-ending, the Haitian Revolution sparked fear among Americans. The Haitians were first led by a man named Boukman. When he died, they were led by a former slave named Toussaint L'Ouverture. It was the second war for independence that had taken place in North America. American newspapers, however, reported on it as a kind of killing frenzy. Jefferson called the Haitians "cannibals." Between 1791 and 1793, the US sold "arms and ammunition and gave hundreds of thousands of dollars in aid to French planters on the island" (143).

In September 1796, Americans found out that George Washington, then 64, would not run for a third term. The public was astonished. He knew that he would set the precedent that no president should hold office forever. In his Farewell Address, Washington warned about "the danger of disunion" (146). He did not believe that the regions of the United States should see their interests as disparate or competing. He also warned that political parties were the "worst enemy" of any government, as they only worked to agitate communities and kindled animosity. The American experiment would survive, he believed, as long as the American public were religious and moral and well educated.

As the Washingtons prepared to leave the nation's capital, some of their slaves escaped to the North. One of them, Ona Judge, had been intended as a gift to Martha Washington's granddaughter. When the Washingtons were unsuccessful in returning her by slave catcher, Judge sent word to Washington that she would only return to Mount Vernon if she were freed. Washington refused, believing that, by granting her manumission, he would set a "dangerous precedent."

On December 12, 1799, Washington fell ill. Two days later, while lying in his bedchamber, he asked his wife to bring him two wills. In his second will, which he had written that summer, he had decided to free all of his slaves after his wife's death. Washington's will was published in newspapers throughout the union, and everyone on Mount Vernon knew its terms. His wife, knowing that the slaves' freedom was contingent upon her death, feared for her life.

The nation fell into mourning upon George Washington's death. His Farewell Address was reprinted and even stitched into pillows. James Madison, meanwhile, kept safe the notes he had taken at the constitutional convention—"the story of how the Constitution had been written, and of its fateful compromises" (149).

In this chapter, Lepore depicts how the Constitution is key to the United States' foundational narrative—arguably, more so than England's Magna Carta, as the United States' beginning is marked by the Constitution's ratification. Two key protagonists in the nation's founding are James Madison and George Washington. Lepore presents the former as a meek intellectual, while the latter is depicted as a hero who was lauded for both his military prowess and towering physical presence.

Early debates on the construction of the federal government focused on the statuses of white women, enslaved Black people, and the property requirements for white male suffrage. The abolition of slavery in Northern states led to key political and ideological distinctions between the regions. A central question, too, hovered over the new republic: Is it possible to have a free nation whose economy is powered largely by slave labor? The Founding Fathers' response was to avoid any mention of slavery in the Constitution—a denial of the nation's foundational hypocrisy by feigning ignorance.

During this period, the two-party system also arose. Ideological differences between the Federalists and Anti-Federalists ensued, leading to arguments over a large, centralized government versus a smaller one that retained state autonomy, and the inclusion of a bill of rights in the Constitution. The national character also emerged through its early architecture and the planning of the new capital, which had a strong French influence. There was less organization, however, concerning the formation of the Supreme Court.

While the United States was recognized by Europe, the West was unable to see Haiti's freedom struggle as congruous with those of the American colonists and the French poor. This denial of Haitian independence and disrespect for its people underscores the inextricability of race from emerging ideas about citizenship, freedom, and political autonomy.

President Washington's aversion to political parties may have been connected to a wish to avoid anything that would sow national discord. This, too, may have partly explained his aversion to dealing with slavery as a political issue, despite his increasing ambivalence about the feasibility and righteousness of maintaining the institution. Here, Lepore also briefly describes Martha Washington's own power as a slaveholder. Martha had first been married to man named Daniel Parke Custis who was one of the wealthiest planters in Virginia before his death. Slaves who belonged to the Custis estate were returned to that family after Martha's death. She did, however, own one slave on her own whom she refused to manumit. After her death, he became the property of a grandson. The elevation of Washington to an almost sacred status, despite his seeming indifference to the well-being of the hundreds of men, women, and children who labored for him and his family on Mount Vernon, reveals the nation's willingness, since its nascence, to overlook and even tolerate serious moral flaws in its leadership.

Part 2

Part 2: The People (1800-1865)

Part 2, Chapter 5 Summary and Analysis: "A Democracy of Numbers"

Thomas Jefferson worried that the language of the Constitution allowed a president to serve again and again until death, like a king. John Adams, on the other hand, liked that idea. In 1796, when Washington decided not to run again, Adams and Jefferson each sought to succeed him. The two men faced off again in the next election, which Jefferson nicknamed "the revolution of 1800." The election was the climax of a decades-long political debate between the men, which caused a constitutional crisis. Adams and his running mate, Charles Cotesworth Pinckney, ran as Federalists, while Jefferson and his running mate, Aaron Burr, ran as Democratic-Republicans. Jefferson had heard that, if Adams lost, the Federalists would suddenly change the law in favor of Adams, and would allow him to serve for life. Rumor had it that some Federalists would have risked civil war rather than elect Jefferson.

Four years earlier, in 1796, in seven out of 16 states, the citizens elected delegates to the Electoral College. In the other states, it was the state legislatures who elected delegates. Two parties had emerged by then, and party leaders believed that delegates ought to satisfy the demands of the men who had them elected.

Under the Constitution, the candidate with the greatest number of electoral votes was to become president, while the runner-up was to become vice president. In the 1796 election, Adams got 71 votes and Jefferson got 68, while Pinckney got only 59. This made Jefferson Adams's vice president, to everyone's disappointment.

During the Adams administration, the distance between Federalists and Democratic-Republicans widened. Adams tried to outlaw the other party by getting Congress to pass the Alien and Sedition Acts, which Jefferson and Madison believed violated the Constitution. They wrote resolutions objecting to the laws. The growing chasm between the parties also hardened their views on slavery. Jefferson had wanted a remote relationship with a freed Haiti, while Adams wanted to renew trade with the island and recognize its independence.

Meanwhile, the descendants of Africans in America found inspiration in the Haitian revolution. In the summer of 1800, Gabriel Prosser, a Richmond-based blacksmith, led a slave rebellion under the motto "Death or Liberty." The revolt was put down. Prosser and his followers were tried and executed.

Jefferson believed that the election of 1800 would "determine whether republicanism or aristocracy would prevail" (159). Both Federalists and Republicans met early that year to decide on their respective party's presidential nominee, to avoid the debacle of 1796. They called the meeting a caucus, derived from the Algonquian word for "adviser." The Democratic-Republicans again chose Jefferson, while the Federalists again chose Adams—though, Alexander Hamilton tried to encourage the party to support Pinckney instead, due to what he considered severe defects in Adams's character. The candidates did not campaign, as Americans, at the time, viewed direct addresses to the people as "a form of demagoguery" (160).

The Republicans attacked Adams for abusing his office, while Federalists attacked Jefferson for being a slave owner. Jefferson was also a target for his views on religion. In *Notes on the State of Virginia*, he had expressed his support for religious toleration, writing that he was indifferent about whether his neighbors were Christians or even polytheists. The campaigning was long and drawn out, as there was no election day in 1800. Voting was also conducted in public by counting heads. A year earlier, Maryland had passed a law requiring that citizens vote on paper, but most states were slow to follow suit. The paper ballot, however, still had not made voting secret. Out of a population of 5.23 million people, only around 600,000 were eligible to vote. Maryland was the only state in which free Black men could vote, until the state's 1802 constitution outlawed this. Only in New Jersey were white women allowed to vote—a law that persisted until 1807. Most states limited suffrage to property owners or taxpayers.

When the Electoral College met in December, the winner was unclear. It was clear, however, that Adams had lost. Thomas Jefferson and Aaron Burr were tied with 73 votes. The tie was thrown to the House, which was dominated by Federalists. They eventually decided in favor of Jefferson. Timothy Pickering, a Federalist, called Jefferson a "Negro President" because his win was largely due to the Three-Fifths Compromise. Without these fractional counts, Adams would have won.

Thomas Jefferson was elected president on February 17, 1801, and inaugurated on March 4. He was the first president to be inaugurated in Washington, DC. His inauguration was also "the first peaceful transfer of power between political opponents in the new nation" (165). Also, it became clear that the two-party system was healthy for the new republic. Jefferson delivered his inaugural address to Congress in the Capitol, which was still under construction, but his message was for the American people. He brushed off "the bitter bipartisanship" that had characterized the election (165).

Before leaving office, John Adams appointed John Marshall as chief justice of the Supreme Court in 1801. Marshall was a cousin of Jefferson's, a fellow Virginian, and a fierce political rival of the new president. Thus, while Federalists had lost the presidency and Congress, they retained power in the judicial branch. Supreme Court judges were appointed for life, which led one to wonder how the power of the judiciary would be checked. The other solution—the popular election of judges—would subject them "to all manner of political caprice" (165). When the Supreme Court started out, it had no building of its own and appeared weak. It served merely as an appellate court, a trial court, and a circuit court.

Adams, in getting Congress to pass the Judiciary Act of 1801, also got Congress to reduce the number of Supreme Court justices to five. This was only so that Jefferson would have to wait until two justices left to name another to the bench. The newly elected Democratic-Republican Congress repealed the act and suspended the next two sessions of the Supreme Court. While sessions of Congress were then open to the public, John Marshall decided that the Court's ought to be secret.

By 1810, the US population had grown to 7.2 million—"35 percent every decade" (168). By 1800, half a million people had moved westward. Jefferson tied the nation's fate to its expansion. He believed that yeoman farmers were the best citizens due to their independence and the security of their land possessions. Influenced by the English economist Thomas Malthus, Jefferson believed that a new nation needed more land "to supply its growing population with food and to retain its republic character" (168). Ideologically tied to farming, Jefferson feared manufacturing. He looked to England and saw factory workers as less virtuous and more subservient. As Jefferson was committed to westward expansion, Napoleon's offer to sell the Louisiana Territory was a great boon. Federalists, however, argued the purchase would too widely disperse the republic and result in the dissolution of the federal government. Jefferson thought that the purchase would encourage indigenous peoples to move further west.

In 1806, Jefferson signed the Non-Importation Act, "banning certain British imports" (171). The following year, he signed the Embargo Act, which banned all American exports. These laws were responses to Britain's seizure of American ships and seamen during the ongoing Napoleonic Wars between France and Great Britain. Jefferson figured that outlawing trade was the only way that the U.S could stay neutral. Besides, he insisted that Americans could produce all of the goods they required to satisfy their needs. Contrary to this belief, the embargo "devastated the American economy" (171). Congress repealed the act in 1809 when Jefferson left office.

In 1812, the US was no longer able to stay neutral in the Napoleonic Wars and Madison, with the support of the South, declared war on Britain. New England and mid-Atlantic states largely opposed the decision, as it both impacted Northern manufacturing and "threatened an invasion from Canada" (172). The conflict, which came to be called the War of 1812, took place largely at sea and in Canada. Then, in 1813, the British captured Washington, DC, forcing Madison and his cabinet into Virginia. The President's House was nearly burned to the ground. Three clerks from the War Office saved the Constitution from burning with it. The British proceeded to incinerate the capital. After the war, the President's House was rebuilt and painted. From then on, it was called the White House.

In December 1816, a coterie of Northern reformers and Southern slave owners met in Washington, DC, at Davis's Hotel for a meeting chaired by the Kentucky congressman Henry Clay, then Speaker of the House. The men gathered to discuss what they ought to do with the nation's increasing number of free Black people. There was also the matter of the westward expansion, which expanded slavery into the region. Ohio and Indiana had entered the union in 1803 and 1816, respectively, as free states, while Louisiana entered in 1812 and Mississippi four years later. Population growth in free states, however, was outpacing that in slave states. More worryingly, the population of free Black people "was growing at a rate more than double that of the population of whites" (176). The men at Davis's Hotel decided to create the American Colonization Society as the solution to ridding itself of a population it deemed "useless and pernicious" (176).

In 1819, Missouri, which had been settled by Southerners, sought to enter the Union. New York congressman James Talmadge introduced an amendment to outlaw slavery in the state. The Tallmadge Amendment narrowly passed in the House but was killed in the Senate. Madison, now retired in Virginia, believed that Missouri, once it became a state, should have the right to institute slavery. Opponents of Tallmadge also offered that, if Black people were to become free, they could never live among white citizens as equals.

The Missouri question was settled when Maine entered the Union as a free state in 1820. Now, the number of free and slave states were equal, at twelve each. The Missouri Compromise set the standard that any territory south of a defined border would enter the Union as a slave state, while any territory north of it would enter as a free state.

In 1824, Americans faced another election: the choice between the learned John Quincy Adams and the pugnacious Andrew Jackson. Jackson and his brand of democracy, which ushered in populism, would ultimately prevail. The election of 1824 also changed how presidents were elected. Two years earlier, the public had become averse to party's nominee being selected by a Congressional caucus. By the time the election came around, "King Caucus" was dead. Eligibility for voting had changed, too. Twenty-one out of 24 states had eliminated property qualifications for voting. Increasingly, poor white men voted and were elected to hold office. Party leaders also began to print ballots instead of asking voters to write their preferred candidates on a scrap of paper. Party tickets expanded the electorate even more, as they did not require that a voter needed to know how to read or write. Each party ticket was a different color with the party's special symbol.

Andrew Jackson won the popular vote in 1824, but not the required majority of the electoral vote. The House, including Henry Clay, chose John Quincy Adams. Furious, Jackson resigned from the Senate the following year and returned to his home, the Hermitage. Meanwhile, the electorate grew from 400,000 in 1824 to 1.1 million in 1828. In the latter year, Jackson ran again and defeated Adams. In this election, four times as many white men cast a ballot. Those men also voted "for an entire slate of Democratic Party candidates" (186). Jackson was inaugurated on March 4, 1829. He told the American people that the majority was to govern, then bowed to the people. After he mounted his horse and departed, the crowd followed him—a motley crew of country people, gentlemen, Black and white people. Some worried that their force might crush the new president to death.

In this chapter, Lepore explores the debates that ensued regarding the limitations of executive power. In that context, she details the pivotal events of 1800. While the Founding Fathers debated the extent of executive power during the Revolution of 1800, a Richmond-based blacksmith named Gabriel Prosser attempted to lead an uprising in Virginia. Debates over the character of the early republic were inextricable from the moral problem of the US being a slaveholding nation.

Anti-Federalists now called themselves Democratic-Republicans. Led by Thomas Jefferson—a Southern, agrarian slave owner— their party platform was centered both on questions about federal power and on who should determine the national character. Jefferson, particularly in his bid for westward expansion, believed that yeoman farmers were the noblest Americans and those most fit to populate the growing republic.

John Adams, a New Englander who had been sympathetic to the Crown, led the Federalist Party. Adams seemed to distrust the public and was not averse to the establishment of a form of executive power that was akin to monarchical rule. Adams and Jefferson, lifelong political rivals, had divergent views on race, too, which were epitomized by their reception of the Haitian Revolution. If Jefferson had recognized Haiti as an independent nation, this may have jeopardized his position as a slaveholder.

He did not see himself, it seems, within the context of the kind of aristocracy which he claimed to abhor.

The rise of Andrew Jackson, as well as the populist movement that he ushered in, is a result of the Jeffersonian legacy. Jackson was a presidential candidate in the molds of both Jefferson and Washington. Like both, Jackson was a Southern planter and slave owner, and like Jefferson, he disliked centralized government. Like Washington, he was a skilled military leader. During his tenure, white male suffrage expanded—the results of both the legacy of Bacon's Rebellion and the party ballot, which eliminated the necessity of literacy.

According to Lepore, Jackson enjoyed popularity with a wide swath of the American public, including Black people. One wonders if African Americans hoped that Jackson's populist message would also be more inclusive. Or was the general public simply drawn to Jackson's charisma and accessibility, despite the fact that he was a wealthy planter? In either case, Jackson's election helped prove that image could override the facts of one's personal history and political platform when selling a candidate to the public.

Part 2, Chapter 6 Summary and Analysis: "The Soul and the Machine"

Democracy was celebrated at the start of the 19th century. The public generally agreed now that the majority had a right to govern, and that all white men should enjoy voting rights. By the 1830s, the United States had "the first large-scale popular democracy in the history of the world," which Americans celebrated "in campaigns and parades, rallies and conventions" (191). The two parties had their own newspapers, and the electorate was educated "in a new system of publicly funded schools" (191).

In 1810, Francis Cabot Lowell, an American merchant, toured textile mills in England and sketched what he saw. Back in New England, he used those sketches as models when building his own machines. He also raised money to build his own factory. Lowell died seven years later, but his successors opened mills named after him on the Merrimack River in 1823. Lowell had intended for his system to provide an alternative to the harsh labor conditions in England. The owners of Lowell mills hired young women who worked 12-hour days and attended lectures in the evenings. By the 1830s, however, the mill owners departed from Lowell's vision of using the mills for social reform. They cut wages, sped up production and, when the women protested against the unfair conditions, the managers replaced them with men.

To aid the acceleration of production in factories, canals were constructed to aid transportation. The Erie Canal was completed in 1825. It had taken eight years to dig and covered 360 miles. Wagon trips to transport goods took upward of 20 days, but on the canal, goods could be ferried over six days. As a result of this speed, the price of goods dropped, and the standard of living increased. The nature of work also changed. Before the 1820s, workers were often paid with liquor, not wages. They also operated according to task, not the clock. Later, men earned wages and worked by the clock. "Work" also referred not only to one's responsibilities, but also where one went to perform tasks. "Home" was the place where women stayed and did what was not considered work—that is, wage labor.

Bosses no longer lived in their shops, but moved to new neighborhoods—forming a new middle class. This class expressed concern about drinking among their employees. They formed temperance unions and agreed to stop paying workers in alcohol. They also insisted that their workers join churches. Many of these men were encouraged in their efforts by their wives. It was women who led the temperance movement, largely because drunken husbands were often abusive and wasted their wages on liquor. Since married women could not own property, they had no legal recourse.

The United States, however, was not exactly founded as a Christian nation. The Bill of Rights forbids the establishment of religion and the Constitution forbids religious litmus tests for office holders. However, in 1775, there had been 1,800 Christian ministers in the US; by 1845, there were over 40,000. Due to the absence of an official religion, Americans founded a myriad of sects. The only thing that unified all of them was an apparent belief in the American creed and a kind of worship, which Thomas Jefferson warned against, of the men who had founded the nation.

Conversely, abolitionists did not venerate the Founding Fathers; they criticized them. Admiration for the values in the Declaration of Independence, combined with anger at the founders for their hypocrisies, were views most frequently expressed in Black churches. Aided by the introduction of the cotton gin in 1793, cotton production doubled in the South between 1810 and 1820, and again between 1820 and 1825. Cotton was "the most valuable commodity in the Atlantic world" (202). Though the Atlantic slave trade officially ended in 1808, there remained a booming domestic market in slaves—many of whom were sold from wealthy slaveholding states like South Carolina and Virginia to Alabama, Mississippi, and Louisiana. Another million enslaved people were sold and sent west between 1820 and 1860. When the price of cotton went up in England, the price of slaves also increased. Slaves, like cotton, were sold according to their grades, based on how much cotton they could pick. A healthy man counted as "two hands," while a woman was a "half-hand," and a child was a "quarter-hand."

In 1822, Denmark Vesey, a carpenter who lived in Charleston, South Carolina staged a rebellion with enslaved and free Black people. He was quickly caught and hanged. Slave owners blamed Black sailors who had spread word of "freedom in the North and of independence in Haiti" (202). Thus, the South Carolina legislature passed the Negro Seamen Acts, demanding that Black soldiers be held in prison for as long as their ships were at port.

Abolitionists argued for the immediate emancipation of all enslaved people. As they radicalized, Southern antislavery organizations closed. Before 1830, the number of abolitionist groups "in the South had outnumbered those in the North by more than four to one" (204). Southern antislavery activists were more likely to be supporters of colonization than emancipation, however.

In the summer of 1831, a 31-year-old preacher and slave named Nat Turner planned a slave rebellion to take place on Independence Day. Turner's parents had been enslaved, but his mother had supposedly been born in West Africa, while his father had escaped to the North. The wife of Turner's first owner had taught him to read when he was a boy. He later studied the Bible. By 1828, he claimed that he had had a religious vision: In it, God had called upon him to lead his people in an uprising.

Using signs from nature to guide him, he decided to wait instead until August. In the end, he and his followers killed between 55 and 65 white people. The group was caught, and Turner was hanged.

The Virginia legislature began to consider the possibility of emancipating enslaved people, fearing future rebellions. Thomas Jefferson's grandson, Thomas Jefferson Randolph, proposed a plan for gradual emancipation. Instead, the legislature decided to pass laws banning anyone from teaching enslaved people to read and write and from teaching them about the Bible. When Alexis de Tocqueville, the French political theorist visited earlier that year for a nine-month tour of the US, he declared that, if the nation ever underwent another great revolution, it would be caused by the presence of Black people in the nation and the inequality in which that race lived.

Meanwhile, one effect of Jacksonian democracy and the Second Great Awakening was "the participation of women in the reformation of American politics by way of American morals" (206). Having no access to public political or economic participation, women clung to their role as mothers, which they believed made them morally superior to men—"more loving, more caring, and more responsive to the cries of the weak" (206). They formed abolition societies, vegetarian societies, and temperance societies, among others. By 1837, 139 women-led antislavery societies were formed around the country, especially in Massachusetts and Ohio.

Women worked largely behind the scenes on social reform, while men protested in the streets. There was a great deal of struggle, starting in the 1810s, between business and labor. After the Panic of 1819, factories closed due to bank failures. Workers' wages fell drastically. They soon began to exercise their political power, forming the Working Men's Party in Philadelphia in 1828. Workers demanded shorter hours—10 instead of 11 or 12—and better conditions. They also expressed concern about the "excessive accumulation of wealth and power into the hands of a few" (207). Though Jacksonian democracy dispersed political power, industrialization consolidated power among a minority. Also, native-born workers were forced to compete with immigrants arriving from Europe in great numbers. In 1831, 20,000 people of European descent arrived in the US. In 1854, that number increased to over 400,000. The largest number of immigrants were from Ireland and Germany. Critics of President Jackson, who was of Irish descent, blamed him for "the rising population of poor, newly enfranchised Irishmen" (208). Many of the Irish and German immigrants who arrived were Catholic, which swelled hostility toward the sect, much of it fueled by evangelical Protestants. Samuel F. Morse, an inventor and painter, created a secret code of dots and dashes to be communicated via telegraph, as he believed that Catholics were plotting to take over the nation. Thus, the government would need a secret code to defeat such a scheme.

In Philadelphia in 1844, a riot broke out between Catholics and Protestants that left 20 people dead. Between 1845 and 1849— the years of the Irish Potato Famine—1.5 million Irish people left their homeland for the US and settled in cities along the Eastern Seaboard. They lived in ethnically homogenous neighborhoods and worked for very low wages. They also built Catholic churches, mutual aid societies, and parochial schools. Finally, they looked to the Democratic Party to defend their institutions. By 1850, one quarter of the population of Boston was Irish. Signs in shop windows excluded them from employment by reading "No Irish Need Apply." Germans, on the other hand, endured less prejudice. They usually arrived with more personal funds, allowing them to move further inland, where they farmed. They, like the Irish, sent their children to their own schools and churches. The insularity of these communities gave rise to a movement "to establish tax-supported public elementary schools [...] meant to provide a common education and civic education to all classes of Americans" (209). This American experiment, like that of universal suffrage for white men, made the US more modern than Europe.

Some hoped that common education would diminish partisanship, as common schools also helped nurture "a strong civic culture" (209). This was culture was encouraged, too, by rising nativism. Others argued that schools encouraged regimentation to prepare young people for the demands of industrialism. Worse, Black children were not allowed to attend common schools. Free Black people set up their own schools for their children, such as the African Free School in New York, which, by the 1820s, had over 600 students. In other cities, Black families fought to integrate their local common schools and won. Massachusetts senator Charles Sumner led the charge for integration in his state, but other states responded by outlawing integration.

Education increased literacy, which led to a rise in the number of newspapers and a decrease in their prices. The "penny press" that emerged advocated facts over opinions. In 1833, the new Democratic Party was pitted against the Whig Party. People wanted to know not only how to vote for their preferred party but also what was true and what wasn't.

President Jackson's first major domestic campaign was his policy of removing indigenous peoples, but only in the Southeast.

He focused on what came to be known as the Five Civilized Tribes—the Cherokee, Chickasaw, Creeks, Choctaws, and Seminoles. The tribes lived in Alabama, Mississippi, Louisiana, Georgia, Florida, and Tennessee. Jackson brought his military experience to the campaign. In 1814, he led a group of US and Cherokee forces in an effort to root out the Creeks. The Creeks ended up having to cede over 20 million acres of their land to the US. Two years later, Jackson forced the Cherokees "to sign treaties selling to the United States more than three million acres for about twenty cents an acre" (213). When the tribe protested, Jackson reminded them of what had happened to the Creeks.

In 1816, evangelical Christians attempted to convert the Cherokee, believing it was their mission "to make the whole tribe English in their language, civilized in their habits, and Christian in their religion" (213). The Cherokee responded by declaring both their independence and political equality as a nation. In 1823, they refused to cede any of their land to the US. Three years later, they established a national capital in Georgia. A year later, they wrote a constitution. Then, in 1828, "gold was discovered on Cherokee land" (214). Jackson, soon after he took office, declared "that the establishment of the Cherokee Nation violated Article IV, Section 3 of the US Constitution," which prohibited the formation of a new state within the jurisdiction of another state without the original state's approval (214). He got his Indian Removal Act passed in Congress, with most Southerners voting in favor and New Englanders largely against. Some began wondering if race impacted justice, in addition to facing a difficult reckoning over the cost of settling the Americas. The Cherokees, meanwhile, took their case to the Supreme Court. In *Cherokee Nation v. Georgia* (1831), Chief Justice John Marshall defined the Cherokee Nation as "domestic dependent nations" (215). In *Worcester v. Georgia* (1832), he declared that the laws of

Georgia had no jurisdiction over the Cherokee Nation. Marshall's decision led other tribes in New England to seek their own independence.

In the end, Jackson ignored the Supreme Court and forced the resettlement of indigenous tribes, including Cherokees, west of the Mississippi. By the time they were all removed, Jackson's two terms in office had ended. The election of 1832 rested on the question of retaining a federal bank. Between 1830 and 1837, 347 banks opened up around the nation, and each printed their own money, "producing more than twelve hundred different kinds of bills" (219). Counterfeiting and swindling became common problems.

In 1816, Congress had created the Second Bank of the United States to help the nation financially recover from the War of 1812. In 1819, the Supreme Court declared the bank constitutional. The bank handled all of the federal government's debts and taxes. Jackson, however, hated banks. He believed that the national bank undermined the people's sovereignty and allowed a handful of capitalists access to public revenue.

In January 1832, Nicholas Biddle, the bank's president, requested that Congress renew the bank's charter. Congress agreed, but Jackson vetoed the bill in July, claiming that "the president [had] the authority to decide on the constitutionality of laws passed by Congress" (220). The consequence was the loss of the nation's economic stability. Those who supported the bank insisted on the necessity of the federal government regulating the nation's paper currency. Jackson would have preferred no paper currency at all, as he preferred a gold standard.

Americans, meanwhile, moved further west by wagons and steamboats. Slavery moved with them. In the South, some American settlers crossed into Mexico, which had won independence from Spain in 1821. Certain territories along the Gulf of Mexico, particularly Texas, were attractive to American settlers looking for new places to plant cotton. At the time, Texas also included much of what later became Kansas, Colorado, Wyoming, New Mexico, and Oklahoma.

In 1835, Americans who had settled in Texas, led by Sam Houston, rose up against Mexican rule. The following year, they declared their independence. Houston became president of the new nation. Mexican president, General Antonio López de Santa Anna warned that, if the US government was behind the Texas rebellion, he would march his army to Washington, DC, and plant his nation's flag upon the Capitol Building.

President Jackson ignored Houston's request for annexation of Texas, fearing reprisal from Mexico. Also, he viewed Texas as a foreign nation. Finally, if Texas were to be admitted to the Union, "it would enter as a slave state" (223). John Quincy Adams, aware of this prospect, spent three weeks filibustering Houston's annexation proposal. The American Anti-Slavery Society sent tens of thousands of abolitionist petitions to Congress. Southern slave owners silenced Adams when he attempted to read the petitions on the floor—a triumph for opponents of free speech.

Southern slave owners made up only 1% of the population, but they relied greatly on the federal government to help them uphold slavery. They also worked hard to suppress dissent on the matter in Congress.

President Jackson, meanwhile, had decided not to run for a third term, but he was determined to choose his successor. He called for a Democratic nominating convention in 1835 "to assure the nomination of [his] handpicked successor, Martin Van Buren" (224). The Whigs, which had become a disorganized party, did not hold a nominating convention and could not choose a candidate. Four ran for the presidency, creating a wide path for Van Buren, who took office in March 1837. Five weeks later, the nation fell into a financial disaster. By the fall, "nine out of ten eastern factories had closed" in what came to be called the Panic of 1837 (225). It led to "a decade of despair" called "The Hungry Forties" (225). Whigs blamed Van Buren, though the depression was the result of Jackson's policies—largely, his decision to leave the banking industry unregulated. However, the panic did democratize bankruptcy protection and abolished all debtors' prisons. Americans came to see those who fell into debt as "victims of the business cycle" (226). Still, Van Buren, who had been nicknamed "Martin Van Ruin" stood no chance at reelection in 1840.

The Whigs nominated William Henry Harrison as their candidate and "ran him as a war hero" and "a frontiersman," which was not true (227). Harrison had been governor of Indiana Territory and was sired by a Virginia plantation owner who had signed the Declaration of Independence. His campaign biographer, however, portrayed him as a humble farmer of modest origins. Harrison said little publicly, earning the moniker "General Mum." Whigs called him the "Log Cabin Candidate" because he "campaigned in log cabins mounted on wheels" and "hand[ed] out mugs of hard cider along the road" (227).

Neither the Whigs nor the Democrats addressed the question of slavery. As a result, new parties were founded to do so. The

Whigs, however, welcomed white women into their ranks, while the Democrats banned them. More men were now voting. Voter turnout was up to 80% in 1840. Harrison won in a landslide election. He then died of pneumonia soon after he was elected. His vice president, John Tyler, rose to the presidency.

That December, telegraph wires were "installed along lines cut by train tracks through woods and meadows and even mountains" (229). American began imagining a nation in which railroads and telegraph wires extended across the continent. The telegraph allowed news to spread immediately. Around this time, in Paris, a philosopher named Karl Marx began to imagine the consequences of capitalism. In the US, questions about people and products always led back to slavery and the commodification of people.

Lepore describes the start of the 19th century as an era in which Americans heralded the arrival of popular democracy. This was also an era in which slavery became more deeply entrenched into the national character, while the treaty rights of indigenous tribes were overridden by the ambitions of Manifest Destiny.

Lepore also examines the impact of early industrialism in forming the working and middle classes. In her depiction of the early employment of young, working-class women in Lowell textile mills, Lepore describes how the owners and managers of those factories exploited female labor, but she does not provide any accounts of the dangers that women faced in these factories. With little concern over workplace safety, young women often suffered serious injuries, such as having their hair caught in and ripped out by the machines. The practice among employers of supplying laborers with alcohol coincided with exploitation, as inebriated workers were less likely to be resistant.

Lepore briefly illustrates the division of labor in the 19th century—the Victorian Era—into domestic and non-domestic work. Domestic duties—particularly, cooking and childrearing—were unpaid tasks performed by women who, as a marker of their class status, did not work outside of the home or occupy the public sphere. The middle class, Lepore explains, became a cultural influence during this period, starting with the temperance movement, which would become a plank in the suffragists' political platform.

Criticism of the Founding Fathers also emerged during this period, particularly among abolitionists who pointed out the hypocrisy of sanctioning slavery while claiming to found a nation based on democratic principles. This uproar coincided with the emergence of the African American church as a space in which to voice protest. Indeed, there were chinks in the new democracy's armor: the increased oppression of enslaved peoples, particularly restrictions on their movement and access to printed material; the role of women in social reform, despite the unacceptability of women's presence in the public sphere; classism and the reluctance to absorb immigrants from Germany and Ireland; and concern over the increased presence of Catholics in a Protestant nation. The last point reiterates the establishment of early America as a Protestant refuge from religious oppression in Europe and the religious wars that ensued after the Protestant Reformation. Ironically, Americans would then persecute those who did not follow the common religion.

Education became a key tool in trying to eliminate partisanship and sectionalism, in the interest of forming a common culture. However, the exclusion of African Americans from public schools reveals a concerted effort to marginalize them from the common culture. Generally, there was increased interest among Americans in knowing what was true in current events, as well as the stances of political parties. The populace was becoming increasingly astute about politics.

The eagerness to form a common culture also influenced attempts to assimilate some indigenous tribes. The Cherokee Nation's fight for political and cultural autonomy was overwhelmed by the predominance of white settlers, who exercised their demographic, political, and military power to drive the Cherokee and other tribes westward. Additionally, the introduction of the telegraph was also instrumental in forming a common culture. The telegraph both succeeded and surpassed the printing press as the key means of communication in the century, connecting Americans faster and across great distances.

Part 2, Chapter 7 Summary and Analysis: "Of Ships and Shipwrecks"

The US Senate was preparing "to vote on a treaty to annex Texas" (232). Mexico, however, still regarded Texas as one of its provinces. Abel Upshur, John Tyler's secretary of state, knew that if the Senate approved Sam Houston's request for annexation, Mexico might declare war on the US.

Tyler had banked his presidency, which had been weak from the beginning, on annexation. He was a Southern aristocrat who disliked Jacksonian populism. He had no true party. He was nominated as William Henry Harrison's running mate, as he had been a vociferous critic of both Jackson and Van Buren. No one questioned him on his politics, and no one knew much about them. The Whigs simply hoped that he could carry his critical home state of Virginia.

President Tyler, however, was a strong believer in states' rights and disliked anything that was nationalized, particularly the federal bank. After Congress twice passed legislation to renew the national bank's charter, Tyler twice vetoed it. By September, everyone in Tyler's cabinet, except for his secretary of state, Daniel Webster, resigned in protest. Two days later, 50 Whigs gathered in front of the Capitol and banished Tyler from the party. Some protestors gathered in front of the White House. Concerned for his safety, Tyler set up a police force that later became the Secret Service. After Webster finally resigned in May 1843 to protest plans to annex Texas, Abel Upshur became secretary of state.

Upshur, like Tyler, was a Southern aristocrat. He also believed that slavery was useful in that it helped even the lowliest white man feel better about his circumstances. Tyler and Upshur both believed that the nation's stability rested on its expansion. At the time, both Britain and the US claimed the Oregon Territory. Upshur worried that Britain would try to extend its borders to the south. The foreign nation had been selling Mexico steam-powered ships, and offered to purchase California. Upshur also believed that Britain offered loans to Texas, in exchange for its promise to abolish slavery. Tyler then decided to annex to Texas and have it join the Union as a slave state, while Oregon would be admitted as a free state. Tyler and Upshur avoided language related to slavery, however, and focused on notions of liberty. They reasoned that the acquisition of new territory would offer economic opportunities to the poor, as anyone could be employed to clear the land. More people also talked of the west as a "safety valve"—a place to relieve the pressures that existed in other places. One Democratic senator from South Carolina declared in 1844 that Texas would relieve the current slaveholding states from his overabundant slave population.

Abel Upshur died on February 28, 1844, during an accident aboard the USS *Princeton*. Tyler appointed John C. Calhoun to replace him. John Quincy Adams, now 76, warned that the North might secede if Texas were annexed. Calhoun, in a riposte, said that the South might have seceded if Texas were not annexed. The Senate ultimately failed to ratify the treaty to annex Texas "by a vote of 35 to 16" (236).

Tyler, unwanted by all parties, decided to run for reelection, wedding himself to the fate of Texas's annexation. Still, he hoped to convince the Democrats to nominate him at their convention. Andrew Jackson, who still controlled the party, had changed his mind about annexing Texas. He endorsed James K. Polk, a loyalist from the Southwest. Formerly a Speaker of the House and governor of Tennessee, Polk was largely unknown. Tyler dropped out of the race, assured that the Democrats would push for annexation.

Meanwhile, Henry Clay fulfilled long-term presidential ambitions. He had already run three times when the Whigs chose him again. He opposed the annexation of Texas, but his opposition was not strong enough to hold on to Whigs who left the party in favor of the antislavery Liberty Party. The race between Clay and Polk was very close, but Polk won the popular vote.

On January 25, 1845, a majority of the House voted for a resolution in favor of annexation, "having devised a compromise under which the eastern portion of Texas would enter the Union as a slave state, but not the western portion" (238). The Senate narrowly passed it. Tyler signed it on March 1, three days before Polk was inaugurated.

In the 1840s and 1850s, westward expansion, more than abolition, was the question that pressed the public to determine the constitutionality of slavery. While antislavery activists condemned "the annexation of Texas as an extension of the slave power," others, including former congressman and secretary of state Daniel Webster, "called it an act of imperialism, inconsistent with a republican form of government" (241). In the end, however, it was the expansion of the Union, which resulted in its splintering, that helped end slavery. Polk was more determined than any previous president in the nation's expansion. He wanted to admit Florida as a slave state and, hopefully, Cuba. Spain angrily refused to cede Cuba. Polk focused his attention, instead, on Oregon Territory, which then included what would later become Oregon, Idaho, Washington, "and much of what later became Montana and Wyoming" (242). Other nations, including Britain and Mexico, had tried to claim the territory. Americans claimed it by settling there, moving steadily westward along the Oregon Trail. In 1843, around 800 Americans traveled the route, which was a series of old roads that cut through mountains and across valleys.

Polk next sent an envoy to Mexico with $25 million to buy New Mexico and parts of what would later become Arizona, Nevada, Wyoming, Colorado, and Utah. He also sought to purchase the Nueces Strip—a disputed piece of land claimed by both Mexico and Texas. When Mexico refused to make an agreement with Polk's envoys, he sent troops into the Nueces Strip. Zachary Taylor led the soldiers, who settled along the Rio Grande. Polk got the confrontation that he sought to provoke. During one skirmish on April 25, 1846, Mexican soldiers killed 11 US troops.

Polk asked Congress to declare war on Mexico, claiming that they had invaded the nation and shed American blood on American soil. In Congress, Abraham Lincoln, then a representative from Illinois, introduced resolutions in which he demanded to know the exact spot where American blood had been shed. Congress sided with Polk and granted the president his declaration of war.

There were also battles within the halls of Congress between 1830 and 1860. Southern congressman traveled to work with bowie knives and pistols. Northerners arrived at the Capitol unarmed. Meanwhile, questions lingered around Mexico. If, for instance, the US were to acquire Mexican territory, would its inhabitants become American citizens? John C. Calhoun, now a senator, was vehemently opposed to this, insisting that theirs was a "government of the white man" (244). Also, would these former Mexican territories become slave states or free states? David Wilmot, a Democratic congressman from Pennsylvania, lent his name to what became the Wilmot Proviso—an agreement that slavery would not exist in any territories acquired as a result of the Mexican-American War. The Wilmot Proviso passed in 1846.

Both Wilmot and Calhoun were interested in the rights of white men. Wilmot was trying to preserve the integrity of free white labor. The nation began to break apart over its war with Mexico, with some coming to believe that the Union's preservation depended on machines. Railroads and, particularly, telegraphs were essential in connecting people in an expanding nation.

In February 1847, US troops defeated the Mexican army. By the summer, Mexico was ready to negotiate a peace. Polk, knowing that he had the upper hand, thought about trying to annex all of

Mexico. In the end, Mexico gave up over half of its land. Mexican nationals faced the choice between either crossing back into Mexico and retaining their citizenship or becoming American citizens. Around 100,000 Mexicans chose to stay in what became the US, most of them in Texas and California, where they faced increasing racial hostility. Their economy, which was based in ranching and trading, was gradually replaced by commercial agriculture, industrial production, and prospecting. The war ended on February 2, 1848, with the Treaty of Guadalupe Hidalgo. The US population swelled to 23.2 million. With the acquisition of Mexican territory, the nation's size grew by 64%.

Polk, when he ran for president, promised to serve only one term. Democrats were unsure about whom to select as his replacement. They needed a candidate who would attract both Northern and Southern voters. They thought about James Buchanan, who had served as Polk's secretary of state. Buchanan suggested extending the Missouri Compromise westward. Senator Lewis Cass, who had served as President Jackson's secretary of war, believed that each state ought to decide whether it would permit or prohibit slavery. Cass prevailed and became the Democrats' nominee.

The Whig Party chose Zachary Taylor, who only grudgingly joined the party. However, these candidates were unappealing to voters who opposed the extension of slavery into Western territories. In June 1848, some of these voters held a convention in Buffalo at which they formed the Free-Soil Party. They chose Martin Van Buren as their candidate. The Free-Soil movement was also tied to free speech, disputes over interpretations of the Constitution, and the revolutions of 1848 in Europe. The Free-Soilers, like the revolutionaries, were concerned with labor—in the US, this meant the difference between free labor and slave power, which had fostered a decadent Southern aristocracy. The Free-Soil movement got much of its support from working men in Eastern cities and farmers in the West, as well as free Black people. Much of the party's rhetoric came from Transcendentalism.

The attacks from Free-Soilers led Southerners to work more strongly to preserve their way of life. They accused Northerners and their system of wage labor of being more exploitative than slavery. The latter, they argued, was "fundamental to American prosperity" (255). They also argued more vociferously for more stringent notions of racial difference. Many of their ideas came from the pseudoscientific field of ethnology.

The Free-Soil Party held its first convention in Buffalo in the summer of 1848. The party's support among women helped lead to the Seneca Falls Convention, which also took place in Buffalo that summer. A Whig newspaper declared the convention a "shocking and unnatural incident" (257).

By the mid-19th century, the debate over slavery reached the Pacific coast. Then, in 1850, there was a gold rush in California. Migrants came from neighboring Oregon and as far away as Chile and China to prospect. A year before, a state constitutional convention declared that slavery would never exist in the state. In the fall of 1849, California sent Congress a request to enter the Union. It would be admitted as a free state. To appease proslavery factions, settlers of New Mexico, Utah, Arizona, and Nevada were allowed to resolve for themselves whether or not they wanted slavery. In 1851, Free-Soiler Charles Sumner won the Massachusetts senate seat that Daniel Webster, who had devised the Compromise of 1850 that sought to diffuse tensions between slave states and free states, had long held. Sumner, an antislavery advocate, despised the Compromise, which further imperiled enslaved Black people who escaped to the North.

Meanwhile, conversations about a transcontinental railroad, which had been a matter of discussion since the 1830s, continued. Senator Stephen Douglas wanted the railroad to run through Chicago, but "so-called Permanent Indian Territory," the land to which Jackson had displaced indigenous tribes, stood in the way (262). Douglas insisted that, in an expanding and modernizing nation, the maintenance of such a territory was absurd. He insisted that the territory should be removed. It was organized into what became Kansas and Nebraska. The people of those new states would decide whether or not they wanted slavery.

Left to decide the slavery issue for itself, Kansas broke out into war, earning the nickname "Bleeding Kansas." Southerners moved into Kansas to vote for it to become a slave state, while Northerners moved in to vote against it. Soon they began trying to kill each other. In May 1856, Charles Sumner, in a speech entitled "The Crime Against Kansas," condemned slavery and warned of civil war. Two days later, Congressman Preston Brooks, a cousin of the South Carolina senator who had cowritten the Kansas-Nebraska Act with Stephen Douglas, beat Sumner with his cane. It took Sumner three years to recover from his head injuries. While he recovered, his Senate seat remained empty, as Massachusetts refused to elect a replacement. It became clear that the South could not tolerate free speech.

By then, the Whig Party was nearly dead. The Democrats nominated James Buchanan, a proslavery Northerner. He had served as ambassador to Great Britain, which made him seem distant from the violence that had broken out within the US. He campaigned against the explorer John C. Frémont and won by a landslide.

Buchanan's presidential inauguration was the first to be photographed. He was sworn in on March 4, 1857, by Chief Justice Roger Taney. In his address, Buchanan trivialized slavery, claiming that there were more pressing and practical questions to resolve.

In this chapter, Lepore illustrates how American expansion into the West deepened the nation's regional divisions, particularly divergent views about the future of slavery in the growing union. The expansion of the US into formerly Mexican territory was the fulfillment of the nation's ambitions of Manifest Destiny. Many viewed the West as a "safety valve" that would relieve Eastern cities of their growing immigrant populations and the South of increasing slave populations. These demographic struggles revealed both the Union's difficulty with absorbing new populations and how the South's greed and dependence on slavery overwhelmed them politically and socially.

The acquisition of territory won from Mexico and the inevitable integration of Mexicans into the American populace led to stricter classifications regarding who would qualify as "white." Since the Age of Exploration, the descendants of Spanish colonists had been regarded as lesser peoples by the English and their descendants, due to their embrace of intermarriage.

Meanwhile, controversy ensued over the nature of labor and the desire of some politicians to preserve what they believed was the natural integrity of white male labor—that is, they were averse to policies that would exploit white men of the working class in the ways enslaved Black people and even working-class white women were exploited. White manhood was the default standard for humanity—a view that was supported by the racial pseudoscience invented to justify both slavery and Europe's developing interests in imperialism.

Despite the more intense, and often violent, sectarian strife that erupted in the US, President Buchanan denied that slavery was the root cause of the nation's divisions. This pattern of denial, which helped lead to the Civil War, had existed since the nation's founding (e.g., James Madison's aversion to mentioning slavery in the Constitution) and has continued to impact contemporary conversations about the causes of the Civil War.

Part 2, Chapter 8 Summary and Analysis: "The Face of Battle"

In March 1839, Samuel Morse, on a trip to Europe, visited the Parisian studio of fellow artist and inventor Louis Daguerre. Two months earlier, Daguerre had presented the results of his experiments in photography: pictures that he took by exposing "polished, silver-coated copper sheets" to light (272). The result created a ghostly image. Eight months later, the first photograph seen in the US was displayed in a New York hotel. Studios opened quickly around the country. By the 1850s, 25 million portraits were taken in the US. Photographs were cheap, making it "a technology of democracy" (272). The daguerreotype was quickly abandoned in favor of the paper print. The Civil War would also be the first war to be captured by photography.

On September 1, 1858, New Yorkers held a parade to celebrate the completion of a cable that stretched across the bottom of the

Atlantic Ocean. Morse believed that telegraph technology was the answer to preventing all future wars, which he deemed failures of communication. Several months earlier, the people of Illinois had witnessed the debates between senatorial candidates Abraham Lincoln and Stephen Douglas—what "proved to be the greatest argument over the American experiment since the constitutional convention" (274).

During the Kansas-Nebraska crisis four years earlier, Lincoln and Douglas each gave consecutive opposing speeches, but they never faced each other directly. Around 12,000 people showed up for their first debate on August 21 in Ottawa, Illinois. The audience stood, as there were no seats, for three hours. The rules were strict: The first speaker would talk for an hour, while the second would speak for 90 minutes; then, the first speaker would provide a 30-minute rebuttal. The debate was largely about Lincoln's opposition to the Dred Scott decision, and the candidates' respective interpretations of the Declaration of Independence and Constitution. Douglas insisted that both documents applied only to white men, and that the nation was made only for white men. Lincoln insisted that he had no interest in interfering with slavery in the states in which the institution existed. He also did not believe in fostering the social and political equality of Black and white people. However, he saw no reason why Black people should not be entitled "to all the natural rights enumerated in the Declaration of Independence" (278).

Crowds watched the debates as though they were at a boxing match. The final debate took place in Alton, Illinois, on October 15. Lincoln narrowly lost the election, but he rose to a position of leadership in the Republican Party.

The year in which the Lincoln-Douglas debates took place, abolitionist John Brown held a constitutional convention in Canada at a final stop on the Underground Railroad. Slave states became more rabid in their determination to hold onto their human chattel, particularly because the price of slaves had significantly risen between 1850 and 1860. Southerners were now less concerned about slave rebellions than they were about "a mass exodus from slave states to free" (280).

Concerned about this mass exodus, some slave states, such as Arkansas, tried to ban the presence of free Black people. Other states, particularly Oregon, tried to adopt a whites-only policy, restricting the increasing number of Chinese immigrants. To profit from the exorbitantly high price of slaves, some white Southerners tried to reopen the African slave trade. South Carolina and Louisiana led the charge.

Most Americans, by mid-century, agreed with Lincoln that the country "would either be one thing or another" (282). John Brown, too, insisted that the conflict between slavery and freedom was unavoidable, and believed that he should ignite it. On the evening of October 16, 1859, Brown and 21 men attacked Harper's Ferry, Virginia, and captured it. Passengers on a train speeding toward Baltimore tossed notes out of the windows, warning people about the rebellion. Half a day after the raid started, a telegraph went across the continent, spreading news of the insurrection. Brown had hoped that the news would prompt Black people to take up arms, resulting in a revolution throughout the South. However, enslaved people, largely isolated from telegraph technology, were unaware of any uprising. Soldiers led by Robert E. Lee took back the arsenal, captured Brown, and captured or killed all of his cohorts. Lee concluded that Brown was either "a fanatic or a madman" (283).

Northern abolitionists who had funded Brown's effort denied involvement, but many believed that Brown's death signaled the beginning of another American Revolution. On the day of John Brown's funeral, Mississippi congressman Reuben Davis told Congress that the South would sever ties with the Union if that was what would be required to protect their honor and secure their rights.

Several weeks after Davis's warning, Abraham Lincoln posed for a photograph at Mathew Brady's studio in New York. Later that day, he gave a speech at Cooper Union that launched his presidential campaign. His new portrait was used in a presidential campaign button. Lincoln made the interpretation of the Constitution a fundamental plank on his platform, arguing that Stephen Douglas's interpretation was incorrect. He next edited and published his debates with Douglas as *Political Debates Between Hon. Abraham Lincoln and Hon. Stephen A. Douglas*, first advertising the volume 11 days before the Republican National Convention. When he was invited places to speak, audiences often asked Lincoln to read from *Debates* instead. Douglas often complained that his speeches had been "mutilated" by Lincoln.

In April, the Democratic Party held its national convention in Charleston, South Carolina. Several state delegations, including those of Alabama, Texas, and Florida walked out "in protest of the platform's failure to include a guarantee of the rights of citizens to hold [slaves]" (286). Unable to nominate a presidential candidate, they held a second convention in Baltimore two months later.

The Republican Party held its convention in Chicago in May. Lincoln won the presidential nomination to thundering applause.

Poet William Dean Howells, then only 23, was commissioned to write a campaign biography for Lincoln. He completed *Life of Abraham Lincoln* in weeks, though he had never met Lincoln and knew little about him. Predictably, he told numerous tall tales that offered a grandiose vision of the presidential candidate.

The second Democratic National Convention was even more disastrous. One delegate pulled a pistol on another. The convention was deadlocked yet again on the nomination. Then the party split, with the South walking out. Ultimately, Stephen Douglas become the nominee of the Northern Democratic Party, while the Southern Democratic Party nominated John C. Breckinridge, a US senator from Kentucky. During the election, Lincoln won every Northern state and all four states in which Black men could vote. He hardly won any votes in the South. In the North, his election led to attacks on abolitionists. Southerners began to support secession more fervently. In February 1861, seven Southern states, led by South Carolina, formed the Confederate States of America and elected as president a former US senator from Mississippi, Jefferson Davis, who argued that only the Confederacy had remained "true to the original Constitution" (289). When they adopted their own Constitution, they created one that mirrored the Articles of Confederation— that is, a document that allowed states to remain largely sovereign. Alexander Stephens was the Confederacy's vice president. He emphasized the new government's foundational idea: Black people were not the equals of white people, and that slavery is the "natural and moral condition" for those of African descent (290).

Lincoln was inaugurated on March 4, 1861, and sworn in by Chief Justice Roger Taney. In his inaugural address, Lincoln addressed the rift that had divided the nation and rooted its cause in slavery—"the only substantial dispute" (290). He retained hope that the dispute could be resolved through debate. However, slave owners had long opposed free speech. They had enforced gag rules, postal bans, antiliteracy laws, and the suppression of public speakers. Censorship was key to building and maintaining support for the "modern, proslavery, antidemocratic state" they were attempting to build (291). The strongest supporters of secession were wealthy planters while the least fervent supporters were poor white men who did not own slaves. The latter comprised the majority of white male voters, and the way to persuade them to support the interests of the former was to remind them that the existence of slavery spared them from the most demeaning work. Georgia passed a law that enforced the death penalty for those who dissented. Four states in the upper South, including Virginia, did not secede until Confederate forces fired on US troops at Fort Sumter in South Carolina on April 12, 1861. After this occurred, Lincoln had all telegraph wires that connected the capital to the South severed.

By May, 15 states and 12 million people, a quarter of whom were enslaved, made up the Confederacy. The Civil War, when it broke out after the firing on Fort Sumter, ushered "a new kind of war, with giant armies wielding unstoppable machines" (293). Both sides expected the war to be brief. Instead, 200 battles occurred over four years. Over 750,000 Americans died. Twice that number died from battle wounds. Their misery was captured, for the first time, on camera.

The Civil War's turning point came on July 1, 1863, at the Battle of Gettysburg in Pennsylvania. By the third day, each side had lost over 20,000 soldiers. Robert E. Lee began his retreat. Four months later, Lincoln traveled to Gettysburg. He saw thousands of corpses, barely covered by soil. The War Department provided caskets and ensured that every corpse was "uncovered, sorted, and catalogued" (295). Lincoln was invited to dedicate the burials of the fallen men. He spoke for only three minutes, focusing not on slavery, but on his insistence that the dead did not die in vain.

On September 22, 1862, Lincoln announced that he would free every enslaved person held in the Confederacy on New Year's Day 1863. Lincoln read a draft of the Emancipation Proclamation on December 29. The declaration did not free slaves in states that had remained in the Union. Lincoln signed the Emancipation Proclamation on January 1, as promised. Shortly thereafter, formerly enslaved Black people left plantations and began to look for long-lost relatives.

On March 2, 1863, Frederick Douglass called on Black men to fight for the Union army. The year before, Congress had lifted a ban on Black men joining the military. After emancipation, Douglass began traveling through the North, recruiting for the 54th Massachusetts Infantry—an all-Black regiment. The Confederacy, meanwhile, had instituted the first draft. They called upon 85% of men, most of whom were married, leaving their families at risk of poverty and famine. The Confederate government then passed a "one-tenth tax" that required citizens to give the state 10% of everything they grew or raised on farms. Still short on both manpower and supplies, the Confederate army began to enlist slaves as soldiers, "to the great dismay of many Confederate soldiers" (300).

The Union followed suit with the draft. In July 1863, white New Yorkers protested "during five days of violent riots that mainly involved attacking the city's blacks" (300). They lynched 11 Black men and set the Colored Orphan Asylum on fire.

The Civil War expanded the government's powers through precedents set in both the North and the South. These powers included conscription, income taxes, welfare programs, and the printing of currency. In 1862, Lincoln signed a law that established an Internal Revenue Bureau, which was in charge of "administering an income tax" (300). The Confederacy, however, was reluctant to levy taxes, leaving them unable to raise enough money for the war. This was one reason why they lost.

While Confederate soldiers claimed that they were fighting to protect their homes and wives, Confederate women entered the political arena to petition the government for relief. Arguing that they had sacrificed their men to the war cause, hundreds of female mobs, "armed with knives and guns" took part in around 12 riots in Atlanta, Mobile, and Richmond, demanding bread (302). Their protests resulted in a system of state welfare, which led to the modern welfare state. The foundation for modern welfare was established by white, Southern women.

In the first years of the Civil War, Lincoln had insisted that the war's purpose was to save the Union. By 1864, he believed that the abolition of slavery was essential to the Union's victory. He realized that the nation would need a constitutional amendment. Elizabeth Cady Stanton and Susan B. Anthony were among those who knocked on doors and gathered signatures for passage of the 13th Amendment, which fell 13 votes short of the necessary two-thirds majority required in the House.

Lincoln decided to run for reelection. His opponent, George McClellan, was weak, allowing Lincoln an easy victory. He won

55% of the vote. After he was reelected, Lincoln pressed the House to pass the 13th Amendment and lobbied senators from border states. It finally passed on January 31, 1865. At his inauguration in March, Lincoln acknowledged slavery as the cause of the war, but hoped that "the scourge of war" would pass speedily (304). On April 9, Confederate General Robert E. Lee surrendered to General Ulysses S. Grant. On April 14, John Wilkes Booth, a well-known Shakespearean actor, shot and killed Lincoln at Ford's Theatre. He had been present at Lincoln's inauguration and was outraged by Lincoln's allowance of Black citizenship. Lincoln died the next morning, the first president to be killed while in office. His body went into a casket and onto a funeral train that went around the country. Meanwhile, states ratified the 13th Amendment on December 6, 1865.

In this chapter, Lepore describes how the emergences of new technologies and reforms impacted both the Civil War and its aftermath. Photography was key in helping marginalized groups, particularly African Americans and indigenous peoples, represent themselves as they were, instead of being reduced to white stereotyping and caricature. Lincoln was particularly adept at using photography to form his public image. He used his photo to self-advertise during his campaign. He also commandeered his published debates with Stephen Douglas and turned them into a campaign tool. He took an impersonal stance on slavery, centering it as a Constitutional argument. Finally, his campaign biography was filled with grandiose legends—a form of mythmaking that placed him alongside the Founding Fathers, particularly Washington.

Lincoln rooted his arguments against slavery in the nation's founding documents and the incongruity between what the country professed to believe about itself and what it practiced.

Contrary to popular belief, Lincoln seemed to have little interest, publicly anyway, in social equality as a principle. Meanwhile, the South worked harder to enforce control of its already enormous and growing Black population. Their solution was to suppress dissent and to restrict the presence of those whom they believed would adversely influence their human chattel.

The inhabitants of Oregon, which became a state in 1859, tried to create a "white utopia"—that is, an environment that effectively excluded African American and Chinese settlers, particularly. The relative dearth of populations of color in the West to date is the result of a legacy of racially hostile practices. Thus, while the South may have codified racial discrimination to maintain its lucrative slaveholding system, it was not unique in its desire to uphold white supremacy.

The Confederacy was founded on the premise that the Southern states ought to remain largely autonomous. The emphasis on states' rights, both before and after the region's secession, was rooted in its desire to conduct slaveholding without interference from a federal government. The entry of Black men into the Civil War as soldiers corroded the myth of docility. By enlisting, they demonstrated their awareness of freedom and their desire for it. Confederates, meanwhile, were dismayed to see enslaved Black men in their ranks, despite the South's desperation for manpower. The rebels' aversion to the presence of Black soldiers reiterates that the goal of most was to fight for a system of white supremacy. Even poor white men had the racial benefit of knowing that they were free men and that their labor had value.

Lepore also shows the reader how welfare benefits originated in aid to Confederate widows. The program was continued during the Progressive Era to benefit white women who were widowed. It enjoyed popularity for as long as it was limited to this group. Welfare would not become a political bogeyman until the mid-20th century when Black women made use of the program.

Part 3

Part 3: The State (1866-1945)

Part 3, Chapter 9 Summary and Analysis: "Of Citizens, Persons, and People"

For many years before and after the Civil War, the government had no clear definition of what a citizen was. The nation wondered about what made people citizens and under what conditions residents were not citizens. Additionally, one wondered about "the privileges and immunities of citizenship" (313). In the 19th century, political theorists and politicians began to interpret citizenship within the contexts of human rights and state authority. Other questions, however, also emerged: Were women citizens? Was suffrage a right available only to certain citizens? Were the Chinese immigrants populating the West citizens like "free white persons" or "free persons of color?" Or were they something else entirely?

After the Union defeated the Confederacy, it set about guaranteeing civil rights to newly freed Black Southerners. Edwin Stanton, Lincoln's secretary of war, established the American Freedmen's Inquiry Commission in 1863. Later, the Bureau of Refugees, Freedmen, and Abandoned Lands, best known as the Freedmen's Bureau, provided food and clothing to refugees. The bureau also aided in their resettlement. Rumors spread that the bureau also intended to provide those formerly enslaved with 40 acres and a mule. As for the Confederacy, Congressman

Thaddeus Stevens insisted that the South had to be treated as conquered territory—thus, its foundational institutions would have to be reformed. Lincoln instead proposed a 10% plan that would pardon Confederate leaders and allow each state to reenter the union after 10% of their voters took a pledge of allegiance. Radical Republicans rejected that. They drafted the Wade-Davis Bill at the end of 1864, demanding a majority of Southerners swear that they had never supported the Confederacy, thereby disenfranchising "all former Confederate leaders and soldiers" (317). Lincoln vetoed the bill. He did, however, agree to install military rule in the former Confederacy. After Lincoln's assassination, Andrew Johnson turned course. He wanted to bring the Southern states back into the Union as quickly as possible. He allowed them to decide for themselves on matters of citizenship and civil rights.

In the winter of 1865-66, Southern legislatures began to pass "black codes," or race-based laws that perpetuated de facto slavery through "indentures, sharecropping, and other forms of servitude" (318). In South Carolina, Black parents who refused to teach their children to conform to these systems risked having them taken away and placed with white families, where they were forced to labor. Later in 1866, the Ku Klux Klan formed in Tennessee. Founded by Confederate veterans, they dressed in white, to appear as "ghosts" of the Confederate dead. Lepore likens them instead to "the armed militias that had long served as slave patrols that […] had terrorized men, women, and children with fires, ropes, and guns" (319).

On February 2, 1866, the Senate passed the Civil Rights Act, which was "the first federal law to define citizenship" (319). It declared that all citizens had "a right to equal protection under the law" (319). It also extended the Freedmen's Bureau. A month later, President Johnson vetoed the act. Congress then overrode his veto. Johnson was unable to triumph over the Radical Republicans who dominated Congress. That coterie of politicians next set to work on the 14th and 15th Amendments, which would prevent the disenfranchisement of the newly freed and guarantee equal protection under the law. While drafting the 15th Amendment, however, its architects attempted to include a provision that specified voters as male. Women protested it. Senator Charles Sumner claimed that the nation's leadership knew how Black men would vote, but not Black women. The matter would be revisited a century later, when Congress debated the Civil Rights Act of 1964. Meanwhile, the fight for women's rights became one over women's suffrage.

Additionally, Radical Republicans passed four Reconstruction Acts. President Johnson vetoed all four. Congress overrode all four. The acts "divided the former Confederacy into five military districts, each ruled by a military general" (322). Each former secessionist state had to draft a new constitution to be sent to Congress for approval. Also, each state had to ratify the 14th Amendment to be readmitted to the Union; and, while former Confederate soldiers could not vote, formerly enslaved men could.

However, as the Ku Klux Klan grew, Black enfranchisement was compromised. Black men often went to the polls in groups. Black men also began to fill public offices. In Louisiana, a Black man served, briefly, as governor. In South Carolina, for a time, the legislature was almost entirely Black, as was the ancillary staff. The House initiated impeachment proceedings against Johnson, the first time a president had ever been impeached, "charging him with violating a recently passed Tenure of Office Act" (323).

The 14th Amendment was ratified in the summer of 1868. Black men voted in droves for the Republican presidential nominee Ulysses S. Grant. In 1868, Black and white women, partners in a plan called New Departure, went to the polls and tried to vote. They were arrested. As the decade ended, it became more difficult for Black men to vote.

While Black people, newly freed, sought to become citizens, newly arrived Chinese immigrants sought to achieve the same goal. They had begun arriving in the 1850s, shortly after the gold rush. Most of them were men. They first landed in California, then moved into the Mountain West. They initially worked in mining, but many were forced out of the industry. Some mined into the 1880s, often working at sites that had been abandoned. The Chinese began to settle Boise in 1865 and made up both "a third of Idaho's settlers and nearly 60 percent of its miners" (325). Their rights, however, were often limited. A provision in Oregon's 1857 constitution forbade the Chinese from owning property, while California barred them from testifying in court. An 1854 California Supreme Court opinion declared them inherently inferior. Their population, however, continued to grow in the 1860s.

In 1869, the 15th Amendment, intended to guarantee African Americans suffrage, was drafted. It also inspired questions about Chinese citizenship and voting rights. Ultimately, the amendment "neither settled nor addressed the question of whether Chinese immigrants could become citizens" (327). Congress simultaneously passed acts that made it illegal to interfere with Black suffrage. In response, the Ku Klux Klan only stepped up its efforts to restore white supremacy in the South. The 15th Amendment also didn't address the question of women's suffrage, though it inspired women to "test the limits of female citizenship not only by voting but also by running for office," starting with Victoria Woodhull, the first women to run for president (327).

Reconstruction had failed. President Grant, who had served two terms, ended all bids for the presidency in 1876. White Democrats, who called themselves "Redeemers," succeeded in taking back power in the South, thereby ending Black men's disenfranchisement through terrorism. Over 3,000 Black men and women were lynched throughout the South between 1882 and 1930. Meanwhile, legislatures passed the first Jim Crow laws, segregating Black people from white people in most public spaces. Tennessee passed the nation's first Jim Crow law in 1881, enforcing segregated railcars.

Men's electoral politics became domesticated in this era, while those of women moved into the public arena. At their marches, suffragists used "the sermon, the appeal, the conversion," all of which would become features of "the modern conservative movement" (332). Republicans hastened to bring the West into the Union, speedily creating new states and passing the Homestead Act, the Pacific Railway Act, and the National Bank Act in 1862. The last paid for the Pacific rail line that would be constructed from Omaha to Sacramento. To open land for the railroad, the federal government suppressed insurrections by indigenous people. The railroads allowed for the cattle industry to grow, as it became possible to carry herds to major Midwestern cities, including Chicago and St. Louis.

These land and railroad projects required massive spending, which led to excessive borrowing, as well as corruption. In 1873, there was a financial disaster. Farmers banded together in response, forming a populist revolt. They demanded "cooperative farming and the regulation of banks and railroads," as well as "an end to corporate monopolies" (335). They formed the National Farmers' Alliance in Texas in 1877, but they excluded African Americans, who formed their own alliance—the Colored Farmers' Alliance.

Finance capitalism was ushering in the Gilded Age, an era of massive economic development in railroads, steel, and agriculture. White workers who revolted against capitalists also raised their fists against Chinese immigrants, resulting in the Chinese Exclusion Act. There were labor strikes in response to wage cuts. President Rutherford B. Hayes sent in federal troops to put them down, resulting in the first use of federal power to support business interests. Between 1881 and 1894, there was typically one massive railroad strike each week. Ironically, corporations began to use the 14th Amendment to define themselves as persons protected from government regulation.

As the suffering of laborers and farmers increased, the populist movement grew. The People's Party, formed by Henry George and Mary Lease, held its first convention in Kansas in 1890. It became the most successful third party in American history. Their platform was an opposition to monopoly. By the turn of the century, the wealthiest 1% of Americans owned more than half of the nation's wealth. Despite its advocacy for the lowly, the People's Party still sought to exclude anyone who was not white from full citizenship. Anti-Semitism was also rife within their ranks. They instituted numerous reforms with the intent of disenfranchising Black people and immigrants, who were less likely to be literate in English. One such reform was the introduction of the Australian ballot—or the secret ballot. Kentucky was the first to adopt it in 1888. Massachusetts adopted it the following year, with the likely intention of trying to suppress the votes of new immigrants who tended be Democrats. Mississippi, in 1890, passed an "Understanding Clause," which demanded that new voters be well versed in the Constitution. The assumption was that Black voters would not be. Of course, white voters were not either, but they were not required to undergo the oral examination. Suffrage tests and intimidation in the South resulted in stark drops in Black enfranchisement.

Another major populist reform, this one led by William Jennings Bryan, was the income tax. The tax was a means of addressing income inequality. Other planks on the populist platform included the eight-hour workday, public ownership of railroads, and the direct election of US senators, who were then still elected by state legislatures. Female suffrage was not a party concern. In 1892, the Kansas People's Party, in an effort for survival, merged with the Democratic Party, despite Mary Lease's opposition. She began leaning further toward socialism anyway. In 1894, Bryan included an income tax amendment in a tariff bill, which passed. The following year, the Supreme Court declared the tax unconstitutional, with one justice calling it an attack against the rich.

As populism rose, the state became a matter of academic study. By the 1860s, universities became secularized and based their construction on the German educational model, which divided colleges and universities into departments and disciplines, instead of having branches of scholarship guided by religion, as they had been previously.

Populism changed the press, too. By the 1880s, the journalist had become a kind of political scientist. Joseph Pulitzer and

William Randolph Hearst turned newspaper journalism into a major business.

Bryan, meanwhile, ran for president against former Ohio governor William McKinley. McKinley ran a new-style campaign, using massive campaign funds, including a donation from John D. Rockefeller, to advertise. Bryan ran an old-style campaign marked by public appearances. McKinley won.

In 1893, American celebrated the anniversary of Columbus's first voyage to North America with "the largest-ever world's fair, the Columbian Exposition" (353). A major feature of the fair were human zoos in which 400 indigenous people were on display. There were Black people featured there, too, some of them former slaves. Either they "sold miniature bales of cotton" as souvenirs or were "posed in a fake African village" (355). Three years later, the Supreme Court decided in *Plessy v. Ferguson* that Jim Crow laws did not violate the Constitution.

This chapter deals with the question of citizenship, particularly the importance of race and gender in determining one's citizenship and participation in American society.

The Union struggled, particularly, with the integration of African Americans, long viewed as both property and semi-human, as citizens with rights under the law. Lepore undoes a common myth by explaining that the promise of "40 acres and a mule" as reparations to newly freed Southern Black people seemed to be a rumor and not an official Reconstruction policy. While "40 acres and a mule" was supposedly only a rumor, President Lincoln had signed the Homestead Act on May 20, 1862. On January 1, 1863, Daniel Freeman, a Civil War veteran from Illinois, made the first land claim under the act, which allowed

American citizens and future citizens up to 160 acres of land. They would receive this parcel of land in exchange for living on the land, cultivating it, and paying a small registration fee. The fee likely eliminated many newly freed African Americans who were penniless. Again, in the Homestead Act, the question of citizenship arose. Who were American citizens, and who were likely to become citizens?

To open land for the Pacific Railroad, the federal government allowed for the slaughter of the buffalo herds on which Western indigenous tribes depended for survival. Lepore does not mention this, but it is implied in her mention of insurrections by indigenous peoples, which were a backlash to encroaching white settlements and flagrant indifference to the treaty rights of indigenous peoples.

President Lincoln's choice to veto the Wade-Davis Bill was the result, perhaps, of not wishing to dishonor and humiliate the South or to take away the citizenship of former Confederates. Instead, he seemed to treat the Confederacy as wayward children who were to be accepted back into the national fold with forgiveness. This stance aligns with Lincoln's expressed view on the campaign trail that his wish to end slavery was not the result of any malice toward the Southern way of life, and certainly not the result of a wish to treat Black people as the equals of white people, but to help the nation more faithfully live up to its democratic principles.

Conversely, Lincoln's successor, Andrew Johnson, demonstrated an allegiance to white supremacy that included a wish to remain as faithful as possible to the antebellum social order. Johnson, who had worked as an indentured servant before becoming a slave owner, professed that he was an advocate for the "common man." He, like many poor white people, resented the wealthy planters and distrusted Black people. He believed in the formation of a society in which the lowliest white man on the social ladder would still be regarded as "superior" to a Black man of any class. He also believed that the Constitution protected white people's presumed right to own slaves. Contrary to the Confederates, Johnson disfavored secession and supported Lincoln's intention to emancipate slaves only as a deterrent to civil war.

The South's swift institution of the Black Codes in response to Reconstruction underscores the region's stubborn interest in preserving the antebellum social order—that is, its commitment to hold to a past that it would mythologize and come to revere as idyllic. Lepore describes how Black people were reassimilated into a system of coerced labor with the threat of having their children taken away from them. These forced adoption programs coincided with those that were foisted upon members of indigenous tribes. While the latter policy was aimed at assimilation into the white mainstream, the former policy's intention was to get Black people to internalize the belief that they existed only to perform manual agrarian labor. To help enforce this system of keeping Black people in place, white vigilante groups, particularly the Ku Klux Klan, arose to instill fear in Black communities and to swiftly punish those who did not abide by the rules of white supremacy.

Meanwhile, women, particularly white women, some of whom had been abolitionists and activists for Black suffrage, now advocated for their own right to vote. Suffragists formed New Departure—a political strategy which claimed that the Constitution granted women suffrage rights. This strategy was ultimately defeated by the Supreme Court, which ruled that, while women were citizens, not everyone who had citizenship was entitled to suffrage rights.

Efforts to disenfranchise the growing Chinese population mirrored oppressive measures used against Black people. The Chinese were refused legal protections and the right to own property—a key building block to prosperity—as they steadily populated the West. In the South, a group of Southern Democrats went by the moniker the "Redeemers" because they sought to redeem the former Confederacy from the control of the federal government and the Radical Republicans. The Redeemers became representative of the Southern Democrats and hastened the failure of Reconstruction as a civil rights initiative.

The People's Party, a conglomeration of the working class and rural voters, expressed a wish to expand the economic participation of citizens as long as those citizens were white. William Jennings Bryan's failure to become president was due to either an inability or an unwillingness to modernize his campaign. Additionally, large donations were either inaccessible or objectionable to him, as that would have departed from his image as a simple man of the people. McKinley's win due to the large donations of men such as Rockefeller was a harbinger of the overwhelming role that big money would come to play in both the course and outcome of campaigns.

Lepore ends this chapter on the rise of modern citizenship with the Columbian Exposition of 1893, which was attended by Frederick Douglass and a then unknown young poet named Paul Laurence Dunbar. The displays that Lepore describes reveal the influences of both scientific racism and imperialism, as well as national nostalgia for the antebellum South. The exposition's transformation of human beings into spectacles mirrored the human zoos that had become popular in Europe. The convention of dehumanizing nonwhite peoples likely impacted the thinking that led to the *Plessy v. Ferguson* decision.

Part 3, Chapter 10 Summary and Analysis: "Efficiency and the Masses"

During the final decades of the 19th century, a handful of people became enormously wealthy due to industrialism; the middle class received cheaper goods; and a wide swath of people became mired in poverty and misery. The power of the federal government grew as corporations grew. So much of American life became "mass." The term "mass production" was created in the 1890s. There was also "mass immigration" at the turn of the century, "mass consumption," and, by 1927, "mass communication" with the invention of the radio. New agencies were formed, including the Coast Guard and the Forest Service. To meet the challenges of the new age, which became known as the Progressive Era, activists created reforms. Their greatest failure, Lepore contends, was the Progressives' unwillingness to address Jim Crow. Arguably, they supported the system of legal segregation.

Progressivism was rooted in 19th-century populism, but "was the middle-class version: indoors, quiet, passionless" (364). They also championed the same causes as Populists, particularly where big business was concerned. Yet, while Populists advocated for less government, Progressives wanted more, believing that government agencies were essential to reform. Much of the Progressivist ethos came from a Protestant movement called the Social Gospel, which was influenced by Henry George's book *Progress and Poverty*.

After losing the 1896 election, William Jennings Bryan devoted himself to the protest of American imperialism. Bryan believed that imperialism was antithetical to "both Christianity and American democratic traditions" (366). Meanwhile, other Progressives, particularly Protestant missionaries, saw opportunities in Cuba and the Philippines to gain more converts.

In 1898, the Spanish-American War began. Newspaper barons William Randolph Hearst and Joseph Pulitzer sided with the Cubans, who had been trying to throw off Spanish colonial rule since 1868. They sent journalists and photographers who worked not only to report on the war but to stir it up. In February 1898, President McKinley sent the USS *Maine* to Cuba. It exploded in Havana, killing 250 US sailors. Though the explosion was later revealed to be the result of an accident, both Hearst and Pulitzer informed Theodore Roosevelt, then assistant secretary of the navy, that it was no accident. Newspaper readers demanded war. Pulitzer later regretted his role in causing the Spanish-American War, but Hearst did not.

After the war, Cuba became independent, and Spain ceded Guam, the Philippines, and Puerto Rico to the US. Filipinos, however, revolted against American colonial rule after throwing off Spanish rule. McKinley, refusing to recognize Philippine independence "fired on Filipino nationalists" in 1899, thereby initiating the Philippine-American War (367). Bryan organized the Anti-Imperialist League in response. Other members included Andrew Carnegie and Mark Twain.

The Philippine-American War was brutal and involved "the slaughter of Filipino civilians" (367). The annexation of the Philippines caused representatives in Washington to debate citizenship questions once again. Those who favored imperialism in the Philippines argued that Filipinos were unable to govern themselves. Black soldiers who fought in the war saw the connection between colonialism in the Asian country and Jim Crow in the South. Meanwhile, in the North and the West, cities and counties "passed racial zoning laws, banning blacks from the middle-class communities" (369). In Montana, in 1890, Black people had lived in all 56 of the state's counties. Forty years later, they lived in only 11. In Atlanta, W. E. B. Du Bois saw that the knuckles of Sam Hose, a Black farmer who had been lynched, burned, and dismembered, were being sold as souvenirs in a store window. In response to racist terrorism, hordes of Black Americans decided that they could no longer live in the South. They left the South in what became known as the Great Migration.

When McKinley won the 1896 election, the Democratic Party blamed Bryan, who had failed to account for the fact that an increasing number of people were moving to cities and working in factories and offices. Bryan, who had focused on the rural vote, had not taken account of demographic changes. In 1901, an anarchist shot and killed McKinley in Buffalo. Theodore Roosevelt, who was 42 at the time, "became the nation's youngest president" (375). Reelected in 1904, Roosevelt moved further to the left and pursued a reformist agenda, which included regulation of the railroads, food and drug laws, and the cessation of child labor. He also endorsed an income tax. Despite the Supreme Court's decision to overturn the income tax law in 1894, public support for the measure came in 1906 when a massive earthquake in San Francisco resulted in major infrastructural damage and the collapse of the insurance companies, due to their inability to pay all claims. The debts spurred a national financial panic.

Roosevelt chose not to run for a third term, and William Howard Taft was elected president in 1908. Taft, who had been a federal judge and would later serve as chief justice on the Supreme Court, supported a constitutional amendment for the income tax which went to the states to be ratified in 1909. The 16th Amendment passed easily and became law in February 1913.

Between 1880 and 1910, over one-quarter of the federal budget went toward welfare payments. Reformers, such as Jane Addams, began "leading a fight for legislative labor reforms for women," which included limitations on work hours, minimum wages, and the abolition of child labor (377). Critics called these reforms unconstitutional and the Supreme Court often agreed, frequently ruling against Progressive labor legislation. Leftist critics contended that "the courts had become an instrument of business interests," while conservatives insisted that the courts were just to protect business interests (378). Market forces, the latter believed, would eventually care for the sick and enfeebled. Those who died, as Social Darwinists reasoned, were too weak to survive. For these reasons, Progressivist universal health insurance campaigns were far less successful than those in Britain. Germans had invented the first state health insurance plan in 1883. However, after the US went to war with Germany in 1917, those who were against national health insurance used anti-German sentiment to dissuade the public from embracing the policy.

The simplest way, at the time, to advocate for social welfare was to center the effort on women and children. Women held one-fifth of all manufacturing jobs. Still unable to vote, they relied on the state for protections. State courts had made rulings that protected women as a class, particularly in response to labor exploitation. Usually, these protections focused on women being weaker than men.

As the nation grappled with concerns over the expansion of corporate power and the mechanization of labor, more Americans became socialists. In 1908, over 400,000 people voted for Socialist Party candidate Eugene V. Debs. Three years later, 18 cities had a Socialist mayor, and over 1,000 Socialists held offices in 30 states. The election of 1912, in which Woodrow Wilson won the Democratic nomination, was largely influenced by women and motivated by a Progressivist agenda. Women had achieved suffrage rights in eight states. The word "feminism" had entered the English language in the 1910s, as had the term "birth control," coined by New York–based nurse Margaret Sanger. Theodore Roosevelt hoped to win the Republican nomination by appealing to women. He mainly availed himself of another Progressivist reform—the direct state primary, which was first held in 1899 and gained popularity in 1905.

Roosevelt's campaign was a turning point: The focus was on the candidate, not the party. He also used modern advertising to gain a following. Roosevelt won 27% of the vote. However, most of his votes were drawn from Taft supporters, giving Wilson, the ultimate winner, an edge.

In 1914, war broke out in Europe on a scale never before seen. It was a war managed by experts in efficiency "and waged with factory-made munitions" (389). World War I marked the end of Europe as the center of the Western world. The United States would, after the armistice, take the continent's place. In 1916, 800,000 were killed at the Battle of Verdun over several months; 1.1. million were killed during the Battle at Somme. Civilians were killed, too. For the first time, bombs were dropped from airplanes. Before the end of the war, almost 40 million people had been killed and another 20 million injured. In the aftermath of the war, there was increased anticolonialist sentiment, as well as more conversion to fundamentalism, due to an aversion to the horrors modernity had wrought.

It was fundamentalism that instigated the rejection of Darwinism. Fundamentalists argued that the purpose of a church was "to convert people to Christ by teaching the actual, literal gospel" (390). Progressives mocked fundamentalists for their anti-intellectualism. Fundamentalists argued that intellectuals suppressed conservative opinions.

Meanwhile, women marched for suffrage and for peace. Those who could vote awarded Wilson, who had promised to keep the nation out of the war, a narrow victory: He won 10 out of 12 of the states in which women had suffrage rights. Wilson ignored suffrage during his second term, leading to a vigil outside of the White House. Public support for women's voting rights dropped. As the nation neared war, criticism of the president began to look like disloyalty. Several days after Wilson's inauguration, German U-Boats torpedoed three American ships. At the beginning of April, Wilson went to Congress for a declaration of war, saying that the world had to be made safe for democracy. Congress obliged. All American men between the ages of 18 and 45 were to register for the draft; about 5 million were drafted to serve.

To gain public support for the war, Wilson established a propaganda department, the Committee on Public Information, headed by the muckraking journalist George Creel. In 1918, Congress passed a Sedition Act. Dissenters of war, including pacifists, feminists, and socialists, were jailed. Eugene Debs was among them. W. E. B. Du Bois, who had argued that the First

World War was rooted in colonial rivalries in Africa, was reined in by Creel, who called 31 Black editors and publishers to Washington and "warned them about 'Negro subversion'" (396). Du Bois promised not to make any public comments about race relations for the duration of the war. He used his magazine, the *Crisis*, to encourage Black people to stand "shoulder to shoulder with [their] white fellow citizens," encouraged Black men to fight, and asked Black people to delay protests against lynchings (396).

The First World War also expanded the powers of the government, which included new powers over the bodies of citizens. A "social purity" movement, geared toward diminishing the spread of venereal disease, started and led to military ordinances. In December 1917, Congress prohibited the sale of alcohol.

By the end of the war, Americans had suffered only 116,000 casualties, while those in France and Germany were nearly 2 million. Europe, which comprised 17 countries before the war, became a continent of 26 nations. All of them were deeply in debt, mainly to Americans. In 1918, an influenza epidemic took 21 million lives globally but only 675,000 in the US.

The Armistice was signed on November 11, 1918. Wilson led the Paris Peace Conference in January 1919. Wilson was particularly well received by delegates from "stateless and colonized societies," including a young Ho Chi Minh, who unsuccessfully tried to meet with him (399). Wilson promoted a rhetoric of self-determination, which fueled the anticolonial movement. W. E. B. Du Bois traveled to Paris four days after Wilson. He was mainly present to attend the Pan-African Congress.

The treaty both suppressed German industry and deprived the nation of managing its own affairs. Additionally, it demanded $33 billion in war reparations. Wilson believed that the newly established League of Nations could address any shortcomings in the treaty. Two days after he returned to the US, Wilson "delivered the Treaty of Versailles to the Senate and explained its provisions, including for the League of Nations" (400). Finding little support for the treaty in Congress, he decided to gain public support by going on a 17-state train tour. One day, in Colorado, he stumbled while climbing onto a stage. He lost the use of his left side after a stroke and lay infirm in the West Wing of the White house for five months. His wife kept his condition secret. In March 1920, the Senate rejected both the Treaty of Versailles and the League of Nations.

In August 1920, the 19th Amendment, "the last constitutional act of the Progressive Era," was ratified (401). The Equal Rights Amendment was then introduced three years later, leading to a division between early feminists who wanted equal rights and those who supported the maintenance of women under protective legislation.

In the 1920 presidential election, Republican Warren G. Harding triumphed easily over his relatively unknown running mate. Harding rode a conservative wave to the White House. He led a movement to make the Constitution sacred, taking the parchment out of storage and placing it in "a national shrine" (403). Harding also pushed for administrative efficiency in government and lighter tax burdens. He wanted to eliminate government interference in business and peopled his cabinet with conservative businessmen, including industrialist Andrew W. Mellon. Herbert Hoover was secretary of commerce. Harding's cabinet led the nation during "some of the most prosperous years in American history" (404). Industrial production had risen by 70% between 1922 and 1928. Wages and income had also significantly risen. In the 1920s, more American homes gained electricity. Americans' faith in progress was wedded to consumerism. The US economy became the world's largest, as well as the world's biggest lender. The nation also began to turn inward, placing harsher restrictions on immigration. This left Europe unable to send excess workers across the Atlantic, in addition to being unable to sell their manufactured goods to the US, making it difficult to pay their war debts. European countries responded by raising tariffs, which punished American farmers and manufacturers.

Meanwhile, between 1890 and 1920, around 1.5 million Mexicans entered the US. They were fleeing from the dictator Porfirio Diaz, against whom many had revolted in 1910. Many of them took jobs picking produce after Japanese immigration ended in 1908. In Congress, legislators argued over their immigration, with some contending that they were not easily assimilated and therefore should return to their native country, while others said that no one else would perform the work that Mexican laborers did. Thus, Mexicans were allowed to enter the US on temporary visas, but they were denied a path to citizenship. Their status became closely tied to the "new legal, racialized category of 'illegal alien'" (410). The US Border Patrol formed in 1924 after the deportation of "illegal aliens" became a policy measure.

The Ku Klux Klan, which had seen a resurgence in 1915, was vocally supportive of immigration restrictions. While white supremacists rewrote the nation's history as one of white people, Black intellectuals of the Harlem Renaissance drew critical attention to the place of Black people in the nation's past.

By 1926, American politics had become divided, particularly over interpretations of the Constitution. In 1923, US Army veterans Henry Luce and Briton Hadden decided to found a magazine, which they initially intended to call *Facts*. They settled instead on *Time*, which was modeled on Frederick Taylor's idea of efficiency. The magazine was to save readers time, as all of its articles were to be read in an hour. Luce and Hadden also sorted the magazine into sections, which was unprecedented. Subjectivity in journalism, however, led to errors in print. *Time*, therefore, established the process of fact-checking. They hired young women, newly graduated from college, to perform this work. Fact-checking was an intense practice at the offices of *Tim e*'s chief rival, *The New Yorker*, edited by former city newspaper reporter Harold Ross. However, *The New Yorker* was not designed to save readers time.

As part of the nation's growing divide over matters of fact, a year earlier, Tennessee became the first state to ban the teaching of evolution. John Scopes, a biology teacher, was found guilty of teaching it. The ACLU had been looking to challenge Tennessee's law, the Act Prohibiting the Teaching of the Evolution Theory, which infringed on free speech. They initially intended to defend Scopes. That plan changed when William Jennings Bryan joined the prosecution, leading Clarence Darrow to agree to defend Scopes.

The Scopes Trial led to a media circus, as well as "dozens of preachers and psalm singers" (416). Bryan sought to put the theory of evolution on trial. The judge sided with him and refused to allow the testimony of biologists. Darrow called Bryan to the witness stand and subjected him to a rigorous cross-examination. The judge later ordered to have Bryan's testimony expunged from the public record. The jury found Scopes guilty.

109

Five days later, Bryan died, leaving in his wake a legacy of fundamentalism, despite reporters' mockery of both him and his followers. For Walter Lippmann, the battle between Bryan and Darrow was rooted in how people decided on facts. Did truth arise from faith or reason? More importantly, what happened when the citizens of a democracy could not generally agree on what was true? Would majority rule take precedence? Lippmann stumbled upon a quandary: People of faith could not accept reason "as the arbiter of truth without giving up on faith," while the person of reason could not accept "that truth lies outside the realm of reason" (419). If citizens disagreed over matters of fact, they would disagree over how to educate their children in public schools.

In this chapter, Lepore describes two key periods of rapid social progress—the Progressive Era and the Roaring Twenties, also sometimes referred to as the Jazz Age. During the Progressive Era, the US experienced mass industrialization and the introduction of federal agencies specifically dedicated to the preservation of natural resources. Negative consequences of this period of reform most notably include the rise of the eugenics movement and, shortly thereafter, the mechanization of war. As Lepore notes, Progressivists failed to address Jim Crow, leading to a rise in lynching as a terrorist tool. She overlooks, however, the relationship between Progressive reform and imperialism. Both the paternalist sentiments of Progressive Era reformers and a common belief in social Darwinism likely led to the notion that some peoples were better off being led by Western nations than being allowed to remain autonomous. Undoubtedly, the exploitation of some countries, particularly in Africa, for their mineral wealth, fomented the growth of industry during this period.

During this time, there was also a shift of many citizens from rural areas to cities. In addition to the African Americans who left the South during the Great Migration—the results of both a desire to escape from racist violence and the devastation of cotton crops due to the boll weevil—many Americans left farms for jobs in offices and factories. The employment of white women in some of these positions led to the use of the 14th Amendment to ensure their protection as a class. The potential problem with this argument, as Lepore suggests, is that these legal protections were rooted in essentialist ideas about sex. Instead of reforming labor protections so that they would address general concerns about workplace safety and the exploitation of labor, particularly when women were the employees, reformers cast women as relatively weaker than men—a position that would be used decades later to stall the ratification of the Equal Rights Amendment.

Compromises, such as those that white women may have made for workplace safety at the expense of their civil rights, were also made in racially marginalized communities. W. E. B. Du Bois's compromise during the First World War, which backfired, may have influenced his later radical politics.

An offshoot of the suffragist movement, the social purity movement was also largely influenced by soldiers returning from the First World War, some of whom had contracted venereal diseases. This resulted in programs to instill uniformity in hygiene and daily habits, which were unprecedented before this war. Industries also catered to the daily needs of deployed soldiers.

The 1920s was a period of both pulsing innovation and social regression. The Harding administration sought to make the

Constitution sacred, as though the nation's prosperity was connected to its foundational principles. Additionally, the US became more inward-looking, reverting to the isolationist stance it took before World War I. The treatment of Mexicans during this period mirrors their contemporary struggles to achieve citizenship status, as well as the nation's willingness to exploit their labor without offering them a path to citizenship.

The Harlem Renaissance flourished both despite and in response to the rise in white supremacist violence and oppression. Figures from the Harlem Renaissance, who were also often active politically, sought to highlight the integrality of Black culture and Black people to the national heritage while organizations such as the Ku Klux Klan were dedicated to historical erasure and mythologizing. Their efforts to manipulate the national historical narrative were aided by the popularity of D. W. Griffith's 1915 film *The Birth of a Nation*, which portrayed the vigilante group as underdogs turned heroes.

Part 3, Chapter 11 Summary and Analysis: "A Constitution of the Air"

By the end of the 1920s, the nation's optimism seemed limitless. While accepting the Republican presidential nomination, Herbert Hoover declared his belief that poverty would one day come to an end on Earth. American economic growth was an engine that never stopped running. Privately, Hoover worried that Americans mistook him for a kind of superman.

Europe, on the other hand, had fallen into a depression by 1928, still saddled with the consequences of the First World War. Four years later, New York governor Franklin D. Roosevelt stumped for the Democratic nomination, promoting "a new brand of liberalism that borrowed as much from Bryan's populism as from Wilson's Progressivism" (428). Roosevelt later heard at the governor's mansion in Albany that he had secured his party's nomination for president. He called the convention hall in Chicago and announced that he'd be arriving soon. It was the first time a presidential nominee had ever appeared to accept the nomination. In his acceptance speech, Roosevelt promised Americans "a new deal" (429).

In November, Roosevelt defeated Hoover resoundingly, earning huge margins in both the popular vote and the Electoral College. Roosevelt's success was partly due to the stock market crash of 1929, which led to the Great Depression. The public seemed to blame Hoover for this economic turndown. After his election, the parties arranged themselves according to their respective position on the New Deal—blue-collar workers, farmers, nonwhite people, liberal intellectuals, and some women and industrialists formed the New Deal coalition. Together, they marked the arrival of a new form of liberalism. Both parties feared that newly enfranchised women would form their own voting bloc; predictably, both set about recruiting women by forming divisions dedicated to that bloc. Carrie Chapman Catt, head of the League of Women Voters, encouraged other women voters to join one of the major political parties instead of forming their own party, believing that it would be easier to get things done by working within existing frameworks. More women became Democrats than Republicans, however.

The nation, sinking under the Great Depression, collectively believed that the economic crisis was so serious that only a president with "the powers of a dictator," thereby overruling congressional obstructionism, could address it (433). On the matter of dictators, the world watched Germany. American reporters had not initially taken Hitler seriously. On January 30, 1933, he proved them wrong when he was appointed chancellor of Germany. Joseph Goebbels, the head of the newly established Ministry of Propaganda, noted in his diary two months later that broadcasting in Germany was controlled completely by the state. Hitler next outlawed all political parties except for the Nazi Party and withdrew from the League of Nations. Jews who tried to flee to the US were burdened by a German law that forbade them from withdrawing more than a few dollars, and American immigration laws that forbade the entrance of anyone who might become the citizenry's responsibility.

In the US, bank and business failures were at their zenith. Both the New York Stock Exchange and the Chicago Board of Trade suspended trading. The Emergency Banking Act declared that banks would only be opened once they proved to be financially sound.

High rates of unemployment ensured that more Americans would be at home listening to the radio. Some also became more attracted to distributive economic policies. During the Great Depression, around 75,000 Americans joined the Communist Party. Also in the 1930s, bipartisan concern rose over arms manufacturers. Americans had always owned guns, and states had regulated their production, sale, and storage. It was illegal to carry concealed weapons in many Southern states, including Florida, Texas, and Louisiana. In the West, sheriffs routinely collected visitors' guns.

In 1871, the National Rifle Association (NRA) was founded "as a sporting and hunting association" by a former *New York Times* reporter (445). In the 1920s and 1930s, the NRA both supported and sponsored firearms regulation by lobbying for state gun control laws that

> [t]axed the private ownership of automatic weapons ('machine guns'), mandated licensing for handgun dealers, introduced waiting periods for handgun buyers, required permits for anyone wishing to carry a concealed weapon, and created a licensing system for dealers (445).

Firearms legislation passed in 1934 and 1938 "enjoyed bipartisan support" and was upheld by the Supreme Court (446). Business interests, particularly members of the du Pont family, opposed both gun control legislation and New Deal legislation. In July 1934, they convened with fellow businessmen "in the offices of General Motors in New York, where they founded a 'propertyholders' [sic] association' to oppose the New Deal" (446). This later became the American Liberty League, which particularly objected to Social Security.

Also by 1934, Josef Goebbels, hoping to sow division in the US via radio, broadcast pro-Nazi English- and foreign-language propaganda to parts of Africa, Latin America, East and Southeast Asia, and Australia. In North America, particularly the US, it sent false news in English which focused on claims that there was a Communist-Jewish conspiracy at work in the nation. Newspapers began calling this propaganda "fake news." Roosevelt, too, had been accused of using the radio to propagandize. On June 27, 1936, Roosevelt accepted the Democratic nomination for the presidency.

The failure of Hoover's presidency, as Lepore depicts it, reveals the problem of leadership. By this time, Americans seemed to believe that a president alone could guarantee both prosperity and safety—a myth perpetuated by Warren G. Harding, yet initiated by earlier expansions of executive power, which turned the presidency into a cult of personality.

The ascendancy of Franklin Delano Roosevelt resulted in the creation of a new cult of personality that effectively united the two major political parties. Like William Jennings Bryan, Roosevelt had the ability to connect with those who were ideologically opposed to him. On the other hand, Hoover's choice to continue Harding's legacy of keeping the government out of business affairs, instead of addressing the Great Depression, tarnished his legacy. He failed to tailor his policy platform to the urgency of the economic crisis. This resulted in the creation of a new Democratic Party—one that was less rural, more cosmopolitan, and more diverse. The instability of the era also led numerous Western nations to see comfort, however illusory, in authoritarian power. Roosevelt harnessed the power of the radio, aided by the nation's idleness, to disperse his message and to wield his own overwhelming paternalist authority, however benevolent.

What may be most striking to the contemporary reader is the nation's shift in its attitudes toward gun rights since this period. Ironically, it was the South and the West—that is, the regions that are now most fervently against gun control—that most often sought gun legislation. Lepore illustrates how powerful corporations, even during a period of Big Business's unpopularity, sought to manipulate public opinion. It is possible, too, that growing concerns about communism and a burgeoning civil rights movement among African Americans led to the kind of fears among many white Americans that would have encouraged the ownership of firearms.

In 1939, the World's Fair was held in Queens, New York. The fair's centerpiece was the Perisphere—a globe that stood 18 stories high and was 200 feet in diameter. Inside of the globe was a *Democracity* exhibit, which showed spectators a replica of a world a century in the future, in which highways would carry people from suburbs into cities. RCA, which introduced the new technology of television, announced the opening of the fair on April 30, 1939, on NBC, which had its first broadcast that day. However, the exhibit was obsolete even before it was introduced: Austria and Czechoslovakia, which were featured in the pavilions, no longer existed. In fact, Germany had conquered half of the European nations represented at the World's Fair.

On September 1, 1939, Germany invaded Poland, leading Britain and France to declare war on Germany. Some believed that, had the US joined the League of Nations after the First World War, another war could have been averted. Franklin D. Roosevelt focused on planning for war, despite both Congress and the public preferring an isolationist stance. However, when civil war broke out in Spain in 1936, around 3,000 American citizens volunteered to fight against Francisco Franco's fascist-supported regime. Still, the following year a Gallup poll showed that most Americans had little interest in events in Spain. Ostensible American indifference emboldened Nazi Germany. Moreover, Hitler believed that Americans were too self-centered and easily distracted to notice what he did in Europe.

In 1938, FDR planned for the US to manufacture planes for Britain and France. He also worked toward building an American air force with 10,000 aircraft, believing it was in the nation's best interests to support its allies and prepare American forces. Secretly, the president worried about German chemists' discovery of nuclear fission that year.

Meanwhile, Nazi propagandists sought to align themselves with white Southerners. Radio personality Father Coughlin preached anti-Semitism in 1937 and expressed admiration for Hitler. In turn, the German chancellor expressed admiration for the former Confederacy and lamented its defeat. Coughlin's audience answered his call to form a new political party called the Christian Front. Shortly thereafter, 20,000 Nazi supporters gathered in Madison Square Garden wearing both swastikas and American flags, claiming that they were demonstrating for "True Americanism."

Most of those who favored an isolationist stance were Republican. Some of FDR's opponents worried that, if Britain surrendered, the Germans could seize American munitions. On May 10, 1940, Winston Churchill became prime minister and eagerly worked to court Roosevelt's support, as Britain could not defeat Germany without American backing. Shortly thereafter, Roosevelt was reelected to his third term. He took to the radio and asked manufacturers to put all of their effort into munitions production. Britain, however, was both outgunned by Germany and out of money. To assist them, FDR offered the Lend-Lease Act—the US would lend arms to Britain in exchange for long-term land leases for military bases. Congress passed the act. During his annual address to Congress the following year, he announced that the US had to secure the "'four essential freedoms': freedom of speech, freedom of religion, freedom from want, and freedom from fear" (480). A couple of months later, Hitler ignored his agreement with Joseph Stalin and invaded the Soviet Union. By then, Germany had taken all of Europe, except for Britain and Ireland. Japan, meanwhile, had taken almost half of China. Ohio Republican senator Robert Taft warned prophetically that American entry into the war would mean, ultimately, that the United States "will have to maintain a police force perpetually in Germany and throughout Europe" (482).

Churchill maintained hope that FDR would ask Congress to declare war. That summer, Churchill and FDR released a joint statement saying that they would support a postwar world characterized by "free trade, self-determination, international security, arms control, social welfare, economic justice, and human rights" (483). Their agreement became known as the Atlantic Charter.

On December 7, 1941, the Imperial Japanese Navy "sank four battleships, destroyed nearly 200 American planes, killed more than 2,400 Americans, and wounded another 1,100" (483-84). In doing so, they practically eliminated the entire US Pacific Fleet. Shortly thereafter, FDR gave a rousing speech in which he called on the might of the American people to respond. Congress responded by declaring war on Japan. Roosevelt also planned for the nation to declare war on Germany, but on December 11, Hitler preempted Roosevelt by declaring war on the US.

Thirty-one million men between the ages of 18 and 45 registered to enlist; 10 million were deemed eligible to serve. Three million women entered the war effort, too. Some were in the labor force, while others joined the Women's Army Corps and the US Navy's WAVES. By 1945, 12 million Americans were active-duty service members. The nation had been preparing munitions since the 1930s, ramping up a massive supply of military planes, tanks, naval ships, and machine guns. Farm production also increased by 25% to supply both American and Allied forces. The federal budget grew from $9 billion in 1939 to $100 billion in 1945, and the gross domestic product (GDP) doubled.

Following in President Lincoln's footsteps, FDR claimed a range of new, emergency war powers. He removed the secretaries of war and the navy from the military chain of command and placed them under his own authority. Congress next passed the War Powers Act, which gave the executive branch "special powers to prosecute the war, including the power to surveil letters, telegraph messages, and radio broadcasts" (487). In March 1942, a Second War Powers Act was passed, which granted the president authority over special investigations and census reports, in addition to establishing the National War Labor Board and the Office of Price Administration. The act gave the executive branch considerable control over both the economy and the federal government.

In 1943, the Pentagon opened, increasing the number of civil servants in federal government to 3.8 million in two years. More bureaucracy meant more spending, which increased the national debt. To meet costs, the government raised taxes and asked citizens to buy war bonds. The Revenue Act of 1942 broadened the tax base. Memberships in trade unions doubled from 1939 to 1945. The Manhattan Project, a secret federal plan to develop an atomic bomb, started in 1939. It cost $2 billion and employed 130,000 people. FDR then issued an executive order to establish the Office of Facts and Figures, headed by writer Archibald MacLeish, whom the president had earlier named Librarian of Congress. MacLeish focused his efforts on battling Nazi propaganda through a pamphlet issued to the American public.

MacLeish decided to use the Office of Facts and Figures to celebrate the 150th anniversary of the Bill of Rights in 1941 with a radio play entitled *We Hold These Truths*, "broadcast eight days after the attack on Pearl Harbor" (490). It was the first radio show to be broadcast on all four major networks. Roosevelt later replaced the Office of Facts and Figures with the Office of War Information, led by CBS reporter and former Coca-Cola ad manager Elmer Davis, who was more willing to apply mass advertising to the war effort. MacLeish returned to the Library of Congress.

Roosevelt, with an eye toward eventual peace, invited Winston Churchill to the White House for Christmas in 1941. Together they planned a new organization which FDR named the "United Nations." Ironically, it was Republican Wendell Willkie, the future vanquished presidential opponent of Harry Truman, who raised public support for the new organization. China and the Soviet Union joined it with the US and Britain. Together, they became known as the Big Four. By January 2, 26 nations signed the "Declaration by United Nations." The Big Four then planned the military strategy of bombing Germany and then landing in France.

In 1942, much of American fighting in the Second World War took place in the Pacific arena. American forces defeated the Japanese in the Solomon Islands during the Battle of Guadalcanal. On American soil, however, the federal government had begun to place American citizens of Japanese ancestry in internment camps due to a 1934 report from the State Department warning about "the possibility of sabotage by Japanese Americans" (493). Five years later, FDR asked the FBI to gather a list of possible traitors, all of whom were categorized based on their respective level of danger.

On February 19, Roosevelt signed Executive Order 9066, "authorizing the secretary of war to establish military zones" (493). On March 1, the US Army "issued Public Proclamation 1 [...] directing aliens to demarcated zones," entailing curfews and relocation orders (494). Around 112,000 Japanese people, including 79,000 citizens, were forced into internment camps along the Pacific coast and in Arizona. Gordon Hirabayashi, an American citizen and Quaker, refused to obey the curfew, resulting in the Supreme Court case *Hirabayashi v. United States* (1943), which declared that the curfew was constitutional. However, even Justice Frank Murphy, who concurred with the ruling, regretted it, saying that the notion that a group could not assimilate into the national fabric meant admitting that "the great American experiment has failed" (495).

Meanwhile, Fred Korematsu, who had been born in Oakland, California, in 1919, had tried to enlist in the military. He refused to be relocated and lived instead with his Italian American girlfriend. He even got plastic surgery to acquire more ethnically European features, eventually pretending that he was Mexican American. Finally, he went into hiding. The ACLU defended him in the case that became *Korematsu v. United States*. Using *Hirabayashi* as a precedent, the Supreme Court emphasized the potential danger posed "by possible Japanese saboteurs who might aid a Japanese attack on the West Coast" (495).

The Japanese were not alone in the experience of discrimination. While the wartime economic boom lifted many Americans out of poverty, African Americans were excluded from any opportunities to prosper. They also "served in segregated, noncombat units, where they reported to white officers and did menial work" (496). In the US Navy, they served "as cooks and stewards and were altogether forbidden from serving in the air force or marine corps" (496). In response, several sit-ins were conducted in 1939. In May 1941, A. Philip Randolph, the head of the Brotherhood of Sleeping Car Porters, put out a call for a Negro March on Washington set to take place in July. Over 100,000 marchers were expected. Eleanor Roosevelt met with Randolph and Bayard Rustin, his co-organizer, in New York with the hope that Randolph would call off the march. The First Lady then arranged for Randolph to meet with FDR at the White House. The president, too, tried to convince him to call off the demonstration. To appease civil rights activists, FDR signed Executive Order 8802, "prohibiting racial discrimination in defense industries" (498). Randolph relented and called off the march. However, protests continued, particularly when Black men and women refused to obey Jim Crow on buses. Some, such as Martin Dies of the House Un-American Activities Committee (HUAC) and FBI head J. Edgar Hoover, blamed communists for inciting subversion among Black Americans in the South.

In February 1942, white residents in Detroit "barricaded the streets when the first black families moved in to a public housing project, the Sojourner Truth Homes" (499). In August, rumors of a white police officer killing a Black service member led to riots that lasted for two days. FDR, who still depended on Southern Democrats to move civil rights legislation forward in Congress, created toothless measures that left enforcement at the discretion of states. In 1944, Gunnar Myrdal, a Swedish sociologist, published *An American Dilemma*, a study of race in the US. There was, Myrdal found, tension between "the American creed of human rights and personal liberty and, on the other, racial injustice" (500).

By 1943, the tide of the war had turned in favor of the Allied Forces. In July of that year, Churchill, Roosevelt, and Stalin—then called the "Big Three"—met in Tehran to discuss their campaign against Germany and their postwar plan of international cooperation. Roosevelt gave Stalin further details about the United Nations. Churchill began to feel betrayed by FDR's repeated meetings with Stalin. Domestically, Roosevelt spoke more about the UN's developing commitment to human rights. In January 1944, Roosevelt unveiled his Second Bill of Rights. He emphasized certain "economic truths" as "self-evident," declaring that citizens should be guaranteed remunerative work, decent housing, adequate medical care, and a good education (503). By 1943, however, Congress had whittled down many New Deal programs. Others became headed by conservatives.

In 1945, Martin Dies reconvened HUAC and began to search for and investigate more liberals suspected of communism. Conservatism gained strength, particularly in regard to the issue of taxation.

On June 6, 1944, the Allies conducted D-Day to liberate Europe. One million men participated in the invasion on the Normandy coast. It was "the largest seaborne invasion in history" (505). With the help of the French Resistance, the Allies defeated the Germans, while the Soviets pushed them back from the east—in concordance with the plan that had been organized in Tehran. In July 1944, the Allies met to discuss postwar peace, which emphasized Keynesianism, particularly free trade and open markets. The World Bank was established.

By the end of the war, FDR had become haggard. Still, he agreed to travel halfway around the world for a summit with

Winston Churchill and Joseph Stalin. In the end, alongside Churchill, the three men agreed to a division of Germany "into zones of occupation and to the prosecution of Nazi war criminals" (510). Three months later, Germany surrendered. Japan followed suit six months later. However, before both surrenders, Stalin had already started to renege on his pledges at the Yalta Conference. To secure Stalin's support in his fight against Japan, FDR betrayed the principles established in the Atlantic Charter.

On April 12, while sitting for a portrait in Warm Springs, Georgia, Franklin Delano Roosevelt collapsed and then died that afternoon of a cerebral hemorrhage. Three days later, he was buried at his home in Hyde Park, New York. On the same day, CBS reporter Edward R. Murrow delivered his first report of a Nazi concentration camp. The scale of the Nazis' atrocities was virtually unknown in many parts of the West. Six million Jewish people and other ethnic minorities, including Roma people, homosexuals, and the disabled, were murdered in concentration camps. The public would not learn about the extent of the genocide until years later.

As Allied Forces closed in on the Axis Powers, Italian partisans found Benito Mussolini on April 28, "shot him down, and dumped his body on the street, where a mob urinated on it, and hung him by his heels" (513). Hitler committed suicide in a Berlin bunker two days later, and Germany surrendered on May 7. Meanwhile, Josef Stalin began to assert claims over territory that Hitler had conquered. Though he had promised free elections in Poland at the Yalta Conference, he reneged on that pledge by spring. On June 25, President Truman "attended the founding conference of the United Nations in San Francisco" (514). He still had to figure out how to end the war with Japan. He contemplated the use of the atomic bomb, despite the opposition of 70 scientists who had worked on the Manhattan Project. The public had no knowledge of this technology. On August 6, the US dropped an atomic bomb on Hiroshima. Three days later, it dropped another on Nagasaki. Finally, Japan surrendered, thereby ending the war.

In this chapter, Lepore introduces a world that would have been barely recognizable 50 years earlier, one with new and frightening technologies, as well as shifting borders due to the incomplete work of the First World War. In the end, borders would continue to shift, as the Iron Curtain fell at the close of the Second World War, leading to what seemed to be an impermeable division between the capitalist West and the Soviet East. Additionally, this new world order signaled the introduction of the both the military-industrial complex that then general and future president Dwight D. Eisenhower would later warn against and the advent of the World Bank, which would be criticized for its failure to secure the free and fair trade that Roosevelt and Churchill promised in their Atlantic Charter. The Lend-Lease Act, for example, was a prelude to the permanent US military installations that exist to date in foreign nations.

This sense of incompletion was partly due to failed diplomatic and economic policies that facilitated the rise of Nazi Germany, which found sympathizers in the US, particularly in the South. Nazi sympathizers and propagandists, aided by the popularity of Father Coughlin, tried to harness the power of the radio to disperse their anti-Semitic, white supremacist agenda. Conversely, Roosevelt continued to harness the medium to support the war effort.

As part of his war effort, Roosevelt presented an annual address to Congress that was intended to bolster the nation's core values. The irony of these speeches was that the freedoms he delineated did not typically apply to nonwhite citizens. The president's hypocrisy during this period was especially evident in his choice to intern and stigmatize Japanese Americans. His choice to focus on this group and not on German Americans or Italian Americans was due both to the American focus on the Pacific arena and the lingering influence of ideas about race that were established in earlier immigration laws. These laws, some of which had been instituted only 20 years earlier, separated people of non-European ethnic descent from those who were determined to be white. The cruel irony was that American soldiers would soon be liberating concentration camps in Europe, but the nation was maintaining its own camps in the western United States. Lepore correlates the experience of Japanese Americans with the relegation of African Americans to menial work during the Second World War. This included, too, their exclusion from many of the benefits of the G.I. Bill, which was key both in educating veterans and in securing their entry into the middle- and upper-middle classes.

The Second World War and the importance of media, particularly film, were especially key in helping Roosevelt extend his war powers. His efforts to pass New Deal legislation and to convince Congress to go to war, and his dominance of the radio, were markers of his extensive authoritative power. Like Abraham Lincoln, he used war to extend the power of the executive office and to inscribe his personality on the presidency. Meanwhile, Archibald MacLeish, following a precedent established by Warren G. Harding, tried to buoy American spirits by reminding the public of its noble democratic lineage. Unfortunately, the public's means of consuming media had changed and attention spans were shorter, which likely influenced the president's

decision to use an ad man to convey his messages—
increasingly propagandist in nature—to the public.

Part 4

Part 4: The Machine (1946-2016)

Part 4, Chapter 13 Summary and Analysis: "A World of Knowledge"

The bombing of Hiroshima marked the beginning of an
unprecedented political era "in which technological change wildly
outpaced the human capacity for moral reckoning" (521).
Truman found out about the bombing while on board a cruiser.
The White House informed the press the next day. Then, several
days later, Americans celebrated the Japanese surrender. The
Manhattan Project had been classified, as were the computers
that the military had been building. ENIAC, an acronym for
Electronic Numerical Integrator and Computer, was the first
electronic digital computer for general use. It was the size of a
room. The Allied Powers had been interested in computers
during the war for two reasons: to break secret codes and to
calculate weapons trajectories. In 1942, scientists built a
computer with vacuum tubes in the interest of making them
process faster. During the war, FDR created the National
Defense Research Committee and the Office of Scientific
Research and Development, both of which were led by engineer
and inventor Vannevar Bush. Atomic scientists took their
message of using scientific knowledge for industrial progress to
the public, speaking at churches and synagogues, schools,
libraries, and Kiwanis clubs. Others advocated for the federal
government to fund the development of computer science.

The end of the war also signaled the beginning of a new age of affluence. Voters also began to move away from favoring government regulation to preferring individual rights. A new form of conservatism, centered on the fight against communism, emerged. Citizens were consumers and consumerism was a way to express one's citizenship. Some critics bemoaned "the banality and uniformity of consumer society [which] had reduced Americans to robots" (528). Disneyland, which seemed to epitomize the new, prepackaged society, opened in 1955. One park feature, Frontierland, gave visitors the illusion of returning to frontier America, traveling from the Revolutionary era to the settlement of the Southwest, where the park was located.

Most of the new consumers were women, particularly homemakers. The average marriage age dropped after the war and couples began to have more children per family. While claims for equal rights had been steadily made during the war, this activism was largely abandoned afterward. Women who had served during the war were not eligible for G.I. Bill benefits. While men who had served attended colleges and universities, some of which were prestigious, many schools either stopped admitting women altogether or reduced their number to make room for male enrollees. Men who had been giving a "blue discharge" during the war, however, meaning that they were suspected of being homosexuals, were also rendered ineligible for G.I. Bill benefits.

African American veterans had been both denied the G.I. Bill's educational and housing benefits and "were excluded from veterans' organizations," including the powerful American Legion (529). Moreover, most colleges and universities refused to admit Black students, and places at historically Black colleges and universities were limited. Banks refused to extend loans to Black applicants and redlining restricted much new housing in suburbs to white applicants. The result of restrictive housing covenants, which were perpetuated by the Federal Housing Administration despite a Supreme Court decision banning them, was the expansion and increase of ghettos. Lynchings resumed in Georgia and Louisiana.

While FDR did his best to ignore racial discrimination, Truman refused. He established a commission on civil rights. He also prioritized a national health insurance plan. He enjoyed bipartisan support from Republican California governor Earl Warren who had proposed in California compulsory health insurance funded with a payroll tax, the same plan Truman had for the nation. Warren had run for governor in 1942 in a campaign run by Clem Whitaker and Leone Baxter, a married team whose methods of running campaign elections made them highly sought after by Republican candidates for the next two decades. Just before his election, Warren fired the team, and they never forgave him. When the California Medical Association hired Campaigns, Inc., the ad agency that Baxter and Whitaker had founded in California in 1933, they succeeded in torpedoing Warren's state health plan, which had once been popular. Whitaker and Baxter had postcards sent to voters, tying the insurance plan to the nation's enemy, Germany. When Warren's health bill went up for a vote, it failed to pass by one vote. He blamed Whitaker and Baxter.

In 1946, American diplomat George Kennan sent the State Department a lengthy telegram in which he described the Soviets' determination to rival the West, in a battle of communism against capitalism. Two weeks later, Winston Churchill warned of an "iron curtain" falling across the European continent. The Soviets had lost a great deal during the Second

World War: 27 million Russians perished, "ninety times as many casualties as were suffered by Americans" (535). Meanwhile, in Africa, Latin America, and South Asia, nations that had been colonized by Western powers began to fight for their independence. In this new world order, that meant choosing between democracy and totalitarianism, between capitalism and communism, between American influence or that of the Soviets.

Truman began to move to the right on foreign policy, vowing that the nation would help any democracy that was under attack. In March 1947, he announced the Truman Doctrine—the United States' pledge to support free peoples who resisted pressure from anti-democratic forces. Truman aides would later confess that the president was not personally concerned with communism, but was responding to the desires of voters, with an eye toward his reelection chances. Truman also supported the Marshall Plan, which provided billions in aid to rebuild Europe. The US, meanwhile, became a national security state, spending an unprecedented amount on building up its military. A year later, the Soviet-backed Communist Party in Czechoslovakia staged a coup. When the Soviets blockaded Berlin, Truman organized an airlift to ferry supplies to West Berlin.

Several months after the US and Western Europe formed NATO, the USSR tested its first nuclear bomb and China's Communist Party won the civil war in that country. In December 1949, Mao Zedong, chairman of the Communist Party in China, visited Joseph Stalin in Moscow to form an alliance.

Within the US, new spending on defense helped to restructure the American economy, particularly in the South. By the mid-1950s, military spending comprised three-quarters of the federal budget. The New South led the nation in aerospace and electronics manufacturing.

Truman had proceeded with little of his domestic agenda, due to obstruction by a Republican-controlled Congress. In particular, they had stopped proposed labor reforms. At the Democratic convention in Philadelphia, segregationists stormed out to protest Truman's position on civil rights. In response, these Dixiecrats, as they were nicknamed, formed the States' Rights Party and nominated South Carolina governor Strom Thurmond as their candidate.

Truman focused on campaigning against Thomas Dewey and emphasized his chief campaign promise: a national health insurance plan. Dewey was a dull presidential candidate, but, ironically, every major polling organization predicted that he would win. Two days after the *Chicago Tribune* went to press with the headline "Dewey Defeats Truman," Truman smiled for a photograph holding up the newspaper. The pollsters had probably undercounted Black voters. Gallup routinely failed to poll Black people, believing that, in the South, Jim Crow prevented most from voting. However, those who did vote cast their ballots overwhelmingly in Truman's favor.

After Truman's reelection, the American Medical Association (AMA) called Campaigns, Inc., which had defeated Earl Warren's health care plan in California, and rehired Clem Whitaker and Leone Baxter to ensure the same fate with Truman's national health care proposal. The plan's long-term objective was to permanently prevent socialized medicine in the US. The strategy was three-fold: Demonstrate to the American people the danger of government-regulated healthcare, convince the people that private medicine was superior, and stimulate the development of private health insurance to increase the availability of medical care to the American people. Truman was furious about the plan to sabotage his health care plan, which took over three years and cost the AMA nearly $5 million.

Around this time, Richard Nixon worked on investigating the accusation that government official Alger Hiss was a Soviet spy. In January 1950, Hiss was convicted of perjury for denying that he had ever been a communist. He was sentenced to five years in prison. Five days later, Nixon gave a four-hour speech on the floor of Congress entitled "The Hiss Case—A Lesson for the American People." He characterized himself as a detective in the case. He used the speech in his campaign for the Senate, challenging the longtime Democratic incumbent Sheridan Downey. Nixon won, largely because of the reputation he had earned from going after Hiss. In his Hiss speech, he had drummed up the theory that Hiss and others in the State Department were part of a massive communist conspiracy. He later allied with Joseph McCarthy and initiated a campaign against communism that coincided with a campaign against homosexuals.

Joseph McCarthy was adept at manipulating both the press and the public in believing that a network of both communists and homosexuals were undermining "Americanism." The most forceful critic of McCarthyism was Margaret Chase Smith, the first woman to serve in both houses of Congress. Smith, a moderate Republican, expressed her concern that the Republican Party would become marred by a culture of ignorance, fear, bigotry, and smear. As a consequence of her activism, Smith was forced out of the Permanent Subcommittee on Investigations—replaced by Nixon. Later, despite her centrism, Smith joined North Carolina senator Clyde Hoey's committee to investigate homosexuals as potential threats to national security. Despite this overwhelming paranoia, "[m]embership in the Communist Party in the United States was the lowest it had been since the 1920s" (551).

Liberal intellectuals tended to dismiss McCarthyism as an aberration. This assessment, Lepore asserts, was incorrect. McCarthyism was part of "a rising tide of conservatism" (553). The movement's leading thinkers had fled communist and fascist regimes. The most notable among them was Ayn Rand, who had been raised in Bolshevik Russia. Another was the Austrian-born economist Friedrich Hayek.

While it was men who publicly advanced conservatism, it was white housewives who protested and took part in grassroots activism in support of McCarthyism. By the 1950s, most GOP activists were women, while women constituted only 41% of activists within the Democratic Party. Within the Republican Party, party work was regarded as women's work. They even referred to tasks such as "ringing doorbells and filling out registration cards" as housework (557). Their participation helped conservatives characterize the academy as "godless" and the press as "mindless," while defending "women's role as housewives, however politicized the role of housewife had become" (557). The crusade against homosexuality was inextricable from a moral crusade in favor of the traditional, yet newly imagined, American family.

While conservatives sought to root the nation in tradition, the television network CBS claimed that it would predict the winner of the 1952 presidential election using a giant brain called UNIVAC, the Universal Automatic Computer—"the first commercial computer in the history of the world" (557). When used commercially, UNIVAC and subsequent computers helped to cut business costs and streamlined managerial and administrative tasks. Later, it would help businesses track and predict consumer spending.

By 1952, 45% of American households had a television. This was also the first year in which a presidential election would be broadcast on television. General Dwight D. Eisenhower, who had rejected a presidential run four years earlier, was finally convinced that he should run against Truman in an election that became "a referendum on US involvement in Korea" (559). The Korean War had become unpopular and costly. Clem Whitaker and Leone Baxter of Campaigns, Inc. managed Eisenhower's campaign. They made the choice to put the candidate whom voters called "Ike" on television. That year, the Republican Party spent $1.5 million on TV advertising compared to $77,000 spent by the Democratic Party.

Richard Nixon traveled to the Republican National Convention in Chicago "on board a chartered train from California called the Earl Warren Special," supposedly to support Warren's bid for the presidency (561). During the cross-country train ride, however, Nixon got the California delegates to throw their support behind Eisenhower. The general rewarded his favor by offering Nixon the vice presidency. Eisenhower, after the election, made Warren his solicitor general.

On election night, UNIVAC first predicted that Eisenhower would win, then it predicted that Adlai Stevenson, his Democratic opponent, would win by a slim margin. In the end, UNIVAC called the election correctly, as did pollster George Gallup: Eisenhower won in a landslide.

Despite the country's embrace of conservativism, McCarthyism was losing favor. Joseph McCarthy's questioning of the respected army general Ralph Zwicker had stoked Eisenhower's ire. Reporter Edward R. Murrow read a "selection of McCarthy's speeches before the public and during congressional hearings, revealing the cruelty of the man [and] his brutality" (566).

Still, many Americans sought to resist the godlessness of communism and turned in droves toward organized religion. In the 1950s, church membership "grew from 75 million to 100 million" (567). Much of this growth was driven by the ambitions of the Southern Baptists, particularly Billy Graham. Graham united both Northern and Southern white, conservative Protestants, all of whom stood against communism and in favor of Christ. Graham also "romanticized rural America" and was anti-intellectual (568). In 1950, Graham began to hold prayer meetings with senators and socialized with presidents. Eisenhower began to see his non-affiliation with any church as a political liability and decided to convert to Presbyterianism. He became the first president to be baptized while occupying the White House.

While Eisenhower was opposed to national health care, and even equated free polio vaccinations with socialized medicine, he disappointed conservatives due to his ambivalence about the Cold War. Having been raised by pacifists, he regarded war as a sin, despite his illustrious reputation as a general.

In 1956, the first-ever televised debate between two presidential candidates took place. Adlai Stevenson debated fellow Democratic candidate, Estes Kefauver, a senator from Tennessee. The men had a one-hour debate in a Miami television studio. The debate took place the day after the US dropped on the Bikini Atoll in the Marshall Islands "a bomb far more powerful than the bomb dropped on Hiroshima" (571). Stevenson noted during the debate that the future could either be one of great abundance or total destruction. He won the Democratic nomination, as he had four years earlier. He also convinced the nation that presidential candidates should debate each other on TV regularly. He next debated against Eisenhower. Both Democrats and Republicans, however, lamented the confusion that TV advertising had created among American voters. Stevenson tried to remind voters of the media's capacity to create illusions. In the end, he proved to be unconvincing. He lost the interest of Black voters at an event in Los Angeles, at which he tried to subtly persuade them to proceed gradually with civil rights to avoid upsetting "habits or traditions that are older than the Republic" (573). Eisenhower defeated Stevenson again in the Electoral College, this time by a larger margin.

By the mid-1950s, television reporters began to express favor toward civil rights legislation and aired incidents of "southern racial violence and intimidation, long hidden from view outside the South" (576). The Supreme Court, in hearing the *Brown v. Board of Education* case, was aware of how the US looked, calling itself the leader of the free world while maintaining an oppressive racial order at home. Not all civil rights activists, however, supported the legal strategy of the NAACP and its lawyer Thurgood Marshall in overturning *Plessy v. Ferguson*. Not all African Americans wanted desegregated schools, which often caused Black teachers to lose their jobs. Others who wanted desegregation believed that other political goals were more important, particularly better jobs, equal pay, and fair housing. Segregationists, meanwhile, prepared to go to war. They started a campaign to impeach Chief Justice Earl Warren. When the court ordered some Southern schools to desegregate, those in Washington, DC, and Baltimore complied, but the "overwhelming majority did not" (582).

The fight to desegregate public schools often put Black children on the front lines. This was followed by other acts that defied Jim Crow, which took place on buses and at lunch counters. On December 1, 1955, in Montgomery, Alabama, NAACP activist and seamstress Rosa Parks refused to give up her bus seat to a white man. Parks had joined the NAACP in 1943. As secretary of her local chapter, she had worked on both voter registration efforts and desegregation of public transportation. She had purposefully decided to challenge Jim Crow on Montgomery's buses, resulting in Martin Luther King Jr. leading a citywide protest and a boycott of Montgomery's buses four days later in response to Parks's arrest. More than 5,000 people joined the protest. Ninety percent of Montgomery's Black population boycotted the city's buses. King was indicted for violating the state's antiboycott law. On November 13, 1956, the Supreme Court deemed Montgomery's bus law unconstitutional.

Justice William O. Douglas would later blame Eisenhower's silence for the violence that engulfed the South and, later, the nation. If the president, still a national hero, had gone on television and condemned the violence, Douglas insisted, many Americans would have fallen in line and accepted desegregation as the law of the land. Instead, his silence encouraged racist rabblerousers and political opportunists looking to benefit from white supremacist ire. Orval Faubus, governor of Arkansas, had no personal opposition to integration and had even sent his son to an integrated college. However, his nearly all white constituents were firmly opposed to desegregation. Arkansas was also a state that prevented Black people from voting. On

September 2, 1957, Faubus announced that he would send 250 National Guardsmen to Central High School in Little Rock to ensure that no Black child would enter its doors. Elizabeth Eckford, one of the Black students who tried to attend, was attacked with lynching threats and a mob wielding sticks, stones, and weapons.

Congress debated the Civil Rights Act of 1957 while Eisenhower dithered over what to do. The federal government established a Civil Rights Commission. It granted the commission the authority to hear complaints, but not to respond to them. Despite Strom Thurmond filibustering against the bill for more than a day, it was pushed through due to Lyndon Johnson's brokering. On September 25, 1957, federal troops escorted the nine Black students, who became known as the Little Rock Nine, into Central High. About two weeks later, the Soviet Union launched its Sputnik satellite into orbit. Shortly afterward, Eisenhower asked the nation's top scientists what the position of scientific research was in government. The meeting led to the creation of the National Aeronautics and Space Agency (NASA), which established operations in Florida and Texas, and the funding of research in universities across the former Cotton Belt and in the Sun Belt. The Advanced Research Projects Agency would later build what became the Internet.

In this chapter, Lepore focuses on the theme of scientific advancement and moral responsibility. During the postwar years, the first computers, which had grown out of war technology, were introduced for public use. The government started publicity efforts to make the public amenable to the new technology to prevent fear over it, though this technology would later lead to the automation that would displace human labor.

During the years between the end of the Second World War and the end of the 1950s, the US simultaneously became both modern and backward-looking, eager for scientific advancements and technologies, encouraged by the introduction of newer household gadgets and appliances, as well as better automobiles, and eager to embrace traditional American values. The latter was most pronounced by the need to ensure that women would return to the home after being in the workforce during the war. Simultaneous attacks on homosexuals reflected the emphasis on strict gender roles. Women of all races, people of color, and some homosexual men were excluded from the benefits of the G.I. Bill, thereby bolstering the economic dominance of white males. There was, too, a rise of evangelicalism that was reminiscent of the Second Great Awakening. Billy Graham, with his anti-intellectualism and nostalgia for rural America, was a figure in the mold of William Jennings Bryan.

Meanwhile, a new world order emerged. The world was polarized between capitalism and communism, democracy and totalitarianism, wondering which order would prevail and which was more morally sound. Additionally, the American South was transformed after the war, restructuring its economy so that its new base was in manufacturing instead of agriculture. Black people, however, were still largely excluded from these new economic opportunities. In the North, they fared little better, due to de facto segregation, a problem that Lepore does not explore much in this chapter and, in the next chapter, only in the context of civil unrest.

Though politics mattered little to most Americans during the midcentury, political think tanks worked to manipulate the political parties to polarize them and to encourage the public to follow suit. Lepore does not explain the motivation behind this, but a possibility may have been to strengthen the hands of increasingly powerful corporations, bolstered by 1950s consumerism, which would have needed public support, as well as that of Congress, to lobby for their interests. Similarly, the American Medical Association worked with Campaigns, Inc. to prevent the socialization of health care in the interest of protecting their profit margins.

As the political tides shifted, Richard Nixon moved with the current, thereby buoying his political career and, eventually, emerging as a serious presidential contender. Nixon allied himself with figures in the Republican Party according to their respective popularity—first, Joseph McCarthy, then Eisenhower and, finally, Barry Goldwater. At the same time, conservative white women became fervent GOP activists. Long before the Republican Party's realignment, women of all races had been a powerful presence within it. After the realignment, conservative white women emerged as political activists and cemented their roles as protectors of the traditional home. Their ideas were rooted in a racialized idea of femininity, not unlike that of the activism of Confederate women who demanded welfare benefits after the Civil War.

Within the Black community, a political schism formed over school desegregation, which would presage later schisms within the civil rights movement regarding political priorities. Moreover, the placement of Black children on the front lines of the movement did not work in activists' favor. This action merely exposed and reaffirmed white supremacists' inability to regard Black children as children instead of as objects of racial animus, a view that would be crystallized by the Montgomery church bombing of 1963—an event that Lepore does not mention in this chapter or the next, though it illustrates the ruthlessness of Dixiecrats in maintaining Jim Crow.

The chapter ends by meditating on the incongruity between the nation trying to move forward scientifically, both in its space and arms races with the Soviet Union, as well as its development of computers, while it still contended with the unfinished business of the nation's founding and the failures of Reconstruction. In this regard, Lepore reminds the reader that the US, despite its rapid developments and assumption of world leadership and military dominance after the Second World War, was still very much a work in progress.

Part 4, Chapter 14 Summary and Analysis: "Rights and Wrongs"

Since 1940, inequalities of wealth and income had been diminishing. The state's growing power and a progressive income tax had "made possible unprecedented economic growth and a wide distribution of goods and opportunities" (591). By 1960, two-thirds of all Americans owned their own homes. Excepting civil rights, Americans generally agreed with each other about their system of government and shared a theory about politics. However, the general public knew little about politics, "resulting in a very loose and unconstrained attachment to any single set of political beliefs" (593). This lack of sophistication about politics resulted in a more moderate political ideology. Between 1968 and 1972, political polarization and economic inequality increased. By 1974, American liberalism began its long decline, while conservatism entered a long period of ascent. The nation, in subsequent decades, would become as divided and unequal as it had been in the years before the Civil War.

African Americans, meanwhile, continued to press for civil rights. In early 1960, four young college students in Greensboro, North Carolina, staged a sit-in at a segregated lunch counter in a Woolworth's. By the end of the week, over 400 students were involved in the Greensboro sit-in. The nonviolent protest movement quickly spread throughout the South. The Black students' stoicism in response to thuggish and violent white supremacists "even earned the admiration of some hardened pro-segregation southern newspaper editors" (595-96). In April, Ella Baker, acting director of the Southern Christian Leadership Conference (SCLC), invited the student leaders to a meeting on Easter weekend. She balked, however, when the SCLC tried to get her to convince the students to join the organization as a junior chapter. She urged them, instead, to start their own organization. In response, they started the Student Nonviolent Coordinating Committee (SNCC). Baker left the SCLC to join SNCC.

Later that year, when Eisenhower's commission delivered its report, he called for federal action to support voting rights, urged the denial of federal funds to employers who discriminated on the basis of race, and insisted upon the urgency of ending segregation in education (597).

For the 1960 election, the Simulmatics Corporation continued the work of both UNIVAC and George Gallup. Simulmatics's founder, Ithiel de Sola Pool, sought "to both advance and accelerate the measurement of public opinion and the forecasting of elections" by "sort[ing] voters into 480 possible types" (597). One key question Pool asked was, "Which party is better suited for people like you?" (598). The point of Simulmatics's work was that, even if voters did not have core political ideologies, they could still be sorted into ideological categories based on their race, ethnicity, location, income, age, etc. The Democratic National Convention (DNC) found Simulmatics's first report so helpful that they ordered three more reports on Kennedy's public image, Nixon's public image, and on foreign policy as a significant campaign issue. Simulmatics also analyzed how Kennedy should discuss his Catholicism. The corporation concluded that the presidential candidate should be open and straightforward about his religion. Kennedy then "gave a frank and direct speech in Houston on September 12, 1960," in which he affirmed his belief in the separation of church and state" (599). Nixon, meanwhile, won the Republican nomination, despite having no support from Eisenhower.

Richard Nixon agreed to debate Kennedy on television. On September 26, 1960, the candidates met in a CBS TV studio in Chicago. There was no audience. The debate was broadcast by CBS, NBC, and ABC. By the time this debate aired, "nine in ten American households had a television set" (600). Nixon felt ill and had been hospitalized for nearly two weeks before the debate. He was both in pain and unprepared. Sixty-six million Americans ended up watching Nixon scowl and sweat on television. Two days after the candidates' final debates, Martin Luther King Jr. was arrested in Atlanta during a sit-in and "sentenced to four months of hard labor" (600). Robert F. Kennedy intervened and got King released. Nixon, who actually had a stronger record on civil rights than John Kennedy, was unresponsive. He later came to believe that his unwillingness to act cost him "one of the closest elections in American history" (600). Nixon also believed that the election may have been rigged. There was, indeed, evidence of voter fraud in both Illinois and Texas.

When John F. Kennedy was inaugurated on January 21, 1961, he marshalled in a new era. Three days earlier, Eisenhower gave a farewell address in which he warned that the US-Soviet arms race could lead to the development of a military-industrial complex. However, few heeded his warning, particularly as Americans were alarmed by the spread of communism in Southeast Asia. The US, trying to flex its own influence in this region, had "redirected its foreign aid from Europe to Asia and Africa" (602). When French Indochina tried to overthrow its colonial rulers, the US supported France over the Vietnamese. This led to growing anti-Americanism. A treaty divided newly liberated Vietnam. Ho Chi Minh and the Communist Party took power in the North, while Ngo Dinh Diem, an American-backed Catholic nationalist, led South Vietnam. The US engaged in state building in South Vietnam, training its civil servants and police force, and building the nation's infrastructure. Some viewed this as a sign that the US wanted to place Vietnam under new colonial rule.

By the end of 1963, Ngo Dinh Diem was killed in an American-sanctioned coup three weeks before Kennedy's assassination. Soon thereafter, 16,000 American troops were stationed in Vietnam. Not long before his death, the Kennedy administration nearly created a nuclear crisis during a confrontation with Cuba. In April 1961, Castro's army had destroyed the American-backed Cuban exiles that attempted an invasion of Cuba in what became known as the Bay of Pigs invasion. The following summer, American U2s flew over Cuba and observed ballistic missiles that had the capacity of reaching the US Soviet premier Nikita Khrushchev had sent them. Kennedy appeared on television on October 22, 1962, when he disclosed the "existence of the missiles and argued for action" (604). The American government responded by sending the navy to quarantine Cuba. Two days later, 16 Soviet ships went to confront the blockade before turning back. Khrushchev sent the White House two contradictory messages: The first promised that the Soviet Union would withdraw its missiles if the US would end the blockade; the other conveyed something stern, which Kennedy urged his advisers to ignore. Kennedy responded to the first message, and Khrushchev withdrew the missiles.

Meanwhile, the Congress of Racial Equality (CORE) sent 13 volunteers, both Black and white, to the Deep South on buses. Eight days later, white supremacists attacked a Greyhound bus on which the so-called Freedom Riders had been passengers. They shattered the windows, slashed the tires, and then set it on fire. The riders barely escaped. When the second bus arrived, the KKK were waiting at the train station in Birmingham. Attorney General Robert Kennedy ordered that the riders be evacuated. CORE sent in more riders from Nashville, who were met at the bus station and jailed by the troops of Birmingham police commissioner Eugene "Bull" Connor. Alabama dared the federal government to act. Robert Kennedy convinced his brother to call Alabama governor John Patterson, who had supported Kennedy's campaign in 1960. Patterson, however, refused to take the president's call. The governor did reluctantly agree "to provide a police escort for the [Freedom Riders'] bus on its trip from Birmingham to Montgomery" (605). However, when the bus reached the station, another white mob was waiting. They beat the riders. Still, the Freedom Riders and 1,500 other Black civil rights activists met at First Baptist Church to decide on their next strategy. Three thousand white vigilantes surrounded the church and were eventually dispersed by the Alabama National Guard. The Freedom Riders decided to ride all summer long.

In April 1963, Dr. Martin Luther King Jr. led a protest in Birmingham, which was "the most violent city in the South" (607). When fellow clergyman, all of whom were liberal and white, denounced him in the town's newspaper and declared that the protests were "untimely," King wrote what became a famous letter from a Birmingham jail, where he had been placed in solitary confinement. Meanwhile, George Wallace, who succeeded Patterson as governor, said that "if black students tried to enter the campus of the state university in Tuscaloosa, he'd block the door himself" (607). President Kennedy decided that it was time to address the public. He urged white Americans to sympathize with Black people who were denied "the full and free life" that everyone wants (608). He then talked about military service, and how Black citizens have always served loyally.

To mark the centenary of the Emancipation Proclamation, civil rights activist Bayard Rustin began organizing a march on Washington, scheduled to take place in August 1963. The Kennedy administration prepared for possible violence by arranging "for military troops to be kept on alert" (609). Three hundred thousand people gathered. It was the first time that most Americans, including Kennedy, had ever seen Dr. King deliver a speech. Three months later, President John F. Kennedy was assassinated in Dallas. Less than five years later, King, too, was assassinated in Memphis. Riots ensued that Easter Sunday in what came to be known as the Easter Riots.

The day after Kennedy's assassination, Lyndon Johnson, who had assumed the presidency, began to make it clear that he was not a conservative. On November 27, 1963, he encouraged Congress to act on civil rights. During his first State of the Union address in January, he also pledged an "unconditional war on poverty" (611). When Congress debated the civil rights bill, both

Dr. King and Malcolm X traveled to Washington to witness the debates, which had split both parties. Eventually, the bill passed and Johnson signed the Civil Rights Act into law on July 2, 1964.

The fight for voting rights caused dissent within the Democratic Party. The party's delegation at the nominating convention was all white. SNCC set up the alternative Mississippi Freedom Democratic Party. Ella Baker operated its Washington office and "delivered the keynote speech at its state nominating convention in Jackson" (621). At the convention in Atlantic City, "party leaders refused to seat the Mississippi Freedom Democratic Party delegation" (621). This led Freedom Rider Stokely Carmichael to give up on party politics in favor of radicalism.

George Wallace's bid the for the presidential nomination ended when Barry Goldwater entered the race. The Republican National Convention nominated him eleven days after the Civil Rights Act was signed. Conservative white women flocked to Goldwater's campaign. The 1964 presidential race "was the first in which as many women voted as men" (616). Overall, women were likelier than men to vote against Goldwater.

After winning the presidential race, Johnson decided to use his huge popular vote win and his big Democratic majority in the House to move his anti-poverty agenda forward. According to Lepore, "no unified government in American history was as productive as LBJ's" (617). He pushed Congress to pass an education act that largely benefited low-income students in both primary and secondary schools. He also established Medicare and Medicaid. He flew to Independence, Missouri, so that Harry Truman could witness him signing the nation's first socialized health care legislation. Johnson also passed "the largest tax cut in American history," believing that it would help to ease unemployment. Instead, he ended up with insufficient funding for his programs.

Initially, Johnson's tax cut worked. People used what would have been tax payments to purchase goods. However, his economic reforms could not pay for both the Great Society and the war in Vietnam. After President Kennedy died, his brother Robert pressed Johnson to remain in Vietnam, which Johnson had initially been disinclined to do. By 1965, however, Johnson realized that he couldn't withdraw without admitting defeat. He decided to conceal from the public his escalation of the war. By the end of the year, 184,000 troops were stationed in Vietnam, most of them people of color and poor white people. To pay for the war and avoid raising taxes, Johnson cut funding for his Great Society programs. His choices led to his becoming so unpopular that he publicly announced his decision not to run for a second term in 1968.

In 1965, Dr. King went to Selma, Alabama, "where demonstrators had pledged to march all the way to Montgomery" (621). The marchers walked through a county that was over 70% Black, though hardly any African Americans had attempted to vote since the rise of Jim Crow in the early part of the 20th century. Malcolm X flew to Selma and spoke in support of the protestors, despite the reservations of some SCLC members. On February 21, he was assassinated in Harlem. On March 7, 500 Alabama state troopers awaited the marchers "on the far side of [Edmund] Pettus Bridge, ordered by George Wallace to arrest anyone who tried to cross" (621). As marchers tried to cross the bridge, state troopers beat them. The spectacle was televised. Johnson addressed Congress on March 15, calling on them to pass the Voting Rights Act. A week earlier, Johnson sent Congress the Law Enforcement Assistance Act, which led to a war on crime that militarized the police. Money that had previously gone into anti-poverty efforts now went toward anti-crime efforts. As a result of Johnson's war on crime, which would be expanded by his successors, "[m]ore Americans would be sent to prison in the twenty years after LBJ launched his war on crime than went to prison in the entire century before" (622). Black people and those of Latin descent would make up most of the prison population, and the US "incarceration rate would rise to five times that of any other industrial nation" (622-23).

Johnson signed the Voting Rights Act on August 6, 1965. Four days later, riots broke out in Watts, a neighborhood in South Central Los Angeles. King flew to the city to preach nonviolence, though his entreaties fell on deaf ears. In the summer of 1967, riots began in Newark, New Jersey, sparked by an incident of police brutality. The riots, which were broadcast, appeared to some American viewers like scenes from Vietnam. Conservatives believed that the only response to the rioting was to "govern with a will of iron" (624). Ronald Reagan, who was running for governor of California, blamed the riots on overreliance on government. He particularly blamed college students for rousing discontent and criticized the University of California, Berkeley, for inviting Robert Kennedy and Stokely Carmichael to speak. Reagan won the governor's race in a landslide. He began to replace Goldwater as the star of the Republican Party. His agenda was to "[dismantle] the New Deal" (627).

In May 1967, while the California state legislature debated gun control, 30 Black Panthers, led by Bobby Seale, entered the California State House, carrying various firearms. Reagan who signed the measure the legislature voted into law, told the press that he saw no good reason why a citizen should ever carry loaded weapons around.

Johnson, meanwhile, organized a commission to investigate the riots. The resulting Kerner Commission, named for its chair, Illinois governor Otto Kerner, released a 426-page report that requested $30 billion in urban spending on public housing and jobs programs to ameliorate the conditions that had sparked the riots. It also called for the government to commit fully to the desegregation of public schools. Conservatives read the report as blaming white people for violence in Black communities. With the exception of a recommendation to expand policing, Johnson largely ignored the commission's findings.

The escalation of the war in Vietnam "galvanized the New Left" and "[brought] together the free speech and civil rights movements" (628). Dr. King joined the antiwar movement in 1967, thereby severing his alliance with Johnson. That year, around 500,000 troops were stationed in Vietnam and 9,000 Americans died. The war had taken $25 billion out of the federal budget. In January 1968, during the Vietnamese new year known as Tet, the North Vietnamese raided South Vietnam, including the US embassy in Saigon, during what came to be known as the Tet Offensive.

Robert Kennedy entered the presidential race that year as a Democratic candidate. He had changed his position on Vietnam and now characterized it as "Johnson's war." George Wallace had entered the race, too. On March 31, Johnson announced that he would eschew another presidential run to focus on ending the war. Four days later, Dr. Martin Luther King Jr. was killed on his hotel balcony in Memphis. Riots erupted in 130 cities. Two months later, Robert Kennedy was killed while leaving the ballroom of a Los Angeles hotel.

Kennedy's death, as well as increasing national unrest, provided an opening for Nixon who ran on a platform of anti-liberalism and the restoration of law and order. He also ran a campaign based on a "southern strategy," which involved abandoning civil rights in favor of winning Southern Democrats. Instead of speaking with overt racism like George Wallace, Nixon chose subtler language.

The 1968 Republican National Convention took place in Miami, while the Democrats held their national convention in Chicago, where antiwar protestors, including Students for a Democratic Society (SDS), clashed with "12,000 Chicago police, 6,000 National Guardsmen, 6,000 army troops, and 1,000 undercover intelligence agents" (633). Johnson's vice president, Hubert Humphrey, who had not run in a single primary, won the party's nomination, "defeating Eugene McCarthy and arousing the ire of the party's left flank" (633).

Election Day, Nixon defeated Humphrey by winning the votes of Americans who believed that his promise to restore law and order spoke directly to them. They became known as the "Silent Majority." In 1960, around three out of five white, blue-collar voters had voted for Kennedy. By 1968, that ratio voting Democratic had dwindled to one in three.

Nixon's 1968 campaign had been uniquely divisive. He also began to think of his reelection soon after he entered the White House. His chief of staff, H. R. Haldeman, encouraged him to court ethnic white people—those of Polish, Italian, and Irish descent, but not Jewish voters. Haldeman also eschewed Black voters. Nixon criticized nonwhite people who voiced concern about social and economic inequities rooted in a legacy of racism. He accused them of wanting success handed to them instead of "start[ing] at the bottom of the ladder the way [white people] did" (637). He spoke directly and singularly to disaffected white voters. The GOP moved further to the right, "to capitalize on backlash against civil rights," while the Democratic Party went further to the Left (637).

Aside from encouraging strife, Nixon had little interest in domestic policy. His main domestic initiative, announcing in the summer of 1969, was the Family Assistance Plan which aimed to eliminate the welfare system, social works, and many social programs in favor of cash payments dispensed to those below a certain income level.

Nixon became especially notorious for recording conversations in the Oval Office, though all previous presidents since Franklin Roosevelt had done the same. He also maintained tapes that he wanted to serve as a chronicle of his presidency. While Haldeman had Nixon's new recording system installed, defense analyst Daniel Ellsberg tried to figure out how to release "a 7,000-page, 47-volume study of the war in Vietnam that had been commissioned by Robert McNamara in 1967," shortly before his resignation (640). The report, which became known as the Pentagon Papers, chronicled the lies and errors of several administrations in pursuing the war in Vietnam. The *New York Times* began to publish excerpts on June 13, 1971. The Pentagon Papers, however, caused no harm to Nixon, as the report ended in 1968. Still, Nixon was paranoid that his own presidency would come under fire. He asked the Justice Department to forbid the *Times* from publishing any additional portions of the report. The *Times* took its case to the Supreme Court. Meanwhile, the *Washington Post* continued publishing the report. The Supreme Court ruled that the publication of the Pentagon Papers could proceed.

On Saturday, June 17, 1972, G. Gordon Liddy, a former aide of Nixon's White House counsel John Ehrlichman, "directed five men to break into the offices of Lawrence O'Brien, the DNC chairman, at the Watergate Hotel" to steal documents and restore phone wiretaps (641). After completing those tasks, the men were to go to George McGovern's campaign headquarters and do much of the same. They never got there, however, because they were arrested at the Watergate. Nixon had not known about the burglary plans, but he had found out about it several days later and "was captured on tape discussing a cover-up with Haldeman" (641). On Election Day in 1972, Nixon won 61% of the vote and 49 states—the first presidential candidate ever to do so.

In January 1973, he announced that he would end the war in Vietnam. The following month, the Senate voted to organize a special committee to investigate the Watergate break-in. Nixon was soon forced to turn over 1,200 pages of transcripts to 46 of his tapes. The public soon discovered the nature of his character. Nixon tried to withhold transcripts in which he discussed the Watergate break-in. The case that ensued against him went to the Supreme Court in *United States v. Nixon*. The Supreme Court ordered the White House to release the tapes. To avoid inevitable impeachment after the content of the tapes was released on August 6, 1974, Nixon resigned two days later.

In the years after the Second World War, the US endured a moral reckoning for its inaction on civil rights and its hubristic, paranoid pursuit of anti-communism during the Cold War. The nation did, however, enjoy an era of political consensus—that is, politics mattered little in daily life for average Americans who identified less with a particular party than with an individual candidate. This absence of party stratification, which has characterized politics in the late 20th and early 21st century, may have contributed to the sense of relative peace, among white people anyway, during the 1950s.

There was a marked division, however, between how white and Black people lived. Lepore focuses less on how other groups were affected by mid-century segregationist policies in favor of focusing on those who were targeted by the legislation. Middle-class white people lived in comfortable suburbs that Black people were often forbidden to move into due to restrictive covenants. This contributed to the rise of impoverished ghettos. White people's preoccupation with consumerism contrasted, particularly in regard to its frivolity, with Black people's efforts toward resisting Jim Crow and pursuing civil rights. The great irony of the US fighting ardently for democracy abroad, as Lepore noted in Chapter 12, was that it failed to live according to its own values at home. The threat of communism was rooted in the sense that increasing interest in it would diminish American values—that is, eliminate the nation's legacy of white, patriarchal supremacy and its emphasis on Christian faith.

Lepore reminds readers that John F. Kennedy, who has been touted in public historical memory as attentive to civil rights, did not see the urgency of the matter until the end of his presidency. Like Nixon, he led a presidency that concerned itself primarily with foreign policy, though Kennedy managed this less successfully than Nixon. Meanwhile, Johnson's Great Society continued the New Deal's legacy of building the nation's social safety net. Unlike the New Deal, it was marred by bad fiscal policy. Johnson, likely increasingly concerned about domestic discord and a worsening war in Vietnam, wanted to placate the public with tax breaks, at the expense of his most promising and important programs. Worse, he redirected the money into anti-crime efforts, which would have been less necessary if the president had remained faithful to his Great Society programs, particularly those, such as Head Start, which funded child care.

Both the Vietnam War and the Black nationalist movement that grew out of the civil rights era galvanized the New Left and the New Right. Robert Kennedy, despite his past as a McCarthyist and his efforts to convince Johnson to stay the course in Vietnam, associated himself with the New Left. Johnson's newly militarized police force clashed with New Left antiwar protestors and further enraged the New Right, or Silent Majority, that later delivered Nixon the presidency. Nixon capitalized on the rancor expressed by middle-aged white voters who were both concerned about violent national unrest and likely longed for the peace and sterility of the 1950s. However, Nixon's air of paternal authoritarianism, which appealed to those white voters, coincided with a controlling and paranoid personality. Nixon's legacy has been obscured by these revelations of his character, as well as the Watergate scandal. Part of this legacy, as Lepore notes, relates to his advances in foreign policy. There are, too, his creation of the Environmental Protection Agency (EPA) and his support of Title X as part of his Public Health Service Act (1970), which guarantees access to family-planning services, particularly to low-income people.

Part 4, Chapter 15 Summary and Analysis: "Battle Lines"

The public, from the 1960s to the 1980s, was divided over many issues concerning women. However, those divisions, during those decades "did not fall along party lines," though Republicans had historically been more likely to support equal rights and family planning than Democrats (647). Barry Goldwater and his wife had even served on the board of Planned Parenthood in Phoenix. Only in 1980 did both Democrats and Republicans put abortion on their platforms and demonstrate their starkly oppositional positions. By the nineties, abortion had become a major partisan issue. Additionally, gun ownership and gun safety were not partisan issues before the 1970s either (647). Bill Clinton, during his 1992 presidential run, tried to bridge the "guns-and-abortion-divide" by running a campaign solely on economic issues. This proved to be impossible.

It was political strategists and consultants who sowed the division between constituencies, largely with the help of computers. Strategists figured out that, the more emotional the political issue was, the likelier voters were to show up to polls. Abortion and guns turned out to be the most emotional issues.

In 1958, Alan Guttmacher, chief of obstetrics and gynecology at Mount Sinai Hospital, clinical professor of obstetrics and gynecology at Columbia University, and a member of Planned Parenthood's medical advisory board, encouraged New York municipal hospitals "to reverse an institutional policy that forbade doctors from giving out contraceptives or contraceptive information" (649). Efforts to legalize abortion were initiated by the doctors, attorneys, and clergymen who first operated Planned Parenthood. In 1962, Guttmacher ascended to the presidency of Planned Parenthood. During his tenure, he started a campaign to get the poor access to family planning programs, "to overturn bans on contraception, and to liberalize abortion law" (649).

In 1969, President Nixon asked Congress to provide additional funding for family planning. It was George H. W. Bush, a young Republican representative from Texas, who pushed for the legislation. This pressure encouraged legislators in 16 states, including California, where Ronald Reagan was governor, to lift restrictions on abortion. In 1970, Nixon signed Title X, federal family planning legislation, "which included a provision under which doctors on military bases could perform abortions" (650).

Meanwhile, women had become divided over many matters, and the second-wave feminist movement of the 1960s and 1970s had divided into three movements: liberal feminism, radical feminism, and conservative antifeminism. In the Black nationalist movement, there was also controversy over the position of women. Stokely Carmichael once said that "[t]he only position for women in the movement is prone" (651). Despite Carmichael's dismissal, radical feminists had been greatly influenced by the Black Power movement.

In 1971, journalist Gloria Steinem and New York congresswomen Bella Abzug and Shirley Chisholm founded the National Women's Political Caucus. The bipartisan organization sought to get more women elected to political office and succeeded, doubling the number of women in elected office between 1970 and 1975. With that momentum, more women's rights bills were passed and the Equal Rights Amendment (ERA), first introduced on the floor of Congress in 1923, passed the House in 1971 and the Senate the following year. When it first went to the states for ratification, it enjoyed enormous popularity, even in more conservative states, such as West Virginia. In the same year, law school professor Ruth Bader Ginsburg began to argue equal rights cases before the Supreme Court in 1971, "citing Pauli Murray's strategy for using the

Fourteenth Amendment to defeat discrimination by sex" (652). The following year, Ginsburg started the ACLU's Women's Rights Project.

Also in 1971, speechwriter Pat Buchanan told President Nixon that abortion was increasingly becoming an important issue, particularly to Catholics. He suggested that the president's prospects for reelection would improve if he took a stand on abortion. Nixon followed the advice. He changed from having supported abortion to being a candidate who touted the sanctity of all human life, even that of the unborn. Privately, however, Nixon supported abortion in some instances. On tape, he expressed the belief that abortion was necessary in instances of rape and "in case of a pregnancy resulting from sex between 'a black and a white'" (654).

In the mid-1970s, economic malaise set in. However, it first became noticeable to most Americans in 1973, during the OPEC oil embargo. Additionally, Detroit motor companies faced fierce competition from Japanese auto manufacturers. Steel industries closed permanently or moved abroad, turning the formerly bustling Midwest along the Great Lakes into the Rust Belt. Liberals blamed this economic downturn on the abandonment of Johnson's Great Society programs, while conservatives blamed it on the failures of liberalism, particularly taxation and government regulation, which they said had constricted the free market.

Lepore explains past economic growth on the development of technologies, starting with electricity and the automobile. This growth was not sustainable, however, and the pace of innovation had slowed. Few inventions patented after 1970 produced the vast changes and growth that had been enjoyed previously.

Additionally, economic inequality became more common in the last quarter of the 20th century. The advent and rise of the Internet in the 1990s did not bring forth earlier levels of economic growth. It actually contributed to "widening income inequality and political instability" (657). Wages for male workers dropped, causing more married women, particularly white women, to work outside of the household. Many women began to demand government-funded child care. Still, household incomes did not rise much. Typically, liberals blamed conservatives and conservatives blamed liberals, while Phyllis Schlafly blamed feminists.

When the Republican Party was founded in 1854, it "had been the party of abolition and the party of women's rights" (658). By 1896, it was "the party of big business" (658). However, it had remained supportive of civil liberties for women. It was not until 1968, when the ERA was left off of the Republican platform, that feminism experienced its first backlash within the Republican Party. In 1972, feminist Republican women tried to restore the party's pro-ERA plank to the platform. Phyllis Schlafly worked to ensure that they wouldn't gain headway, forming an organization of conservative housewives called STOP ERA. STOP stood for Stop Taking Away Our Privileges. In response, at the 1976 Republican National Convention, 30 GOP feminists formed the Republican Women's Task Force to fight for platform planks in support of the ERA, reproductive rights, affirmative action, federally funded child care, and the extension of the Equal Pay Act (659).

When liberal feminists organized the 1977 National Women's Conference in Houston, Schlafly complained that neither she nor any other conservative women had been invited to help organize the conference. The women, who included anthropologist

Margaret Mead, tennis champion Billie Jean King, and actress Jean Stapleton, met over four days. Lady Bird Johnson, Rosalynn Carter, and Betty Ford were also in attendance. Ann Richards, then a Texas county commissioner, gave a speech about the ERA, in which she invoked her daughter, Ann, who grew up to become president of Planned Parenthood.

In the end, it was race that had divided the second-wave feminist movement, despite the entreaties of some nonwhite activists, such as Coretta Scott King. Nonwhite women made up over a quarter of the women delegates in Houston. However, Schlafly saw more reasons for the divisiveness. The conference's two most controversial proposals were for equal rights for gays and lesbians and government funding for abortion. Feminist Betty Friedan had been hostile to the burgeoning movement for gay rights, believing that it would harm the feminist movement. Some conservative activists, including the singer Anita Bryant, had seized onto the issue, though this only convinced many liberal feminists that they had a moral responsibility to support gay rights.

Schlafly also helped bring together anti-abortion, anti-ERA, and anti-gay rights groups under one political umbrella. Evangelicals, meanwhile, had largely stayed away from politics. This changed in 1961, when the Supreme Court "overturned a Maryland law that required an employee to declare his belief in God" (662). The following year, the court decided that mandatory school prayer was unconstitutional. In 1963, it forbade Bible reading and recitation of the Lord's Prayer in public schools. Finally, in 1971, the court declared that segregated private schools would no longer be tax-exempt. These schools had been a refuge for white supremacists who had opposed school integration. Ultimately, it was religion, not desegregation, that drew evangelicals to conservatives and, eventually, the Republican Party.

Strategists within the Heritage Foundation continued work on building a conservative coalition that would bring in evangelicals. They later recruited Jerry Falwell, who founded the Moral Majority in 1979. The organization's aim was to battle "secular humanism." This included women's liberation, gay rights, the ERA, sex education, government-funded child care, and, primarily, abortion. Prior to Falwell's efforts, evangelicals had actually supported abortion, particularly "under conditions such as rape, incest, clear evidence of severe fetal deformity, and carefully ascertained evidence of [...] damage to the emotional, mental, and physical health of the mother" (664).

By now, Ronald Reagan was the Republican Party's most powerful conservative and he had Phyllis Schlafly's support. Moderates in the GOP, particularly the feminist Jill Ruckelshaus, reminded members of the party that Republicans had long supported the ERA. She and her moderate cohorts were driven out of the party. Reagan won the party's nomination and ran with George H. W. Bush, who adopted a conservative position on both abortion and the ERA, despite having previously expressed support for them.

Strategists knew that the New Right didn't have many ideas, but they did have better technology than the New Left, including computers, telephone marketing, television, cassette tapes, and toll-free numbers from which they asked for both votes and campaign contributions. They used census records, polls, campaign finance records, and election data to target potential support. They also bypassed the mass media, which they believed was biased against conservatives.

The New Right's rise coincided with the increasing influence of the polling industry. In 1972, political scientist Leo Bogart learned that polls largely manufacture opinion because most Americans know nothing or nearly nothing about many issues that are raised among politicians and, therefore, have no opinion.

In 1980, the New Right finally elected their ideal candidate, Ronald Reagan, who, at his 1981 inauguration, declared that government was not the solution to people's problems but the problem itself. He encouraged Americans to rebuild the nation's defenses, to protect unborn children, and to permit Christian faith in the classrooms. Part of Reagan's support had come from voters who were fed up with the complicated tax code. Thus, Reagan made tax cuts a key plank on his campaign platform. He also cut federal spending to social programs, claiming that they promoted dependency and immorality and eroded traditional family life by discouraging marriage. During the Reagan era, over 1 million people lost food stamp benefits. However, Reagan protected Social Security and Medicare.

Reagan's other policy measures included increasing military spending by 35%, which tripled the national debt during his eight years in office. The federal government also expanded, as did financial irresponsibility due to deregulation that "allow[ed] savings-and-loan banks to sell junk bonds and high-risk securities" (671).

In March 1981, John Hinckley Jr. shot Ronald Reagan with a revolver that he had bought at a pawn shop in Dallas. In the early part of the 20th century, the National Rifle Association (NRA) had actively sought out state and federal gun safety measures. It had supported the 1968 Gun Control Act, which had banned mail-order sales, kept high-risk people from owning firearms, and "prohibit[ed] the importation of military surplus firearms" (672). The 2nd Amendment received little attention. It was Black nationalists who first began to invoke the 2nd Amendment in the 1960s, while some conservatives, including Nixon, loathed gun ownership and found the idea that it was "a constitutional right to be absurd" (673).

Gun rights emerged as a conservative political movement, "a rights fight for white men" and a "backlash against both feminism and civil rights" (673). The movement also coincided with a rising White Power movement, which was a response to both the post–civil rights era and an increase in the number of immigrants arriving in the US. While the number of Mexican immigrants remained the same, the number of legal immigrants from Mexico declined. Since the 1960s, Mexican American intellectuals had been pursuing immigration reform as part of a civil rights struggle. With the rise of the Chicano movement, that effort "turn[ed] toward ethnic separatism and nationalism" (674). Eventually, the two strains of the movement—elders had focused on labor rights, while the younger Chicano activists wanted restrictions on immigration lifted—came together in the mid-1970s, seeing that it was important to protect the rights of undocumented workers. However, by the 1990s, the US-Mexican border had become a kind of military zone (674).

Meanwhile, in 1975, the NRA created a lobbying arm led by Harlon Bronson Carter, a marksman and former chief of US Border Patrol who had been convicted of murder in 1931. The NRA had endorsed Reagan's presidency, and Reagan, despite his attempted assassination, had become so opposed to gun laws that he supported abolishing the Bureau of Alcohol, Tobacco, and Firearms. Reagan's press secretary, James Brady, "had been shot in the head with a bullet designed to explode on impact" during the incident and "was permanently paralyzed" (676). He and his wife later created the Brady Campaign to Prevent Gun Violence, leading to the passage of the Brady Bill, which mandated background checks. President George W. Bush later allowed the law, passed in 1994, to expire.

To aid the gun rights argument, conservatives developed originalism as a new mode of constitutional interpretation and focused on the 2nd Amendment. By 1991, more Americans were familiar with the 2nd Amendment than they were with the First. The originalist argument flourished in law schools. Supreme Court Justice William Brennan found the idea that modern judges could ascertain the intentions of the Founders patently absurd. The public, however, didn't believe him. Conservatives had used talk radio, cable television, and direct mail to convince them otherwise.

Reagan's election had also been partly aided by the Iranian hostage crisis in early 1979, when rebels held 66 Americans hostage at the US embassy and Foreign Ministry offices, demanding the return of the tyrannical shah from his exile in the US. The rebels did not release the hostages until Reagan took office, allowing the new president to take credit, though Carter had negotiated the peace.

During the Reagan era, fear of nuclear holocaust coincided with fear of "global environmental catastrophe" (679). There was increasing concern about pollution. A decade earlier, Nixon had established the Environmental Protection Agency (EPA), expanded the Clean Air Act, and signed the Clean Water Act. Environmentalists, noting that pollution knows no borders, advocated for global measures. When Reagan ascended to the presidency, he emphasized defense instead of the environment, unveiling the Strategic Defense Initiative (SDI), which was nicknamed "Star Wars," in March 1983. Its intent was to defend the US from a nuclear attack "with a network of satellite-based missiles" (681). This, to Reagan, would make a nuclear war "winnable."

The scientist and popular host of the TV science series *Cosmos*, Carl Sagan, raised concerns that "even a very limited nuclear war could lead to the end of all life on the planet" by initiating a "nuclear winter" (681). Some environmentalists challenged this idea, finding the science inconclusive. Conservatives then worked to roll back the 1949 Fairness Doctrine, which had been amended a decade later, requiring broadcasters to offer Americans various opinions on major issues. Conservatives advocated for a market-based rule that declared, if people liked something, broadcasters could air it. Reagan also set about trying to undo the Fairness Doctrine and eventually succeeded.

In 1984, the economy of the Soviet Union was in shambles. In the same year, Reagan won 60% of the popular vote and every state's Electoral College except for Minnesota—the home state of his opponent, Walter Mondale. As communism began to fall and the USSR began to open up and restructure its economy, it seemed as though Reagan had led the world into capitalist democracy. By 1991, the Soviet empire had collapsed and, the following year, the Cold War ended.

Reagan used his political capital to change the judiciary at home, looking to appoint judges to lower courts whom he believed embraced "family values." In 1986, he named Antonin Scalia to the Supreme Court—one of the "most learned and eloquent proponent[s] of originalism" (684). The originalist argument came to a head, however, in 1987 during the debate over the

166

nomination of well-known conservative legal theorist Robert Bork, who had been supported by the Federalist Society. Bork believed that "[n]o fundamental rights exist[ed] outside of those listed in the Constitution" (687).

Meanwhile, the gay rights movement was growing, largely in response to the federal government's inaction on HIV and AIDS, a medical condition that first appeared in the early 1980s. Gay men made up three out of four cases. Reagan did not speak about AIDS until 1985. Like arguments in favor of reproductive rights, legal cases involving gay rights had long been fought on privacy grounds. Gay rights activists became frustrated with this method, focusing instead on visibility—that is, coming out—and seeking equal rights.

The Democratic Party had long been the party of the working class—that is, until Republicans began to court prospective blue-collar white male voters "who'd lost their manufacturing jobs" (693). The Democratic Party had largely abandoned the working class in favor of "knowledge workers," particularly those who belonged to the emerging information and technology industry. They also began to see racism as less of a structural problem than one derived from ignorance (694). The 1992 Democratic nominees, Bill Clinton and Al Gore, called themselves "New Democrats" and declared their predecessors' support for unions old-fashioned.

The computer would become the dominant technology in the 1990s. Childhood friends and Seattle natives Bill Gates and Paul Allen had founded Microsoft in 1975. The following year, in Cupertino, California, Steve Jobs and Stephen Wozniak founded Apple Computer. Four years later, Apple's IPO "broke a record held by the Ford Motor Company since 1956" (695).

When Bill Clinton became president in 1992, he made health care reform his first priority. Insurance companies and conservative groups "spent hundreds of millions of dollars in advertising and lobbying campaigns to defeat the proposal" (698). Hillary Clinton advised her husband to stay the course and fight for universal health care. By the midterm elections in 1994, when Republicans took control of both houses of Congress, the legislation failed. On the other hand, a crime bill passed, leading many liberals to take credit for being "tough on crime" (699). The crime bill brought in an era of mass incarceration that disproportionately affected nonwhite people and gave the US the highest incarceration rate in the world.

In 1996, Clinton sought common ground with his conservative enemies by trying to "end welfare as we know it" by rolling back benefits for those who remained trapped in poverty (700). After Clinton's repeal of the Glass-Stegall Act, the securities industry saw record profits. By the end of the decade, the average corporate CEO "earned nearly four hundred times as much as the average worker" (700).

The 1990s were a boom time "for dot-commers and hedge fund managers, for Hollywood moguls and global traders" (702). Incomes rose across the board during the Clinton years, but the middle class, particularly "the rural white middle class," still saw wage decline (702). Conspiracy theorists, notably Alex Jones, blamed elites. He also made the claim that the government was behind Timothy McVeigh's bombing of a federal building in Oklahoma City in 1995. Jones was among several right-wing radio talk show hosts to emerge in the nineties. The most popular, however, was Rush Limbaugh, "who began broadcasting nationally, on fifty-six stations, in the summer of

1988" (704). The Republican political strategist and TV producer Roger Ailes began producing a TV show for Limbaugh soon after meeting the media personality in 1990. Though the show failed, Ailes was convinced that there should be a television network for conservative news.

Meanwhile, CNN had been producing 24-hour news programming since it was launched in 1980. MSNBC, a network dedicated to the liberal perspective, started in July 1996. Later that year, Ailes started Fox News, which was owned by the Australian media tycoon Rupert Murdoch. Ailes had no background in journalism and often expressed his dislike of journalists. He claimed that he had started Fox News "to rescue journalism" (707).

For many years, the only TV channels were the major networks. The news was broadcast every night at 6:30. Those who were less interested in politics—moderates—still tended to watch. However, with the rise of cable, they had other viewing options. As a result, these voters became less engaged in politics and, thus, less likely to vote. Television had also become more salacious, particularly where the Clintons were concerned. In March 1994, the major networks aired 126 news stories about the Clintons' Whitewater land deal, but had only aired 42 stories about the Clintons' proposed health care plan (709). In the last years of the decade, the electorate developed less faith in the ability of the federal government to accomplish anything.

The American economy, however, continued to thrive. Dot-come stock was high. By the end of Clinton's second term in 2000, "unemployment had fallen to 4.1% and the United States was producing nearly a quarter of the world's output" (714). By comparison, the British Empire, at its height, had produced only

8% of the world's output in 1913 (714). Still, Americans without a college education, and especially those without a high school diploma, floundered in a culture in which worship of the rich was predominant. Around this time, the real estate tycoon Donald Trump had been hinting at a possible presidential run, though no one took it seriously. Despite his personal wealth and business career, he identified with "the workers, the construction workers, the taxicab driver" (714). He also decried both parties' inability to speak to working people and centrists.

In 2000, George W. Bush, son of the 41st president and governor of Texas, won the Republican presidential nomination. The younger Bush, who was a born-again Christian, coined a new slogan: "compassionate conservatism." It was based on the notion that conservative values and conservative ideas could aid in fomenting "justice and opportunity" (716).

The 2000 election, however, was extremely close. Even after it was over, it remained unclear who had won an election that had hinged on Florida and the possibility of corruption. The networks had first announced that Gore had won. Fox News countered that prediction. Several minutes later, the major networks followed Fox's lead and named Bush president. Gore contested the results. He had won the popular vote by over 500,000 ballots. The Florida Supreme Court supported Gore's call for a recount. For weeks, the election was undecided. Then, on December 12, the Supreme Court called off the recount. The 5-4 decision had been led by judges who were appointed by Reagan and Bush. They rested their decision on the 14th Amendment, which "had been written and ratified to guarantee the rights of African Americans" (717).

On the final day of his presidency, Bill Clinton admitted to having lied under oath about an affair with White House intern Monica Lewinsky, "in exchange for immunity from prosecution" (717). It was the end of a presidency that had been marked by both national prosperity and seemingly endless scandal.

Lepore covers a broad expanse of history in this section, from the end of the Nixon era, which resulted in China opening itself up to the West economically, to the end of the Clinton years, a time of unprecedented prosperity that was partly due to the economic reforms of some of Clinton's conservative predecessors. Though Clinton was an object of conservative ire, his economic policies, Lepore notes, continued the Reagan era and pursued centrism, particularly after the 1994 midterm elections.

The death of communism, marked by the fall of the Soviet Union, had encouraged already deeply polarized Americans to move farther apart politically. Lacking foreign enemies abroad, they turned on each other. Voters fell along party lines regarding abortion and guns. Thus, moral issues and identity politics defined both parties, with the Republican Party increasingly becoming the haven of the disaffected white male voter. Both sides in the abortion and guns debates—that is, antichoice activists and antigun activists—cast their respective opponents as immoral, even evil, and used less factual evidence than impassioned rhetoric to support their positions.

Lepore also notes, however briefly, the lack of cohesion in the second-wave feminist movement—a problem that has impacted contemporary understandings of feminism. Lepore describes how the movement could never reconcile its disparate strains, as it had during its first wave when suffragists passed the 19th

Amendment, and during the Progressive Era, when they pursued reforms that protected women and children from labor abuses. Lepore notes, even more briefly, the sexism that also existed in the Black nationalist movement, as exemplified by Carmichael's comment, which both objectified women and discounted the pivotal role that Black women played in both the civil rights movement and the Black Power movement. Some women in the Black Panther Party, including Elaine Brown and Kathleen Cleaver, had leadership positions within the organization.

The ERA's initial success is a testament to the popularity of liberalism, which had persisted since the 1930s, despite the communist witch hunts of the postwar era. The fact that the legislation had sunk by the end of the decade is a testament to Phyllis Schlafly's political acumen and, possibly, feminists' underestimation of her and her cohort. In a previous chapter, Lepore mentions that white Republican women had become the foot soldiers of the GOP, and Schlafly was very much in that mold.

She, like Ronald Reagan, perpetuated an idealized conservative myth of an America that had never existed, one in which everyone knew their rightful place and stayed within it. It provided comfort to those who were reeling from the tumult of the 1960s and 1970s. Reagan had encouraged an erosion of faith in the federal government that has persisted in contemporary discourse. This was not, however, rhetoric that he applied to his governance, as defense spending increased significantly during his administration and more employees were added to the Department of Defense. It was an era in which, yet again, foreign policy was prioritized over domestic needs; and military brawn mattered more than the care of the nation's most vulnerable.

On the morning of September 11, 2001, two airplanes crashed
into the World Trade Center in New York City. Around 50,000
people worked in the Twin Towers. The planes had been
hijacked by 19 members of Al Qaeda, a terrorist organization
formed by the wealthy Saudi Osama bin Laden. A third hijacked
plane crashed into the Pentagon about an hour after the attack in
New York. Hijackers were also aboard a fourth plane that they
intended to crash either into the Capitol Building or the White
House, but their plan was foiled by passengers who decided to
tackle the hijackers, thereby causing the plane to crash in
Pennsylvania.

Shortly after the attacks, George W. Bush decided to wage a war
against terrorism. He characterized this war as an inevitable one
"that was part of a clash of civilizations" (721). The fault line,
according to Bush and his cohorts, fell between the West and the
Islamic world. There were precedents to this new war. The US
was dependent on Arab oil and "the rise of Islamic
fundamentalism had already led to the 1979 US hostage crisis in
Iran" (722). There were also the Soviet invasion of Afghanistan
and the Gulf War in 1990. Bin Laden had accused the US of
violating the Islamic world and undermining Muslim faith by
causing wars between Muslims. He called for a fatwa against all
Americans in the name of a global Islamic front. Bush claimed
that the US was targeted because the nation was a beacon of
freedom. Barack Obama, then a law professor and Illinois state
senator, believed that the tragedy stemmed from the attackers'
absence of empathy, which had been born out of "poverty and
ignorance, helplessness and despair" (722). Public intellectual
Susan Sontag blamed the attacks on bad US foreign policy in

the Middle East. The attacks, she surmised, were the result of the US supporting tyrants, the CIA toppling other leaders, and the incessant bombing of Iraq (722). Jerry Falwell blamed the attacks on feminists and gays. Some, including Alex Jones, claimed that the bombing was orchestrated by the US government.

In 1999, Jones started Infowars, a website that promoted what he called "the truther movement, a faction of conspiracy theorists" (724). The movement would first theorize that the US had been responsible for the September 11 attacks and would later make other claims. When Barack Obama ran for president, Jones and other "truthers," as they called themselves joined the "birther" movement, which claimed that Obama had not been born in Hawaii, but in Kenya. Donald Trump, who occasionally toyed with the idea of a presidential run, joined the birther movement. He used his Twitter account to promote his ideas. Part of the suspicion toward Obama may have from the similarity between his surname and the given name of Osama bin Laden, as well as his middle name—Hussein—which likely reminded some voters of the Iraqi tyrant Saddam Hussein. Bin Laden and Hussein were the nation's biggest enemies at the time.

New sources of news and opinion were emerging in the early 2000s. Blogs, webzines, and digital newspapers were more prevalent. Social media would also significantly impact public discourse. Websites rolled out in rapid succession. Facebook emerged in 2004. YouTube started a year later. Twitter launched in 2006, and the Apple sold the first iPhone a year later. Finally, Twitter had 1 million users by 2008 and 284 million users six years later. The new sources of news, particularly those shared on social media, had unverified facts. The politics on some websites, particularly Tumblr and 4chan, became increasingly unhinged and profited from both hysteria and contempt for those on the other side of the political aisle. Everyone's political thinking became more conspiratorial.

Major Internet companies had been founded over a decade earlier: Amazon in 1994, Yahoo in 1995, and Google and PayPal in 1998. Peter Thiel, a libertarian who hoped that people would one day be freed "from government-managed currency" had cofounded PayPal. The image of the Silicon Valley entrepreneur was usually male, outwardly modest, but astoundingly rich. By the end of the 1990s, 43-year-old Bill Gates had become the world's wealthiest man. His corporation, Microsoft, was the first to be valued at over half a trillion dollars. It was a Second Gilded Age.

The icons of Silicon Valley believed in "disruptive innovation," that is, the idea that certain industries were meant to fail to make room for bigger and better ideas. One of the first casualties of this social Darwinist approach to business was the print newspaper. Silicon Valley was not entirely to blame, however. The deregulation of communications, which Clinton had signed into law, allowed for massive media mergers. News outlets became more accountable to their shareholders than to their readers. Only the *New York Times*, the *Washington Post*, and National Public Radio (NPR) were exceptions.

The Internet was exciting because it democratized information and disseminated it more rapidly than ever before. However, "the engine that searched for [that information] was controlled by the biggest unregulated monopoly in the history of American business" (737). The search engine Google controlled about 90% of this market. Data collected by Google, Facebook, and other websites allowed them to profile users and feed them more information about what they already knew or wanted to know.

When the Bush administration demanded that the Taliban hand over bin Laden, who had been hiding in Afghanistan, the Taliban, which had a history of violently oppressing women, refused. The US decided to go to war with Afghanistan, with the intent of replacing the Taliban government with a democratic one. The war became the longest in American history and did not unseat Taliban power. Military spending nearly doubled between 1998 and 2011 to over $700 billion per year.

By embracing the war on terror, starting in 2001, the US "undermined and even abdicated the very rules it had helped to establish, including prohibitions on torture and wars of aggression" (730). The country not only ignored its founding principles, it also ignored the Geneva Conventions, international law, and human rights when it began to torture suspected terrorists and imprison them without trial. In 2001, Bush signed a military order declaring that suspected terrorists were not American citizens, and that they were to be detained at locations to be determined by the secretary of defense. Military commissions were to try them if they were brought to trial. Bush relied on an expanded view of executive power to carry out his war on terror—a view that would be perpetuated by his successors to pass various measures.

Starting in fall 2001, "the US military dropped flyers over Afghanistan offering bounties of between $5,000 and $25,000 for the names of men with ties to al Qaeda" (745). As suspects were rounded up, Bush wondered where to put them. US prisons were not possible because suspects would be able to appeal their cases in US courts. He settled on Guantánamo, a US naval base in Cuba. Bush administration lawyer John Yoo concluded that international treaties, including the Geneva Conventions, did not apply to the Taliban because the US regarded Afghanistan as a "failed state" and Al Qaeda belonged to no state. The suspects, too, had a new name—unlawful combatants. They were not "imprisoned"; they were being "detained." Torture became "enhanced interrogation techniques." These "techniques" were also carried out at Abu Ghraib, in Afghanistan, at Bagram Air Base, and in a CIA prison in Kabul. In 2006, the Supreme Court ruled in *Hamdan v. Rumsfeld* that the president did not have the authority to create military commissions. Congress authorized the commissions six months later, but the Supreme Court also found this act to be unconstitutional.

Despite the fierce rhetoric that emerged during the war on terror, Bush was careful not to denounce Muslim people themselves and praised their faith. Between 2001 and 2004, both Democrats and Republicans supported the wars in Afghanistan and Iraq. Support for Iraq was more contentious, however, and dwindled significantly among Democrats when it was discovered that Saddam Hussein had not been compiling weapons of mass destruction.

The war on terror was unique in that it was led by people who had never served in the military, let alone in a war. None of their children did either. George H. W. Bush had been the last president to serve in the military. Only 0.5% of Americans saw active duty in either war. Conservative writer Andrew Bacevich argued that, despite not having any military experience, Americans and the American government held "a romanticized view of soldiers" and tended to believe that military power and service were "the truest measure[s] of national greatness" (741).

During Bush's two presidential terms, "income inequality widened and polarization worsened" (748). This trend continued during the Obama and Trump years. A Bush-era tax cut encouraged income inequality by giving 45% of the nation's savings to the top 1% of earners, while the poorest 60% of Americans only received 13% (748). When those tax cuts were extended in 2010, Senator Bernie Sanders of Vermont was one of few members of Congress who protested it.

The culture of Washington had changed, too. Previously, when an administration left office, everyone left town and did other things. By now, people stayed and took jobs as pundits, political consultants, management consultants, lobbyists, or all of the above. The need of cable news TV to fill 24 hours of air time created plenty of work for those willing to be talking heads. The more adversarial they were, the higher a program's ratings tended to be.

The Bush era ended with a global economic catastrophe, initiated by Clinton-era deregulation, and the collapse of "financial services giants Bear Stearns, Lehman Brothers, and Merrill Lynch," all of which had become involved in "high-risk subprime mortgages" (749). Unemployment rose by about 5% and the value of homes fell by 20%. In the final Bush years, nearly 1 million properties had been repossessed by banks.

In 2009, when Obama ascended to the presidency, the nation was in disarray. He promised hope and change in his political slogan, and "swept into office with majorities in both the House and the Senate" (754). The US was entrenched in two costly wars in the Middle East. The economy experienced "one of the worst stock market crashes in American history" (725). Forty years of conservative attacks on the government and the press had succeeded in making the public distrustful of both.

Obama asked Congress for $800 billion in stimulus money, but he did not seek to punish those whose recklessness had created the crisis. He sought to rescue the banks, but did not help the people who had lost all their savings. Executives on Wall Street continued to earn nine-figure salaries.

Obama's most important legislative initiative, the Affordable Care Act, passed the Senate and the House by slim margins. It had been a century since progressives had passed a health care initiative. This win, however, was diminished by the determination of conservatives, particularly the newly formed Tea Party, to defeat it, as well as the complicated nature of the legislation.

Obama, who had been a critic of the Iraq War, the Patriot Act, and the torture of terrorist suspects, had continued the war on terror and, arguably, amplified it. He ramped up surveillance "through a secret program run by the National Security Agency" and "used drones to commit assassinations" in the Middle East (765).

Nationalist and white supremacist movements were growing in both the US and Europe, where some "called for immigration restriction, trade barriers, and [...] the abdication of international climate accords" (726). The Tea Party emerged on the right in 2009, as well as the more extreme alt-right. On the left, the Occupy Wall Street Movement formed in 2011 and Black Lives Matter emerged as the successor of the Black Nationalist movement, directly confronting a legacy of police brutality, as had their forebears. The white nationalist movement had two goals: the preservation of icons of the Confederacy, particularly statues in public squares throughout the South, and discontinuing the immigration of darker-skinned peoples (727).

When Donald Trump ran for president in 2015, his platform was based on a racist, anti-immigrant agenda. His primary campaign promise was that he would "build a wall along the US-Mexican border" (727). When he announced his presidency at Trump Tower in New York, he gave a speech in which he characterized Mexican immigrants as "rapists." He also called for a total ban on the entry of Muslims to the US.

Hillary Clinton ran for the presidency in 2016, as she had eight years earlier, this time winning the Democratic nomination. Her campaign, however, underestimated public support for Trump and "failed to address the suffering of blue-collar voters," while also insulting many of them (727). Mitt Romney, Lepore contends, had done something similar when he was the Republican nominee in 2012 and dismissed "47 percent of the population—Obama's supporters—as people 'who believe they are victims'" (727). Trump used data provided by the British firm Cambridge Analytica to aid in his campaign against Clinton.

By the time of the 2016 election, many young, eligible voters got much of their news from Facebook's News Feed, which had been started in 2006. Trump also continued to use his Twitter account to disseminate information to his supporters. Polling began to lose its influence. Three out of four Americans distrusted polls by 2013, and most distrusted them so much that, when polled, they refused to answer the questions. Thus, the results meant nothing. Polls had also failed to make accurate predictions abroad, including the correct outcome of Brexit—the withdrawal of Great Britain from the European Union—in 2016.

However, both the press and major political parties continued to rely on polls. It was polls, too, that gave Donald Trump center stage in the GOP primaries and that declared him the winner. Polls also called the 2016 election incorrectly by declaring that Clinton would win. Though Clinton did end up winning the popular vote, she lost the Electoral College. According to exit polls, "52 percent of Catholics and 81 percent of evangelicals voted for Trump" (777).

Voters who had gotten their news online during the presidential campaign did not realize that they were reading stories, particularly about Clinton, that were untrue. Some had been written by Russian propagandists. Russian president Vladimir Putin disliked Clinton, while Trump admired the Russian president. Congress would later investigate Trump and his campaign for possible collusion with the Russian government in undermining a US election. Some of the writers of the fake news stories, however, had not been Russians. Some stories were written by robots. Social media sites had no way of filtering what was real and what was not. It had also been incentivizing nefarious forces by providing the private data of over 87 million users to data firms, including Cambridge Analytica. The Justice Department would later indict 13 Russian nationals who had not only undermined Clinton's campaign but also the primary campaigns of Republican candidates Ted Cruz and Marco Rubio. Those nationals had supported the campaigns of Bernie Sanders and Green Party candidate Jill Stein. They had also created "fake Black Lives Matter and American Muslim social media accounts" (780). Facebook's sole interest, it turned out, was to maximize its users and the time those users spent on Facebook. Meanwhile, the 2016 election had reignited old hatreds, stoked new fears, and created even more doubt in American leadership and the future of Western democracy itself.

In this chapter, Lepore once again focuses on a nation that is having a moral reckoning. While old questions about citizenship and equal rights linger, there are also new ones about the position of technology in our daily lives, how it can be used to help us, while being aware of the ways in which nefarious influences, from both outside and within, use it to manipulate a populace that has become increasingly less civic-minded and more partisan.

Worse, the nation's leaders demonstrated less integrity by flagrantly dismissing some of the moral principles on which the nation was founded under the aegis of keeping the nation safe. The targeting of people of color, Arabs and others, during the war on terror is reminiscent of FDR's decision to intern Japanese Americans during the Second World War, as they were suspected enemies of the state. Once again, the US used race to stigmatize and vilify a segment of the population.

Lepore mentions the rise of Rush Limbaugh, Glenn Beck, and, particularly, Alex Jones but does not connect their outlandish conspiratorial ideas to the John Birch Society which, though a fringe movement, had first injected strange conspiracy theories into the public consciousness. One of them, about the supposed harms of fluoride, has retained currency. The difference this time is that Internet technology has made it easier to disseminate false ideas to millions, thereby giving strange and outlandish ideas a sense of legitimacy.

Lepore, arguably, does not go far enough in describing how the volunteer military became even more predetermined by race and class—a trend that continued after the Vietnam War. The nation has idealized the military, as Bacevich notes, and blandly thanks soldiers for their service, but recent generations, starting with the

Baby Boomers, have been the least likely to serve in the military themselves.

Hillary Clinton's failed campaign was, for liberals, one of the greatest disappointments of the decade, while it was probably one of the greatest successes for conservatives, who had loathed Clinton since her earliest years as First Lady. Though Lepore mentions the Democrats' shift to an ethos of meritocracy in the previous chapter, she does not mention how this philosophy may have impacted Clinton's campaign and explained her aversion to working-class voters. On the other hand, there has been a strong suggestion that the working-class people whom Clinton ignored were white males—a view that only reestablishes the false notion that white men are the most important members of the electorate. They are not even the majority of the working class, which is predominately composed of women and people of color, constituencies that Clinton pursued.

The rancor and disappointments unleashed by the Trump presidency also ignited some of the most fervent protest and resistance movements to arise since the 1960s. Though Lepore mentions the Black Lives Matter movement, which was rooted in resistance to police brutality, she does not mention the rise of the Me Too movement, which arose partly in response to Trump's unabashed misogyny and objectification of women. His openness about these qualities, which many abusive men tend to shield from the public, inadvertently encouraged women of all classes and races to speak up about the prevalence of sexual harassment and assault in their daily lives.

Epilogue

Epilogue Summary and Analysis: "The Question Addressed"

The climate had changed in Philadelphia since the Constitutional Convention of 1787: The annual temperature was seven degrees warmer. Not long after Donald Trump announced that he would withdraw the US from the Paris climate accord, "a trillion-ton iceberg the size of the state of Delaware broke off of Antarctica" (785).

The United States itself began with an act of severance, which culminated in an attempt to bring disparate strains together. The Constitution tried to create a more perfect union, though it would be the formerly enslaved and their descendants who would most faithfully bring that vision to fruition. The nation that had been born during an era of revolutions would "forever struggle against chaos" (786). With Trump's election, some commentators announced the end of the republic. Americans seemed to be fighting more than ever, particularly over the prevalence of monuments that reminded the nation of its oppressive past. People again began to question the truths on which the nation was founded and their validity. Conservatives still based their right to power on the supposed failures of liberalism, particularly its obsessive focus on identity politics. They focused on winning elections, while liberals, Lepore contends, have seemed to focus more on winning court cases and carrying out social-justice crusades. Conservatives, meanwhile, wanted to turn back in time, which was especially characterized by their preoccupation with originalism. They regaled a vision of America—white, Christian, idyllic—that had never existed. In this regard, again, the US was not unique. Other nations who sought solace from the difficult questions of the present found refuge in creation myths. Lepore concludes that the responsibility will fall to a new generation to "[reckon with] what their forebears had wrought" (788).

In the Epilogue, Lepore summarizes the book's main themes. She starts with the issue of climate change—arguably the most pressing concern of the moment. This change, fostered by nuclear testing and the excesses of the Industrial Revolution, had drastically changed the atmosphere over the course of three centuries. Meanwhile, strident bipartisanship continues to divide Americans. Lepore's book was published before the January 6 coup attempt in 2021, but her tone anticipates a tragic culmination to years of political rancor and distrust. She ends the book rhetorically on the question of whether future generations will protect the democracy they inherited or create something else.

Key Figures

Jill Lepore

As the author and researcher of *These Truths*, Jill Lepore uses the text to pose some of her own questions about the success of the American experiment. Additionally, her approach to historiography focuses greater attention on how the subjugation of particular groups—indigenous peoples, people of African descent, and women—were key in the formation of the new republic. In the Introduction, Lepore notes that she wrote the book because no one had attempted to write a history of the United States from beginning to end in many years. One reason this is important, for Lepore, is that she regards the study of history as a method of inquiry. Her approach to the writing of this history is humble. She is careful to note that she did not set out to write the entire history of the United States, as no one could do that. Instead, she has confined herself to writing what she believes a nation in the early 21st century needs to know about its past.

Christopher Columbus

Described as "a broad-shouldered sea captain from Genoa," Christopher Columbus, who became a figure of controversy in the last quarter of the 20th century, was an Italian explorer, funded by the Spanish monarchy, who inadvertently "discovered" North America (3). His diary was copied by Bartolomé de Las Casas. That copy was lost until a sailor found it in a Spanish duke's library in 1790. The widow of a librarian sold what appeared to be parchment scraps of the original diary in 1894. The scraps had Columbus's signature and the year 1492 was printed on the cover of the diary. The widow disappeared, as did whatever may have remained from the original diary. Columbus had a son, Ferdinand, who wrote a biography of his father, which remained unpublished when he died in 1539.

Bartolomé de Las Casas

Bartolomé de Las Casas was a priest, scholar, and historian of the Spanish conquest who was present in Hispaniola in 1511. He had copied parts of Columbus's diary and Ramon Pané's *Antiquities*. In 1542, he wrote a book in protest of the atrocities that indigenous tribes suffered due to conquest. Eight years later, the Spanish king summoned Las Casas and other scholars to his court in Valladolid to discuss the nature of the Indigenous Americans. Las Casas "argued that the conquest was unlawful" and dismissed charges that the tribes were cannibals (24). Las Casas's account was later translated into English and "lavishly illustrated with engravings of atrocities" (25). It was usually published under the title *Spanish Cruelties* and, later, as *The Tears of the Indians*.

Edward Coke

Edward Coke was the attorney general who prepared Virginia's first charter. Coke was an investor in the Virginia Company and "the leading theorist of English common law" (34). He became a member of Parliament in 1589 at the age of 37. In the early 1600s, he prosecuted Walter Raleigh for treason based on a supposed plot against the king. Raleigh's conviction allowed King James I to establish the settlement of Virginia on his own terms—a plan conducted "under Coke's watchful eye" (34).

In 1621, Coke "had emerged as James's most cunning adversary" and "claimed that Parliament had the right to debate on all matters concerning the Commonwealth" (40). James had Coke arrested and dissolved Parliament. In the 1620s, Coke revived the Magna Carta—a document from 1215 in which King John "pledged to his barons that he would obey the 'law of the land'" (40). The Magna Carta granted to all free men in King John's realm all the liberties in the document to be enjoyed by them and their heirs. It was also King John, son of Henry II, who had attempted to resolve the question of whether a law can exist if it was never written down. Unwritten laws, he decided, were still laws, forming what he called "common law." When Coke was 76, he returned to Parliament, claiming that the king's authority was constrained by the Magna Carta. At his suggestion, Parliament delivered to King Charles, James's successor, a Petition of Right, "which cited Magna Carta to insist that the king had no right to imprison a subject without a trial by jury" (42). In 1629, King Charles forbade the publication of Coke's study of the Magna Carta and dissolved Parliament, which led many of his subjects to flee to the Americas.

John Locke

English Enlightenment-era philosopher John Locke was a key influence on the formation of the United States. Locke's best-known work, *Two Treatises on Government* (1689), established the concepts of natural rights and sovereignty, which inspired American colonists to seek independence, and ideas about property that the colonists used to justify both the usurpation of lands from indigenous peoples and the enslavement of African peoples. Borrowing from Christianity, Locke claimed that "all men were born into a state 'of equality, wherein all the power and jurisdiction is reciprocal, no one having more than another'" (34).

Locke, who had "a hollow face and a long nose," like a bird of prey, was a tutor at Christ Church, a college at Oxford University

(51). One of his students was the son of the Earl of Shaftesbury—the sickly chancellor of the exchequer. Locke had never married and, in 1667, left Oxford to work as the earl's personal secretary and caretaker. He moved into Exeter House, the earl's London residence. Shaftesbury was deeply involved in American colonial affairs, particularly the establishment of "various councils on trade and plantations" (52). Locke later became the secretary of the colony of Carolina. In this role, Locke "wrote and later revised" Carolina's constitution soon after he wrote *Letters Concerning Toleration*. He was simultaneously drafting *Two Treatises on Government*, in which he attempted to explain how governments developed. He imagined a state of nature in which all men had the freedom to organize their actions and dispose of both their energies and possessions however they chose. From this state of natural equality, Locke believed, men created civil society—or government—for the sake of order and the protection of personal property.

In his constitution for Carolina, Locke established freedom of religion, while barring Jews, atheists, and agnostics from settling in the colony and owning land. However, in the document he argued against seizing land from the indigenous tribes simply because they were not Christian. Kings or chiefs like Powhatan, however, had no sovereignty because they did not cultivate their land, but only lived on it. Government, Locke insisted, largely existed to protect and maintain property. Locke's argument was partly motivated by a desire to distinguish English settlement from that of the Spanish. The latter had justified the seizure of indigenous peoples' land by marking their religious difference. Locke determined that their lack of cultivation, based on European standards, was a better justification.

In *Two Treatises on Government*, Locke condemned slavery, arguing that all men were born equal "with a natural right to life, liberty, and property" (54). Governments existed to protect those natural rights. Thus, slavery existed at variance with civil society. However, Locke's constitution read that all free men of Carolina—that is, white men—were to have "absolute power and Authority over [their] Negro slaves" (55).

Thomas Paine

Author of *Common Sense* (1776), a book that was a key influence on the development of the United States, Thomas Paine was the English-born son of a grocer. He immigrated to Philadelphia from England in 1774 and published his famous pamphlet anonymously in January 1776. His intention was to make his 47-page argument easy for the less educated to understand. Paine was a staunch anti-monarchist who believed that monarchs had no inherent right to reign, arguing that their origins were likely as common as everyone else's. Paine asserted the "plain truth" that "all men [were] originally equals" (34). He believed that America's cause was "the cause of all mankind" (94). In a rejection of British imperialism, he also pointed out the absurdity of an island governing an entire continent.

Paine reappropriated Locke and revised the English philosopher's idea about a state of nature, making it more digestible for less learned readers. He claimed that distinctions between rich and poor, and the presumed right of some to rule over others, were unnatural. They were merely the results of actions and customs. He encouraged the colonists "to argue not from precedent or doctrine but from nature" (95). When a government ceased to support a people's safety and liberty, that people retained the natural right to depose that government and forever retained that right. Paine also invoked the Magna Carta, which he cited as a document that contained laws insisted upon by the people, not the Crown. He then urged Americans to write their own Magna Carta.

Paine's next book was *Rights of Man* (1791). He wrote the second part of the book in France, where he went after fleeing from England. Paine was in Paris during the Reign of Terror, when Louis XVI and Marie Antoinette were beheaded. Paine was arrested and penned much of the second part of his book from prison.

Benjamin Franklin

Franklin was the eldest of the 75 men who had been elected to represent 12 states at the Philadelphia convention. He was 81, hunched, crooked, and suffering from gout when he signed the American Constitution in 1787. Franklin was against slavery, a sentiment he expressed to his sister in their frequent letters. He had been a signatory of the Declaration of Independence, the Treaty of Paris, and the Constitution. His final public act was to urge the new nation to embrace abolition.

During the colonial era, Franklin had been a fierce advocate for freedom of the press. Franklin was the youngest of ten sons. He also had seven sisters, including Jane. Franklin taught himself to read and write, then he taught Jane. He aspired to become a writer, but his "[f]ather could only afford to send him to school for two years" (59). One of his brothers, James, became a printer and published the *New-England Courant*. At 16, Benjamin worked as his apprentice and when James was imprisoned for sedition, Franklin took over the printing of the newspaper. He printed excerpts from Cato's Letters—"144 essays about the nature of liberty, including freedom of speech and of the press"

(60). In 1723, after his brother was released from prison, Franklin left the apprenticeship and settled in Philadelphia. There, he printed his own newspaper, the *Pennsylvania Gazette*, in 1729. In 1731, he founded the first lending library in the nation, the Library Company of Philadelphia. The following year, he started printing *Poor Richard's Almanack*. In 1736, he was elected clerk of the Pennsylvania Provincial Assembly. The following year, he was made postmaster of Philadelphia and worked to improve the postal service. Franklin also established the American Philosophical Society, the colonies' first intellectual organization, and took the nation's first census.

In 1751, he wrote an essay about population entitled "Observations Concerning the Increase of Mankind, Peopling of Countries, &c." In the essay, Franklin wanted to know what would happen if the colonies were to grow bigger than the countries the colonists had come from. Land was cheap, making it possible for someone to buy a parcel of land that could be turned into a plantation. In the essay, he also wrote about a people who were "white," while Africans were "black"; Asians and indigenous peoples were "tawny"; and Russians, Swedes, Germans, the French, Italians, and Spaniards were "swarthy." The English were, in Franklin's view, the only true "white" people in the world. In the essay, he admitted to his partiality. Franklin owned several of his own slaves. He promised to free two of them, a husband and wife named Peter and Jemima, upon his death. Some years later, in 1763, Franklin visited a school for Black children. The visit changed his mind about the intellectual capacities of people of African descent.

In 1754, he printed the "Join or Die" woodcut in the newspaper, which he had used to illustrate an article about "the need for the colonies to form a common defense—against France and Spain, and against warring Indians and rebelling slaves" (65). He believed that the colonies lacked cohesion. The newspaper business had made Franklin rather wealthy. In April, the governor of Pennsylvania appointed him commissioner of a meeting set to take place in Albany, New York, in June. There, delegates from the colonies were to negotiate a treaty with a confederation of Iroquois called the Six Nations at what came to be called the Albany Congress. Franklin proposed a Plan of Union there, which would designate representatives for each of the 11 colonies based on the size of their respective populations. The new government would meet in Philadelphia and exert power to pass laws, make treaties, and raise money for defense. The plan, however, was rejected.

Jane Franklin

One of seven sisters of Benjamin Franklin, Jane was, unlike most white women of her time, semi-literate. Under her brother's tutelage, she received a slightly better than rudimentary education, allowing her to maintain an epistolary correspondence with Benjamin, particularly during the years of revolution and the constitutional convention. Lepore uses Jane as the lens from which she can explore what life might have been like for a middle-class Northern woman in the 18th century. Gender determined much of the outcome of Jane's life. While her brother was educated and allowed to realize his full potential, Lepore intentionally prods the reader to wonder what Jane's life might have become if she were given similar opportunities. In her correspondence with her brother, Jane expressed her views about politics and current events. Like many Americans, she had suffered from the Revolutionary War. One of Jane's sons died as a result of being wounded during the Battle of Bunker Hill, while another had become mentally ill. She was fervently against violence, encouraging her brother to "support an end to the draft and capital punishment" (120).

John Adams

In addition to being one of the drafters of the American Constitution and the second president of the United States, John Adams was also one of the delegates and chief author of the state constitution for Massachusetts, which was ratified in 1780. In Article I of the Massachusetts Constitution's Declaration of Rights, Adams had written about the natural rights and freedom of all men, in addition to the right of "seeking and obtaining their safety and happiness" (113). A Black woman named Bett (later, Elizabeth Freeman), enslaved in Massachusetts, cited this clause in a suit for her freedom and won her case.

Adams was born in Braintree, Massachusetts on October 19, 1735. He had a reputation for being argumentative, vain, learned, and fervently opposed to the development of political parties. Alexander Hamilton believed Adams to be unfit for the presidency, due to his vanity and jealousies. He had cofounded the American Academy of Arts and Sciences and wrote the three-volume *Defence of the Constitutions of Government of the United States of America* (1797).

During the constitutional convention in 1787, Adams served as minister to Britain. From there, he maintained an epistolary correspondence with his friend and political adversary, Thomas Jefferson, who was simultaneously serving as minister to France. Together, the statesmen had crafted the Declaration of Independence. Adams was concerned about the Constitution giving the legislature too much power. Like Jefferson, he worried about the outcomes of elections. Unlike Jefferson, he preferred the idea of strong executive power and a president who could serve until death, like a king. He sought to restrain majority rule. Adams believed that, in every society in which the rich and poor coexisted, there could never be equal laws. One side, he insisted, would always seek to take advantage of the other.

Adams was married to Abigail. One of their sons, John Quincy, became the sixth president of the United States. Thomas Jefferson was Adams's political rival and his opponent in two elections in 1796 and 1800. Adams narrowly won the first, while Jefferson won the latter. By 1800, Adams was 64 years old. After he retired from politics, he resumed his friendship with Jefferson. John Adams died at age 90 on July 4, 1826, when the United States celebrated the fiftieth anniversary of the Declaration of Independence. Thomas Jefferson, his friend and political rival, died on the same day.

Thomas Jefferson

Thomas Jefferson was third president of the United States, a drafter of the Declaration of Independence, minister to France, the nation's first secretary of state in George Washington's cabinet, and vice president to John Adams. Like fellow Founding Fathers Washington and James Madison, Jefferson was a Virginian and the owner of a large estate on which enslaved Black people labored. He was known to be moody, frantic, and inconsistent. Like Adams, he was exceptionally learned and regarded as an excellent writer. However, like the other Founding Fathers, particularly George Washington, Jefferson expressed deep ambivalence over the question of slavery. He went further than others in seeking to rationalize his democratic ideals with his commitment to slaveholding. On March 4, 1815, the day after Congress delayed a resolution to eliminate the three-fifths clause from the Constitution, Jefferson created an equation that attempted to calculate "how many generations would have to pass before a child with a full-blooded African ancestor could be called 'white'" (175).

Jefferson was married to Martha Wayles, who had died in 1782, when Jefferson was 38 years old. Swearing to his wife on her deathbed that he would never remarry, he took Wayles's much younger and enslaved half sister, Sally Hemings, as a concubine. With Hemings, Jefferson conceived at least seven children. The last was born in 1808. Hemings remained with Jefferson, despite having had the opportunity to obtain her freedom during a trip to Paris, after he promised that, in exchange for her companionship and labor, he would manumit all of their children. Newspapers scrutinized Jefferson's relationship with Hemings, much to his irritation. Jefferson eventually allowed his two oldest children with Sally—Beverly and Harriet—to leave Monticello, providing Harriet with funds and transportation to Philadelphia.

John Adams was Jefferson's political rival and his opponent in two elections in 1796 and 1800. By 1800, Jefferson was 57 and president of the American Philosophical Society. Jefferson, unlike Adams, believed in the rule of the majority. After the men retired from politics, they resumed their friendship. Thomas Jefferson died at Monticello on July 4, 1826, the year of the nation's fiftieth anniversary. He was 83. His friend and long-term political adversary, John Adams, died about five hours later. In his will, he arranged to free the youngest of his two children with Sally Hemings—Eston and Madison. He did not arrange for Hemings's freedom. After Jefferson's death, Hemings, who was 53, quietly left Monticello and went to live in Charlottesville, where she later died. Jefferson had 130 enslaved people on his estate when he died, all of whom were sold at auction to cover his debts.

James Madison, nicknamed "the sage of Montpelier," was the fourth president of the United States. Previously, he had served as secretary of state in Thomas Jefferson's cabinet and was a key draftsman of the Constitution. He was married to Dolley Madison.

Madison was raised in Montpelier, the Madison family's plantation in the Piedmont region of Virginia, east of the Blue Ridge Mountains. His grandfather, Ambrose Madison, had settled Montpelier. Ambrose was 36 in 1732, when he was murdered by enslaved Africans who poisoned him. Madison graduated from Princeton University and spent his youth at home, educating his younger siblings. He studied religious liberty particularly carefully. He revised George Mason's Virginia Declaration of Rights and Form of Government to include "the first-ever constitutional guarantee of religious liberty" as a fundamental right (96). In response to the passage of the Coercive Acts in 1774, Madison began to think of war. He wrote to his friend William Bradford, a Philadelphia-based printer, and asked if it might be time for the colonies to develop their own defense.

Studious and modest, James Madison presented a contrast to George Washington, the other Virginian leader present at the convention in Philadelphia. He "spoke softly and haltingly" (109). He was a secularist who respected religion, believing, as most Americans did at the time, that religion could only thrive if it existed separately from government, and that government could thrive only if it did not coexist with religion. Madison drafted the Bill of Rights and invented the Three-Fifths Compromise. In April 1787, Madison drafted an essay entitled "Vices of the Political

System of the United States" in which he listed 11 deficiencies in the new nation, including the failure of states to abide by constitutional requirements, encroachments of the states on federal authority, and treaty violations. He believed that the people themselves committed these vices, suggesting that the majority sometimes posed a danger.

In 1791, Madison penned an essay called "Public Opinion" in which he detailed the ways in which the public might be deceived. Though Madison believed that a large republic was superior to a smaller one because a candidate would have to appeal to a large number of voters, thereby having to prove their qualifications, he also thought that the larger a country was, the harder it would be to ascertain its collective opinion. Its populace could also be misled by dishonest yet persuasive people. The wide circulation of newspapers, he believed, was the only viable solution to this problem.

After retiring to his native Virginia, Madison continued to answer questions about constitutionality, including Congress's potential power to make the prohibition of slavery a condition of entering the Union. Madison was also a member of the American Colonization Society. Madison died in 1836, after collapsing at his breakfast table. He was 85 and the last delegate from the constitutional convention to die. In his will, Madison did not free his slaves. Instead, he devoted a sizeable portion of the proceeds from his much anticipated *Notes*, an account of the debates at the constitutional convention, to go to the American Colonization Society. The book was published in 1840. Instead of settling the question of whether the Constitution sanctioned slavery, Madison's *Notes* only gave both proslavery and abolitionist factions more ammunition for their respective sides.

George Mason

George Mason, a Virginian who was 61 during the Philadelphia Convention, is best known as one of several delegates (many of whom were Anti-Federalists) who refused to sign the Constitution until the others agreed to later include a bill of rights, which James Madison drafted. Mason's refusal and opposition to ratification on this ground established "the all-or-nothing dualism" that led to the United States' current two-party system.

Mason was also among those Founding Fathers who had doubts about slavery. In December 1765, he sent George Washington an essay in which he argued that slavery had led to the downfall of the Roman republic and would eventually destroy the British Empire, too. In May 1776, Mason drafted the Virginia Declaration of Rights and Form of Government. In it, he invoked both John Locke and Thomas Paine when arguing that all men were "by nature equally free and independent" and had "certain inherent rights" (96). All power, he wrote, was vested in the people and derived from them.

George Washington

George Washington, the first president of the United States, was born in 1732 in Westmoreland County, Virginia. He inherited his first slaves at the age of 10, traveled to the Caribbean during his youth, and accepted his first military post at age 20. In 1758, Washington was elected to the Virginia legislature, but spent much of his time managing his vast tobacco estate.

Tall, imposing, and serious, he was almost universally admired and received a celebratory greeting when he arrived in Philadelphia for the constitutional convention, for which he played the ceremonial role of president. Much of this admiration came as a result of his resignation of power after the Revolutionary War. Regarded as a strikingly handsome man, Lepore notes that his beauty was spoiled only by his rotting teeth. Washington wore dentures made from ivory. His set of false teeth also included nine teeth extracted from the mouths of his slaves. Washington ran a substantial plantation on his Virginia property, Mount Vernon.

Washington was elected president in 1788 and sworn in at Federal Hall on Wall Street in New York. His speeches, including his inaugural address, were written by future secretary of the treasury Alexander Hamilton. Washington appointed Thomas Jefferson as his secretary of state, Edmund Randolph as his attorney general, and Henry Knox as his secretary of war. John Adams was vice president. Washington served for two terms, though he had initially intended to resign after his first ended in 1792.

Washington returned to Virginia at the end of his presidency and died at Mount Vernon on December 14, 1799. By the time of his death, Washington and his wife Martha owned 317 enslaved Black people at Mount Vernon, most of whom had been owned by Martha. Washington himself owned 123 people, while Martha owned the rest. Several of those whom the Washingtons had enslaved had escaped from the plantation. These included Harry Washington; their cook, Hercules; and a seamstress named Ona Judge. Like other Founding Fathers, including Thomas Jefferson, Washington expressed moral ambivalence about slavery but made no effort to emancipate those whom he had enslaved during his lifetime.

Alexander Hamilton

Appointed Secretary of the Treasury by George Washington, Alexander Hamilton was a New Yorker, a Federalist, and Washington's speech writer. Red-haired and ambitious, Hamilton had not played much of a role at the constitutional convention in 1787, but he penned 51 of the 85 essays in *The Federalist Papers*. Hamilton, however, believed that the Constitution created too democratic a government.

A political rival of Thomas Jefferson, Hamilton supported the institution of a national bank, mirrored on the Bank of England, to pay off the Continental Congress's war debts as well as those of the states. In exchange for the support of James Madison and other key Southerners for this plan, Hamilton agreed that the nation's capital could be in the South. Hamilton believed that the nation's future was in manufacturing. He was antislavery and belonged to the New York Manumission Society, which had been cofounded by John Jay.

John Quincy Adams

Son of the United States' second president, John Adams, and Abigail Adams, John Quincy Adams was the nation's sixth president and the successor to the men who had founded the country. Since his childhood, John Adams had groomed him for the presidency. At the age of 12, when he accompanied his father to Europe on a diplomatic mission, John Quincy began to keep a diary. He studied to be an attorney, then served as George Washington's minister to the Netherlands and Portugal. During his father's administration, John Quincy served as minister to Prussia. He was later James Madison's minister to Russia. He was a polyglot who spoke 14 languages. As secretary of state under James Monroe, he drafted the Monroe

Doctrine. He also served as a US senator. In his duties as an academic, he had been a professor of logic at Brown University and a professor of rhetoric and oratory at Harvard.

During the 1824 election, future president Andrew Jackson was his opponent. Adams was the learned candidate who could write, while Jackson, who had been a general, was styled as the one who could fight. Adams won the election and the South Carolinian, John C. Calhoun, who had been James Monroe's secretary of war, served as his vice president. Calhoun would next also serve as Jackson's vice president. In the 1830s, he was the leader of the Whig Party.

By the time he was 80, Adams was "hobbled and infirm," but still vociferously objected to the Mexican-American War and the annexation of parts of Mexico (251). An opponent of slavery, like his father, he rightly believed that the annexation would expand slaveholding. On the day that President John Polk received the Treaty of Guadalupe Hidalgo, which ended the Mexican-American War, Adams, who had been giving a speech, fell on the floor of the House. He died two days later. The death of John Quincy Adams was the first to be closely reported and turned into a national ceremony. His coffin, which had been covered in glass, traveled 500 miles across the country by train, where thousands of people viewed his body.

Andrew Jackson

Andrew Jackson was the seventh president of the United States. His election heralded a new era—Jacksonian Democracy—born from an expanded electorate and the nation's westward expansion, which Jackson pursued through his displacement of indigenous tribes to Oklahoma Territory. Formerly a general, who became a national hero after the War of 1812's Battle of

New Orleans, Jackson led campaigns against the Five Civilized Tribes, particularly the Seminoles, Choctaws, and Chickasaws. His policy of removal—the first campaign of his presidency—combined treaty-making and war.

Tennessee-born and the son of Irish immigrants, Jackson was also uneducated, provincial, and a ruthless fighter. John Quincy Adams, his opponent in the 1824 election, despised him, referring to him as a "barbarian" who could hardly write his own name. Jackson had served in the Senate for less than a year before he ran for president. Thomas Jefferson declared Jackson the most unfit for the presidency. Despite his lack of sophistication and his cruel policies toward both indigenous peoples and African Americans (Jackson was a slave owner and avidly proslavery), Jackson was a talented politician who used his personal narrative to his advantage. He arranged for the writing of his biography— *The Life of Andrew Jackson* —which omitted any negative details from his past while characterizing him as self-taught, not uneducated; "self-made," not ill-bred. Jackson had also seized on the nation's desire to expand its power and its borders.

Though Jackson lost the 1824 election, due to a failure to seize a majority of the electoral vote (he had won the popular vote), he returned to his property in Tennessee, the Hermitage, and waited while the electorate grew. As new states entered the union and drafted more democratic constitutions, such as the elimination of property requirements for voting, his chances for getting elected increased. Jackson won the election of 1828, which "marked the founding of the Democratic Party, [...] the party of the common man, the farmer, the artisan: the people's party" (186). Jackson received 56% of the popular vote during this election.

During his presidency (1829-1837), he also "dismantled the national bank" and expanded his executive power (211-12). Jackson despised all banks, especially the Bank of the United States, which he believed undermined the people's sovereignty and benefited only a few wealthy capitalists at the expense of the populace. He was the first president to veto laws passed by Congress and, once, rid himself of his entire cabinet. His imperiousness earned him the reputation of a despot. His adversaries nicknamed him "King Andrew." He also believed that the president reserved the right to determine the constitutionality of laws passed by Congress.

William Lloyd Garrison

William Lloyd Garrison was a Boston-based abolitionist and journalist, best known as the editor and publisher of his abolitionist newspaper, the *Liberator*, which was first printed on January 1, 1831. He had apprenticed as a typesetter, worked as a printer and editor, and failed in multiple ventures before founding his radical newspaper. Described as a "thin, balding white man," Garrison was so devoted to his work that "he slept on a bed on the floor of his cramped office" (189-90). Garrison participated in the Second Great Awakening as a supporter of the temperance movement. He next entered the public sphere as a supporter of abolition. He delivered a Fourth of July address to the Massachusetts branch of the Colonization Society in which he criticized the Founding Fathers, calling them hypocrites. He also called the Constitution "a Covenant with Death and an Agreement with Hell." In 1833, Garrison organized the American Anti-Slavery Society.

Garrison later developed a friendship and working relationship with the former slave Frederick Douglass who, under Garrison's sponsorship, became an abolitionist and orator. Douglass eventually broke with Garrison due to the latter's insistence on crafting Douglass's image to suit his own prejudices and those of other white abolitionists.

Henry David Thoreau

Best known as a key figure in the 19th-century Transcendentalist movement alongside his friend Ralph Waldo Emerson, writer Henry David Thoreau was 27 years old in 1844 when he built a log cabin on Walden Pond, on a piece of land owned by Emerson in Concord, Massachusetts. Thoreau moved into the modest cabin on the Fourth of July. Thoreau was resistant to the Industrial Age and worried about what machines would do to the American soul. Telegraph technology had been developing, coinciding with the development of the railroad.

Thoreau lived on little money and almost never bought anything. He worked only six weeks out of the year, spending most of his time reading and writing, and the rest "planting beans and picking huckleberries" (231). In protest against the Mexican-American War, which resulted in the annexation of Texas and the expansion of slavery, Thoreau refused to pay his taxes. He went to jail in 1846 for tax evasion. The experience led to his writing the seminal essay "Civil Disobedience." He argued that the government of majority rule had deterred men from casting votes of conscience. Prison, he believed, was the only house of honor in a slave state.

Frederick Douglass

Formerly enslaved in Maryland, Frederick Douglass was an African American abolitionist, orator, writer, and publisher. Born in Maryland in 1818, he taught himself to read, using pieces of newspaper and old spelling books. At age 12, he read debates in the schoolbook *The Columbian Orator*, which also included "Dialogue between a Master and Slave." His reading of the dialogue led him to question the institution of slavery, its justifications, and its origins.

Douglass escaped from slavery in 1838 by disguising himself as a sailor. While living in New England, he began reading William Lloyd Garrison's newspaper, the *Liberator*. He wrote about his early life as a slave and his journey to freedom in *Narrative of the Life of Frederick Douglass* (1845) and *My Bondage and My Freedom*. The former was translated into French, Dutch, and German. It led to global speaking engagements and to Douglass's reputation as the world's most famous Black person. Douglass was also the most photographed American man in 19th-century America, believing that the photograph eliminated the possibility of being distorted or caricatured by a white portraitist. He sat for his first photograph in 1841 when he was 23. By the 1840s, Douglass had become one of the country's best-known public speakers, with over 100 speaking engagements in 1843 alone. He was known for his "force and eloquence" (248). Douglass bought his freedom in 1847 and returned to the United States to start his own newspaper—the *North Star*.

Though Garrison introduced Douglass to an audience of abolitionists, Douglass disliked how Garrison tried to craft his image, preferring that he appear humbler and simpler—that is, more aligned with Garrison's and other white abolitionists' idea of a former slave. Douglass's insistence on seizing control of his personal narrative, which included challenging the century's stereotypes about Black people, was a key act of agency. His falling out with Garrison, which was also due to a debate over the Constitution (Garrison found the document useless on the question of slavery, while Douglass thought it provided justification to end slavery) also revealed the racist biases of some figures within the abolitionist movement.

On July 5, 1852, Douglass gave his best-known speech in Rochester, New York. "What to the Slave Is the Fourth of July?" criticized the hypocrisy of the holiday—an annual celebration of the nation's liberation from tyranny that occurred while white people continued to tyrannize and enslave African Americans.

After the capture of John Brown, Douglass, whom Brown had told of his plot, fled first to Canada, then, to England, for safety. In December 1860, Douglass delivered his "Plea for Free Speech," in response to a mob that had disrupted a speech he was slated to give at Boston's Tremont Temple in commemoration of John Brown's execution. In the speech, he invoked the Founding Fathers to illustrate the sacred right of free speech, which he knew the defenders of slavery refused to tolerate.

After emancipation, Douglass met with Lincoln's successor, Andrew Johnson, in the White House during what turned out to be a tense meeting. Douglass sought the president's support for the Civil Rights Act of 1866. Douglass later served as US ambassador to Haiti. In 1893, Douglas attended the Columbian Exposition in Chicago, the only eminent African American to appear at the fair. He was 75 and appeared at the fair "to explain the rise of Jim Crow" (353). He gave a lecture on August 25, on what was designated "Colored People's Day" at the fair. Douglass also represented the nation of Haiti at the Haiti pavilion. Douglass had planned to give a lecture entitled "The Race Problem in America," but Ida B. Wells, who was also in attendance, encouraged him to boycott Colored People's Day instead. Douglass ended up writing an introductory essay to a pamphlet entitled *The Reason Why the Colored American Is Not in the Columbian Exposition*, in which he emphasized that, while "he wished he could tell the story of America as a story of progress, the truth was different" (356). He also gave his planned address to an audience that included white hecklers. In his speech, he eschewed the notion of a "Negro problem" and questioned, instead, whether white Americans had enough honor to live up to their own Constitution. Douglass's speech at the Columbian Exposition was one of the last public speeches that he ever gave.

Douglass died from a heart attack at age 77 after collapsing in the midst of a post-dinner conversation with his wife about women's emancipation. He had spent the day attending suffrage meetings with Susan B. Anthony, who was one of his dearest friends. Thousands of mourners attended his funeral.

Margaret Fuller

Margaret Fuller was a journalist, critic, orator, women's rights activist, and Transcendentalist. In 1844, Horace Greeley hired her to work as an editor at the *New York Tribune*, the newspaper he had founded and published. At the time that she was hired, Fuller was 34 and regarded as the most erudite woman in the United States. Arguably, Fuller was one of the most learned figures of her generation of any gender. She was "nearsighted and frail," but "as comfortable writing literary criticism as she was discussing philosophy with Emerson" (252). Ralph Waldo Emerson claimed that her oratory skills put her powerful writing in the shade. Contrary to the conventions of the times, Fuller was one of several white women who spoke publicly and enjoyed debate. She criticized the work of literary figures whom she did not admire, such as that of Edgar Allan Poe, and supported both abolition and equality between the sexes. In 1845, Fuller published *Woman in the 19th Century*, in which she "argued for fundamental and complete equality" (252). The book, which expanded on an essay Fuller had written for the Transcendentalist journal *The Dial* in July 1843, was a hit. One of Fuller's catchphrases when talking about women's abilities was "Let them be sea-captains, if you will," an expression that Greeley often used when greeting her. Greeley sent Fuller to Europe to work as a foreign correspondent for the *Tribune* and she became America's first female war correspondent.

While in Rome, Fuller fell in love, became pregnant, and gave birth to a son. She also wrote about the Italian revolutions of the late 1840s and looked after injured revolutionaries in a Roman hospital. According to Lepore, it was Fuller's work that catalyzed the Seneca Falls Convention of 1848. In July 1850, while returning to the United States with her new family, Fuller, her partner, her infant son, and her manuscript about the revolutions, were lost to a shipwreck a few hundred yards off the coast of Fire Island, New York. Only the body of her nearly two-year-old son, Nino, was found.

Elizabeth Cady Stanton

Elizabeth Cady Stanton was a writer, suffragist, and women's rights activist who was, alongside Susan B. Anthony, one of the chief early advocates of women's suffrage. Stanton was the daughter of Daniel Cady, who first served as a member of the House of Representatives and, later, as a New York Supreme Court Justice. She grew up reading her father's law books. Stanton later married Henry Brewster Stanton, a lawyer and abolitionist who also helped found the Republican Party. Stanton had worked to secure the passage of the Married Women's

Property Act—a New York law that allowed married women to separate their personal property from communal property.

At age 32, Stanton wrote the manifesto the "Declaration of Sentiments" which used rhetoric from the Declaration of Independence. The manifesto outlined how men had oppressed women throughout time. Stanton refused to believe that the battle over the Constitution and the intent of the nation's founders were matters to be resolved only by men. With Susan B. Anthony, Stanton petitioned for signatures to ratify the 13th Amendment.

Harriet Tubman

Like Frederick Douglass, Harriet Tubman was a runaway slave from Maryland. Tubman had first run away from her plantation when she was seven years old. She was key in building the Underground Railroad—a secret network through which abolitionists, allies, and other runaway slaves ("conductors") assisted enslaved people on their journey to Northern states. After the passage of the Fugitive Slave Act (1850), runaways sought to reach Canada, where they could not be hunted and shipped back to the South.

Tubman was five feet tall. She had experienced some of the cruelties that many other enslaved people had endured, including being beaten and starved. Once, a weight had been thrown at her head, leaving a permanent dent. She had escaped from slavery in 1849, making her way to Philadelphia. Nicknamed "Moses" or "Captain Tubman," Tubman made around 13 trips back to Maryland to help approximately 70 men, women, and children escape from slavery. She managed to do this "while working, in New York, Philadelphia, and Canada, as a laundress, housekeeper, and cook" (261).

Abraham Lincoln

Abraham Lincoln was the 16th American president, best known for having emancipated African Americans from slavery. He stood "six foot four and straight as a tree" (276). Lincoln, who was from Kentucky, held numerous professions before initiating a career as a prairie lawyer. He then became a member of the House of Representatives from Illinois—the only Whig from his state. While in office, he had opposed the Mexican-American War and supported the Wilmot Proviso. During his term, he said little about slavery. Lincoln returned to his career in law, but was coaxed back into politics after the passage of the Kansas-Nebraska Act, which he loathed. He was 45 years old at the time. He developed an argument against slavery that was grounded "in his understanding of American history, in the language of Frederick Douglass, and in his reading of the Constitution" (265). When the Republican Party was founded in May 1854, Lincoln joined. Three months later, he decided to challenge Democratic senator Stephen Douglas for his seat. He debated Douglas in Peoria before an enthralled crowd. Douglas spoke for three hours. After a dinner break, the men returned to the debates and Lincoln, too, spoke for three hours. Using language from the Declaration of Independence, Lincoln argued that there was no moral right in making one person the slave of another. He also believed that the maintenance of slavery made the United States appear hypocritical. Ultimately, Lincoln lost the race for the Senate, but he continued to hone his antislavery arguments.

In the summer of 1858, Lincoln and Douglas debated again, and Lepore writes that the debates illustrate, better than any other historical record, the character of the disagreement between antislavery and proslavery factions. This was also the first time in which the two men argued with each other face-to-face. During the debates, Lincoln asserted that he had no intention of interfering with slavery in the states in which it already existed. He also claimed that he had "no purpose to introduce political and social equality between the white and black races," but contended that the Declaration of Independence entitled Black people to all of the natural rights that the document enumerates (277). For Lincoln, quite simply, the discussion over slavery was truly a matter of right versus wrong.

Lincoln narrowly lost the Senate seat to Douglas, but he had emerged as a leader in the Republican Party and its most powerful orator. He later edited and published their debates. Poet William Dean Howells wrote Lincoln's biography as part of the support for the candidate's campaign— *Life of Abraham Lincoln* (1860). Now nicknamed "Honest Abe," Lincoln was inaugurated on March 4, 1861. Since Election Day, he had grown a beard. He ran for reelection—the first president to do so since Andrew Jackson—and won. After he resumed the presidency, Lincoln pressed for passage of the 13th Amendment, which permanently abolished slavery. Lincoln was assassinated at 10:15 p.m. on April 14, Good Friday, at Ford's Theatre, a playhouse just "six blocks from the White House" (305). Lincoln was 56 years old and the first president to be killed while in office. He was quickly apotheosized as a national martyr. His embalmers promised that his corpse would never decay. In the South, many rejoiced in his passing.

John Brown

Militant abolitionist John Brown is famous for his raid on a federal armory in Harpers Ferry, Virginia, on the eve of the Civil War. Prior to this, he worked as a tanner and a sheep farmer. He had also been a failed businessman and the founder of a secret society named the League of Gileadites. Augustus Washington, an African American daguerreotype artist, took his best-known portrait, in which Brown stands beside the flag of the Underground Railroad with his right hand raised, as if taking an oath.

In 1858, the year in which the Lincoln-Douglas debates took place, Brown was 58 and the father of 20 children. He was "lean and fearsome" and "spoke of prophecies and scourges" (279). He and his followers, comprising 44 Black men and 11 white men, wrote their own constitution in Canada, borrowing language from the Declaration of Independence to highlight how Black men were oppressed citizens and that slavery was antithetical to "those eternal and self-evident truths set forth in our Declaration of Independence" (279). Thus, they declared war against slavery and began to hoard weapons.

The following year, in the spring, Brown and a group of his followers went to Maryland. They had planned a military operation that would start with their seizure of a federal arsenal at Harpers Ferry. Brown had sought the support of Harriet Tubman in this venture, yet failed to enlist her. He next sought out the support of Frederick Douglass, whom he met in Pennsylvania. Douglass tried to dissuade Brown, convinced that he would both fail and be killed. On Sunday, October 16, 1859, Brown and 21 men "attacked the arsenal and captured it" (282). They had briefly stopped a train leaving Harpers Ferry, then let it pass. As the train sped to Baltimore, passengers threw notes out the windows of the cars, warning people about the rebellion. The notes led to telegraphs. Brown had hoped that word of the insurrection would lead Black men and women to take up arms and join him and his men in revolt. However, word never reached slave cabins, as enslaved people had no access to telegraph technology. Military soldiers, commanded by Robert E. Lee, retook the arsenal, captured Brown, and captured or killed all of his co-conspirators.

Brown's broader plan was "to lead an armed revolution throughout the South" (283). The soldiers found numerous "boxes of weapons and ammunition, along with [...] thousands of copies of his 1858 constitution and maps of the South [...] with places where blacks outnumbered whites marked with X s" (283). Brown, like Lincoln and Douglass, believed that the nation's founding documents served as proof that slavery was antithetical to the United States' core values. Conversely, Brown's failed plot convinced Southern planters that abolitionists were, indeed, zealots and murderers. After his death, some Northerners, including the writer and Transcendentalist Henry David Thoreau, praised Brown as a righteous hero committed to equality. Brown was ultimately found guilty of murder, conspiracy, and treason. Allowed to speak at his November 2 sentencing, Brown gave a speech in which he agreed to forfeit his life to further justice and the end of slavery. He was hanged on December 2, 1859.

Mary Lease

Mary Elizabeth Lease (née Clyens) was an orator and cofounder of the populist People's Party—the most successful third party in American history. Lease could speak for hours on how the federal government was conspiring with railroad companies, speculators, and bankers to disempower farmers and factory workers. Lease stood nearly six feet tall and had what one writer called "a golden voice" (330). She was born in 1850, the daughter of Irish immigrants. Her father, two of her brothers, and an uncle had died during the Civil War. Her uncle perished at Gettysburg, while her father "starved to death as a prisoner of war" (331). She remained angry at both the South and the Democratic Party for her losses. Lease married Charles Lease in 1873 and had six children—two of whom died while still children. Lease farmed in Kansas and Texas, while also taking in laundry, writing, and studying law. In the spring of 1873, Lease and her family moved to Kingman, Kansas, "onto land they'd acquired through the Homestead Act" (334). The land was free, but Charles had to borrow large sums of money from a local bank to purchase farming tools and to "pay land office fees" (334). The Leases lived in a sod house. After barely getting by for several months, they were unable to pay their bills, leading the bank to repossess their land. The Leases, however, were not alone in their financial suffering. The year 1873 "saw the worst financial disaster since the Panic of 1837" (334).

In addition to fighting for small farmers and laborers, which helped to set off the populist revolt against corporate monopolies, Lease also advocated for women's suffrage and temperance. She entered politics through the Women's Christian Temperance Union (WCTU), believing that women needed the right to vote if they were going "to end the scourge of alcohol," or the abusive and neglectful behavior of men, often triggered by excessive drinking (339).

Despite her and other Populists' commitment to political equality and labor rights, Lease and others within her party embraced white supremacy and nativism. Using the scientific racism of her time, Lease argued in *The Problem of Civilization Solved* that white people were to be the "guardians of the inferior races" (343). She believed that people of African and Asian descent were better suited to perform all manual labor. In the 1880s, she joined the Union Labor Party in Kansas. The party had been formed by Henry George to promote the Australian ballot.

In 1895, Joseph Pulitzer endorsed Mary Lease as candidate for mayor of Wichita. Lease lost the election and her home in the town was foreclosed. She then moved to New York City, which she regarded as "the heart of America," and campaigned for Henry George's next mayoral candidacy. After George died, Lease delivered his eulogy. After the election of William McKinley to the presidency, Lease, repulsed by the infusion of corporate money into politics, left populist politics behind and became a journalist. Pulitzer hired her to work as a reporter.

Henry George

Henry George was a California-based journalist and populist who, along with Mary Lease, cofounded the People's Party. Additionally, George was a political economist who advocated for the single tax. George was also instrumental in introducing the secret ballot into American voting, having previously observed the process of private voting in Australia. George also worked to try to eliminate the influence of money in politics. To promote the Australian ballot, George started the Union Labor Party.

George was born in Philadelphia in 1839. He left school at 14 and sailed to both India and Australia "as a foremast boy, on board a ship called the *Hindoo* " (340). While in India, George noticed the country's remarkable poverty. He returned to his native Philadelphia and worked as a printer's apprentice. He next "joined the crew of a navy lighthouse ship sailing around Cape Horn in 1858" in an attempt to get to California (340). He made it to San Francisco, where he edited a newspaper that quickly failed. By 1865, he had a wife and four children. Impoverished, he begged in the streets for money to feed his family. George eventually found work as a printer. He then worked as a writer and editor for the *San Francisco Times*. He wrote an essay called "What the Railroad Will Bring Us," in which he expressed his belief that it would only make the rich richer and the poor poorer. In 1879, George published *Progress and Poverty: An Inquiry into the Causes of Industrial Depressions and of Increase of Want with Increase of Wealth*, in which he explained his support for the single tax, or land tax—an idea that had some support in subsequent decades before dwindling. Clarence Darrow was one skeptic of George's program, which declared that only economic equality could bring true Christianity to Earth. Darrow believed that George underestimated people's selfishness.

Like Mary Lease, George supported women's suffrage, but he was "vehemently opposed to extending either suffrage or any other right of citizenship to Chinse immigrants or their children" (342). Poor white men were the focus of his activism.

In 1886, George moved to New York City and ran for mayor on the Union Labor ticket. He lost to the Democratic candidate, Abram Hewitt. George beat the Republican candidate, however—28-year-old Theodore Roosevelt. George ran for mayor again in the mid-1890s. This time, it looked as though he might win, but he died of a stroke five days before the election. His body was put on display at Grand Central Station. Over 100,000 mourners went to the station to pay their respects. Mary Lease gave his eulogy. The *New York Times* reported that not even Lincoln's death was met with so much ceremony.

William Jennings Bryan

Best known for his anti-evolution stance during the Scopes Trial, William Jennings Bryan was also a key figure in the populist movement, bringing the political wave "from the Plains to the Potomac," thereby turning the Democratic Party into a people's party (345). Lepore describes Bryan as "[t]all, broad-shouldered, and sturdy" (345) He dressed in the Western style, wearing cowhide boots and a string tie. Nicknamed "Boy Bryan," he was the first presidential candidate to campaign on behalf of the impoverished.

Born in Illinois in 1860, Bryan was fascinated by Democratic Party politics from a young age. He graduated from Illinois College, then attended Union College of Law in Chicago. He trained in oratory. He later moved to Nebraska and settled in Lincoln. At the time, Nebraska was the nation's fastest-growing state. In 1890, when he was 30, Bryan was elected to Congress as a Democrat. Those who heard him speak claimed that he was the best orator they had ever heard. In the summer of 1896, Bryan went to the Democratic National Convention, set to take place at the Chicago Coliseum, "where he would deliver one of the most effective and memorable speeches in American oratorical history" (350). His purpose was to join the People's Party to the Democratic Party—to build a coalition of white Southerners, Western farmers, and Northern laborers—and to turn the Republican Party into the party of wealthy businessmen. Bryan's political style fused together Jeffersonian agrarianism with the revivalist Christianity of the Second Great Awakening. At the convention, Bryan advocated for ensuring the prosperity of the masses, which would eventually benefit every class. The People's Party, including Mary Lease, supported Bryan at the Democratic National Convention. When the party held its own convention in St. Louis, it seconded Bryan's nomination. He also had the support of Socialists, including the labor organizer Eugene Debs. In 1896, Bryan ran against William McKinley, a Republican and former governor of Ohio, for the presidency. McKinley, who had ample funding from wealthy businessmen, won the election.

Bryan later earned the nickname "Mr. Fundamentalist," due to his objection to modern, secular studies at educational institutions. He became a leader of evangelical fundamentalists. Bryan, however, was not an actual fundamentalist—that is, he did not believe in literalizing the gospel and using it to convert people to Christianity. Instead, he believed in the Social Gospel, which promoted the idea of using the example of Christ to perform good works, a position that was anathema to true fundamentalists. Bryan's anti-evolution stance was due to his confusing Darwinism with Herbert Spencer's social Darwinism, and the program of eugenics that would develop out of the latter.

During the Spanish-American War, Bryan formed a volunteer regiment in Nebraska. He then went to Florida to train to fight, though he was never sent into combat. Later, Bryan would position himself as an anti-Imperialist, believing it to be inconsistent with Christian and democratic values. In 1900, Bryan again ran against McKinley for the presidency. Again, he lost. This time, McKinley's running mate, Theodore Roosevelt, outdid Bryan in the latter's strongest area—campaigning. Bryan's second loss was also partly due to changes in American life and politics. Bryan's base were farmers, while, increasingly, more Americans lived in cities and worked in either factories or offices. Despite being a twice-failed presidential candidate, he continued to rail against plutocrats, particularly John D. Rockefeller, and promoted an amendment to the Constitution that would authorize an income tax. The Democratic Party nominated him for a third and final time in 1908. Bryan lost again, this time, to William Howard Taft. In 1912, Bryan endorsed Woodrow Wilson for president. In exchange, Wilson named Bryan secretary of state. Bryan resigned from his post in 1915, due to his inability to stop the nation's drift into World War I.

In 1925, at age 65, he served as prosecutor in the trial of John Scopes—a Tennessee-based high school biology teacher "who was charged with the crime of teaching the theory of evolution" (414). Bryan, still reeling from the horrors of the First World War, decried secular modernity, which he believed determined "the end of sympathy, compassion, and charity" (415). At this point in his life, much of the public regarded the man whom they also called "the Boy of the Plains" and "the Great Commoner" as a relic. His former supporter, the Socialist Eugene V. Debs, disavowed him. Bryan died in his sleep, five days after a jury found Scopes guilty.

Frederick Jackson Turner

Frederick Jackson Turner was a historian, one of the first Americans to receive a doctorate in history. Turner was born in Wisconsin in 1861. He was 31 when he attended the Columbian Exposition in Chicago, where he gave remarks to the American Historical Association, an organization founded in 1884 and incorporated by Congress to collect and preserve key artifacts for the promotion of historical studies. Unlike his predecessor, key historian and national chronicler George Bancroft, Turner used evidence, such as the census, to understand how change occurred. His studies changed how knowledge was organized, and his research led to the abandonment of mystery in favor of objectivity—an intellectual shift that would inadvertently contribute to the rise of fundamentalism.

In the lecture he gave at the Columbian Exposition, "The Significance of the Frontier in American History," Turner chronicled four centuries of American history. Turner was influenced by both Thomas Jefferson and Charles Darwin. He regarded the American frontier "as the site of political evolution"—a wilderness that was, in his view, populated by "savages" (354). In his progressivist vision of history, various forms of settlement, starting with the arrival of European traders and culminating in the development of factories and cities, resulted in a final stage of civilization defined by capitalism and democracy. Turner's ideas developed both out of quantitative analysis and scientific racism. Using information from the 1890 census, Turner argued that the frontier, "which he described as the meeting point between savagery and civilization," had opened in 1492 and closed four centuries later (355). He declared that there was no longer any demarcation between settled and unsettled parts of the North American continent.

Ida B. Wells

Journalist and anti-lynching activist Ida Bell Wells-Barnett was born in Holly Springs, Mississippi, in 1862. Wells, the daughter of formerly enslaved people, started her career as a school teacher. In 1883, she was forced to leave the "ladies' car" on a train and move to a car reserved for Black people. Wells refused, took her case to court, and began writing for African American newspapers. After three Black grocery store owners were lynched, she began writing about the scourge of lynching in the South, which was fostered by the lie that Black men sought to rape white women. Wells encouraged "black militancy and armed resistance against lynching and against Jim Crow" (355).

In Memphis, Wells founded her own newspaper called *Free Speech*. A white mob burned the newspaper's office to the ground, causing Wells to move to New York City, where she continued to publish under the pen name "Exiled." In 1887, Wells was elected secretary of the African American–run National Press Association. Five years later, she published her first book, *Southern Horrors: Lynch Law in All Its Phases* (1892). Frederick

Douglass wrote a testimonial for the volume, "saying that his own voice was feeble by comparison" (356).

Walter Lippmann

Walter Lippmann was a journalist and cofounder of the magazine the *New Republic*. By 1914, when he was 25, he had already written two incisive books about American politics. Lippmann wore three-piece pinstripe suits and was educated at Harvard, where he had studied with the philosophers William James and George Santayana. Though he seemed destined for the quiet career of an academic and philosopher, he decided to become a reporter. He worked for a time as Lincoln Steffens's assistant, while the latter wrote investigative journalism about big-city politics.

Lippmann used his background in philosophy to invent the image of the learned political commentator. This, combined with his appearance as "heavyset and silent," led his friends to call him "Buddha" (361). He lived in Washington, DC, in a row house that he shared with other notable young liberals, including future Supreme Court justice Felix Frankfurter. Its visitors, who included Herbert Hoover, were illustrious. Theodore Roosevelt called Lippmann the most brilliant young man of his age group in the nation. Lippmann was especially adept at taking apart the ideas of his elders by finding their flaws. He wrote with authority and gained mass appeal during the turn of the century. He worried, however, over "the malleability of public opinion," which could shift "into mass delusion" (363). During World War I, Lippmann had advocated for the US to enter the war. When he was 28, he drafted a report entitled, "The War Aims and Peace Terms It Suggests." After the piece was revised by Wilson, it became the president's Fourteen Points. Lippmann was appointed to the London office of an Inter-Allied Board for propaganda, directing his writings at both Americans and the Germans and Austrians in the Central Powers.

In 1922, Lippmann wrote a book entitled *Public Opinion*. Out of this book, which was about the management of public opinion, grew the idea of public relations. After the Second World War, Lippmann brought the phrase "the cold war" into the popular lexicon, as it was taken from his 1947 work *The Cold War: A Study in US Foreign Policy*.

Frederick Winslow Taylor

Frederick Winslow Taylor was a mechanical engineer from Philadelphia who was employed at Bethlehem Steel Works "to speed production" (382). While at Bethlehem, he timed the company's steelworkers, using a stopwatch. Taylor used the example of the fastest worker to calculate the quickest rate at which a unit of work could be completed. All of the factory's other workers were then required to work at that pace or lose their jobs. Taylor called this system "task management," which later became known as "The Gospel of Efficiency" or "Taylorism." Taylor, it turned out, had invented his numbers. Bethlehem Steel eventually fired him for charging too high a fee for himself. Still, his method of efficiency endured and was particularly embraced by Henry Ford, who used Taylor's method on his assembly-line workers. Future Supreme Court justice Louis Brandeis also believed that Taylorism was the solution to problems wrought by "mass industrialism and mass democracy" and encouraged railroad companies to apply it, much to the chagrin of laborers (383).

In 1911, Taylor penned a best-selling book entitled *The Principles of Scientific Management*. In the subsequent decade, his method of efficiency was applied in the Harding White House.

In 1923, Henry Luce and Briton Hadden, the founders of *Time* magazine, applied the principle to their new magazine, working to condense a week's worth of news into a periodical that one could read in an hour. The purpose, as the magazine's name suggested, was to save time.

Theodore Roosevelt

Theodore Roosevelt was the 26th president of the United States and a member of one of the nation's most illustrious families. At age 39, he resigned from his post as secretary of the navy and formed the First US Volunteer Cavalry Regiment. His charge up San Juan Hill during the Spanish-American War made him a national hero. Like Woodrow Wilson, Roosevelt was also a historian who wanted to tell the nation's story. In 1889, he published the first of his four-volume series *The Winning of the West*. Unlike Wilson, he was less interested in political ideas than he was in the history of battles. Still, Roosevelt "read widely and deeply," and was such a great admirer of Lincoln that he wore a ring "that contained a wisp of hair cut from the dead president's head" (375).

Roosevelt had completed a law degree at Columbia University while serving in the New York State Assembly. A large, boisterous man, he spent much of his time on his ranch in North Dakota. After he returned from fighting in Cuba, he was elected Republican governor of New York. Two years later, President William McKinley named Roosevelt his running mate, despite objections from McKinley's adviser, who had called Roosevelt a "wild man." Roosevelt, however, proved to be a tireless campaigner who outdid McKinley's opponent, William Jennings Bryan, on the campaign trail.

In 1901, after William McKinley was shot by an anarchist in Buffalo, Roosevelt "became the nation's youngest president" at age 42 (375). As president, Roosevelt was adept with the press and gave its members a permanent room in the White House. He provided them with stories on Sundays so that they could run their articles at the beginning of the week. His most important legacy is the "establishment of a professional federal government," which included scientific agencies, as well as a "series of wildlife refuges and national parks" (375). Roosevelt served as president for two terms—refusing to run a third time, though he later regretted this decision.

In 1912, he ran for president again as a Republican. After losing the nomination to William Howard Taft, his handpicked successor, Roosevelt formed the Progressive Party, which embraced white women (Roosevelt promised that he would appoint activist Jane Addams to his cabinet), but refused to seat African American delegates. Using the campaign tactics he had learned when campaigning for McKinley, Roosevelt gained a national following by appealing to voters directly with mass advertising. He developed the notion that candidates could foster cults of personality that existed separately from their respective political parties. As a third-party candidate, Roosevelt won 27% of the popular vote, "more than any third-party candidate either before or since" (387). He died in 1919.

W. E. B. Du Bois

William Edward Burghardt Du Bois was one of the United States' earliest civil right advocates and one of the nation's greatest intellectuals. Du Bois, a native of Great Barrington, Massachusetts, earned a doctorate at Harvard in 1895, then studied in Germany at Humboldt University. He pioneered the social survey—a new method of social science research. He applied this methodology to his research in *The Philadelphia Negro* (1899). In the same year that he published the book, Du Bois worked as a professor at Atlanta University. While in Georgia, he observed the chopped and barbecued remains of the Black farmer Sam Hose in a store window, leading Du Bois to believe that he could not adopt the cool stance of a social scientist to write about racism.

In 1903, Du Bois wrote in his seminal work *The Souls of Black Folk* that the problem of the 20th century was "the problem of the color line" (410). Six years later, Du Bois cofounded the National Association for the Advancement of Colored People (NAACP), which developed out of the Niagara Movement—a meeting of African American intellectuals that took place at Niagara Falls in 1905. The following year, Du Bois founded his monthly magazine the *Crisis*, which published both literature and articles about civil rights issues. During the First World War, Du Bois encouraged Black people to align with white people and to abandon, temporarily, their anti-lynching efforts. He also pushed Black men to enlist as soldiers. His reputation suffered after the war, as lynchings increased exponentially after Black soldiers returned home.

In 1929, Du Bois debated the racist and eugenicist Lothrop Stoddard in Chicago. There, he challenged Lothrop's view that the United States was a white nation. Du Bois insisted that the country would not exist if not for the contributions of African Americans. Uncompromising in his devotion to civil rights, Du Bois eschewed both the Democratic and Republican parties in favor of radical third-party politics. He later left the United States for Ghana, where he died in 1963.

Woodrow Wilson was the 28th US president and the first Southerner elected to the White House since the Civil War, after a career as a professor of political science. Wilson, a native of Virginia, studied at both Princeton and the University of Virginia. In 1902, he published the first of his five-volume *History of the American People* and later authored the book *Congressional Government*. As president, Wilson devoted himself to applying the principles of the Constitution to the modern mechanical age. He insisted that the framers of the Constitution could not have predicted mass industrialization, thereby making it imperative that the nation treat the founding document as a living thing that was capable of evolving. He believed that the federal government had to regulate commerce to protect ordinary Americans from the uncontrollable consequences of the Industrial Age. Wilson also believed that Congress had too much power and argued instead for the expansion of executive power, seeing the president as a key unifying figure and the leader of the nation. He used his power to keep the 63rd Congress in session for 18 consecutive months, longer than the legislative body had ever met before. He oversaw their lowering of the tariff; reforms of banking and currency laws; the abolition of child labor; the passage of a new antitrust law; the first eight-hour workday law; and the first federal aid bestowed to farmers. Wilson nominated Louis Brandeis to the Supreme Court, the first Jewish person ever appointed, as well as "a dogged opponent of plutocrats" (388).

Wilson also espoused segregationist politics. He was friends with Thomas Dixon, the Southern novelist whose book *The Clansman* was adapted into the 1915 film *The Birth of a Nation*, directed by D. W. Griffith. Wilson praised the film, which he had viewed at the White House, and believed its content to be true. While speaking on the 50th anniversary of the Battle of Gettysburg, Wilson encouraged his audience to forget that the war had been fought over slavery, instead embracing the notion that it had been a battle over states' rights. Despite his campaign promise to promote equal treatment, which gained him the support of some African American voters, including W. E. B. Du Bois, Wilson imposed segregation in his cabinet, leading to the elimination of many Black civil servants through both demotions and an unwillingness to hire Black employees.

While the First World War raged in Europe, Wilson held fast to an isolationist policy. In 1916, he had campaigned on the promise of keeping the nation out of the war. After German U-boats sank the British liner the *Lusitania* in 1915 and three American ships in 1917, the US entered the war. Wilson later distinguished himself as a key diplomat in establishing peace, particularly with his Fourteen Points and his establishment of a League of Nations—a precursor to the United Nations. Around this time, Wilson signed a tax bill that raised taxes on incomes and corporate earnings to cover the cost of the war. When tax revenue failed to pay the price of the war, the federal government began to sell war bonds.

In 1919, in honor of his leadership after the war, Wilson won the Nobel Peace Prize. After Wilson suffered from a series of strokes, he became bedridden. For five months, he was hidden in a room in the West Wing of the White House. His wife, Edith, refused to allow anyone to see him. He died in 1924.

Henry Ford

Henry Ford was the son of Michigan farmers who opened the Ford Motor Company in Detroit in 1903. He employed the efficiency method invented by the mechanical engineer Frederick Winslow Taylor to speed production. Ford was 40 years old when he opened his factory, where he popularized the use of the assembly line. By 1914, the Ford plant was producing nearly 250,000 cars per year. The automobiles cost one-quarter of the price at which they were sold 10 years earlier.

Ford was also very much involved in the lives of his employees, many of whom were recent immigrants. He sought to assimilate them to American life according to his ideals. Ford's English School taught his employees hygiene, thrift and economy, and how to behave both at home and in their communities. By the 1920s, Ford was the second wealthiest man in America. His son, Edsel, was the third.

Herbert Hoover

Herbert Hoover was the 31st US president, best known for presiding over the nation after it had fallen into the Great Depression. Hoover had previously served as secretary of commerce under President Warren G. Harding.

Hoover had been born in poverty "in the Quaker town of West Branch, Iowa, and orphaned at nine" (405). He enrolled at Stanford University, where he studied geology. He proved to be an organizational genius in his career as a mining engineer, and became wealthy from his efforts in Australia and China. He retired from business at age 37 to devote himself to public service. By then, he had lived most of his life outside of the United States and was working toward humanitarian relief in Europe both during and after the First World War. Some in Europe believed that he, not Wilson, was truly deserving of the Nobel Peace Prize. Reporter and political commentator Walter Lippmann considered Hoover the most interesting man he had ever met. In 1920, both Democrats and Republicans urged Hoover to run for the presidency. He lost the Republican nomination to his future boss—Harding.

Hoover brought his efficiency expertise into the Harding administration. As secretary of commerce, he had "control over the entire American economy" (406). He brought farmers, labor leaders, businessmen, and fishermen to meetings in which they worked out the federal government's priorities. Under Hoover's direction, the department's budget grew exponentially. He also organized "a series of annual radio conferences at the White House between 1922 and 1925" (421). He understood that broadcasting was the future of radio, and that the technology would unify the nation, though he was ill-suited to the medium and failed to use it successfully with the public.

Hoover, who was masterful at managing emergencies, guided the US through the 1929 stock market crash, but he had no incentive to handle the depression that ensued. While Hoover supported charity, he did not support a program of government relief, believing the latter would lead to socialism. Instead, he severed the US from Europe by getting Congress to pass a trade bill—the 1930 Tariff Act, which led to the shrinking of world trade and the decrease of American imports. European debtors, unable to sell their goods to the US, found themselves unable to pay back war debts to American creditors. Between the crash in 1929 and 1932, one-fifth of all American banks failed. The unemployment rate climbed exponentially, reaching 23% by 1932. Twelve million Americans found themselves out of work; a quarter were starving. A drought, which became known as the Dust Bowl, engulfed the Great Plains, leading to death and greater despair. After the stock market crash, Americans overwhelmingly rejected both Hoover and the Republican Party, electing Franklin D. Roosevelt president in 1932.

Franklin Delano Roosevelt

Credited with pulling the United States out of the Great Depression with the New Deal, Franklin D. Roosevelt, or FDR, the 32nd president, was born a patrician into one of the nation's most privileged families. He often wore a wide-brimmed hat and wireless round glasses, in addition to clutching a cigarette holder between his teeth. Roosevelt was born in Hyde Park, New York, in 1882. When he was young, he had so admired his distant cousin Theodore Roosevelt that he adopted some of the latter's expressions. Roosevelt was elected to the New York State Senate as a Democrat in 1910, when he was 28. Three years later, President Woodrow Wilson appointed him assistant secretary of the navy. By 1920, Roosevelt was considered as a vice presidential candidate. The following year, however, when he was 39, he contracted polio and lost the use of both of his legs. Publicly, he disguised his condition by using leg braces and a cane, despite the great pain induced from walking. Privately, he was confined to a wheelchair. His wife Eleanor believed that living with paralysis taught her husband what it meant to suffer. Roosevelt easily defeated Hoover, sweeping up both the Electoral College and the popular vote. Roosevelt was elected to four terms in office and died in the midst of both his fourth term and the Second World War, leaving his successor, Harry Truman, to handle the peace.

Unlike his predecessor, Herbert Hoover, Roosevelt was adept at using the radio. He spoke with such warmth, charm, and sincerity that both Democrats and Republicans found themselves agreeing with his remarks. Roosevelt spoke much slower than most radio announcers, using a pedestrian vocabulary. The

231

technique worked: The entire nation seemed to be tuned in to his fireside chats on the radio. Roosevelt also coordinated with his Federal Communications Commission chairman to prevent newspaper publishers, particularly William Randolph Hearst, from owning radio stations, in an attempt both to prevent Hearst from expanding his empire and to keep a key Republican opponent off the airwaves.

During his first 100 days, Roosevelt met with legislators each day to pass a flurry of legislation that reformed the banking industry, used government reform to regulate the economy, and increased employment through public assistance programs and public works.

Eleanor Roosevelt

Eleanor Roosevelt was the wife of Franklin D. Roosevelt and is one of the United States' most admired First Ladies. Roosevelt was born in New York City in 1884 and was orphaned during her childhood. She married Franklin—her fifth cousin—in 1905, and together they had six children. Less than a decade into their marriage, Eleanor found out about her husband's affair with her social secretary. Agreeing to remain married for the sake of her husband's political career, Eleanor turned her energy toward public service. She worked on international relief during the Second World War and, after her husband became paralyzed, she began a career in public speaking, often working as her husband's surrogate. She became the leader of the Women's Division of the New York State Democratic Party while her husband governed New York and campaigned for the presidency. By 1928, she was head of the Women's Division of the Democratic National Convention (DNC), making her "one of the two most powerful women in American politics" (431).

Roosevelt was tall and lean. She often wore floral dresses and floppy hats. She had little interest in becoming First Lady, a role that she thought would relegate her to a servile domestic role. Instead, Roosevelt revolutionized the role, using it to advance women's rights and civil rights. She wrote a newspaper column, went on a national tour to champion her ideas, and gave a series of 13 national radio broadcasts. Though she was a less gifted speaker than her husband, she gained a devoted audience. She delivered around 300 radio broadcasts from the White House—nearly as many as her husband. She was especially keen on reaching rural women through radio. Roosevelt's efforts helped to make the Democratic Party, a party that had previously dismissed women, one that concerned itself more with women's issues. In the spring of 1933, Roosevelt published *It's Up to the Women*. In it, she argued that only women could pull the nation out of the Depression with hard work, frugality, good sense, and civic involvement.

Malcolm X

Born Malcolm Little in Omaha, Nebraska, in 1925, and raised in Lansing, Michigan, Malcolm X was one of the most pivotal civil rights figures of the 20th century. Malcolm X was born to Louise Little, a native of Grenada, born to a Black mother and a Scottish father. Her husband, Earl, was a Baptist minister. They met at a meeting for Marcus Garvey's United Negro Improvement Association (UNIA) in Philadelphia in 1917. When she was pregnant with Malcolm, a group of Klansmen arrived at the Little home in Omaha, threatening to lynch Earl. The family left for Michigan, where they encountered more racist vigilantes. This time, the family's home was burned to the ground. In 1931, Reverend Little was run over by a streetcar in what was probably the result of another attack from white vigilantes. Due to the insurance company denying Louise her husband's life insurance, the children ended up in foster care and Louise was committed to a mental institution at Kalamazoo State Hospital, where she remained for 25 years. Malcolm left a juvenile home in 1941 and later moved to Boston to live with his older half sister, Ella. There he became a petty criminal before moving to Harlem and becoming a numbers runner and pimp.

During a six-year stint in prison for robbery, Malcolm discovered the Nation of Islam (NOI) and became a Muslim. He also studied Greek and Latin, read history voraciously, and learned how to debate. He would later debate the civil rights activists Bayard Rustin and James Farmer. When he emerged from incarceration, he became the Nation of Islam's most prominent proselytizer and one of Elijah Muhammad's most committed followers. He was featured in the "five-part 1959 documentary narrated by CBS News's Mike Wallace," *The Hate That Hate Produced* (606). Malcolm later compared the documentary to Orson Welles's radio adaptation of H. G. Wells's *The War of the Worlds*.

As Malcolm's star rose and he inadvertently became both the organization's most visible spokesperson and leader, he garnered the envy of fellow NOI members, including that of the leader Elijah Muhammad. Deeper rifts developed as Malcolm spoke out publicly, particularly in the aftermath of President John F. Kennedy's assassination, against the NOI's wishes. Malcolm's subsequent discovery of Elijah Muhammad's sexual exploitation of young women in the organization, as well as his pilgrimage to Mecca, led to a break with the NOI and his development of the Organization for Afro-American Unity (OAAU). Malcolm X's defection from the NOI ultimately resulted in his assassination on February 21, 1965, at the Audubon Ballroom in Harlem, where he was murdered in front of his wife and daughters by a member of the Newark branch of the NOI.

In the late 1980s and early 1990s, there was a revived interest in Malcolm and his espousal of militancy—the opposite of Dr. Martin Luther King Jr.'s advocacy of civil disobedience in response to racist violence. Newly published editions of Alex Haley's *The Autobiography of Malcolm X* (1965) and the 1992 release of Spike Lee's eponymous film spurred renewed interest in Malcolm's life, in addition to solidifying his place within the pantheon of key 1960s civil rights figures.

Lyndon B. Johnson

Lyndon Baines Johnson was the 36th president of the United States, vice president under John F. Kennedy, and a former senator from Texas who was so powerful in his role that his biographer, Robert A. Caro, nicknamed him "master of the Senate." Johnson was adept at "wrangling senators the way a cowboy wrangles cattle," using intimidation, if necessary, to get their votes on key legislation (552).

He displayed this skill most markedly when Congress passed the Civil Rights Bill of 1957. Previously, Johnson had voted against every civil rights bill he encountered during "his career in the House and the Senate, from 1937 to 1957" (585). Privately, he had never been a segregationist, and he publicly supported *Brown v. Board of Education*. By the mid-1950s, he believed that the Democratic Party needed to change its policy direction. More importantly, Johnson was eyeing the presidency. To win, he needed to show that he was a national politician—not simply a Southern one. Due to his ability to court and count votes better than any other Senate majority leader in history, the civil rights bill passed.

Johnson was an enemy of Wisconsin senator and Communist hunter, Joseph McCarthy, and later played a key role in the senator's censure and subsequent fall from power. Johnson is best known for having passed the Civil Rights Act of 1964, which outlawed segregation in public accommodations, and the Voting Rights Act of 1965, which helped bring an end to decades of voter intimidation directed against Black Southerners. He was married to Lady Bird Johnson.

George Gallup

George Gallup, the namesake for the Gallup poll, married journalism and social science to invent political polling, which he believed was "a new field of journalism" (454). Gallup attended the University of Iowa in the 1920s with the intention of studying journalism. Instead, he got a degree in psychology, which was more feasible during that decade. He graduated in 1923, having specialized in Applied Psychology. In his courses, Gallup became interested in measuring public opinion. He first sought "to use the sample survey to understand how people read the news" (454). His dissertation, written in 1928, was entitled "An Objective Method for Determining Reader Interest in the Content of a Newspaper." In it, he argued that the press had once been "the chief agency for instructing and informing the mass of people," but the development of public schools placed newspapers in the field of providing entertainment (454). He developed a method to measure readers' interest, which he called the "Iowa method." This study's purpose was to find out which features and writers readers liked best so that a newspaper editor could eliminate content regarded as dull.

By 1932, Gallup was a professor of journalism at Northwestern University. He used his method of measuring reader interest to calculate the chances of his mother-in-law, Ola Babcock Miller, winning the office of lieutenant governor, for which she was campaigning. After that venture, he moved to New York and both worked for an advertising agency and taught at Columbia. Around this time, "he perfected a method for measuring the size of a radio audience" (454). He continued working in the 1930s on ways to predict elections for newspapers and magazines. He then started a company called Editors' Research Bureau. He renamed it the American Institute of Public Opinion and established it in Princeton, New Jersey, to lend it some academic prestige. Gallup began to survey public opinion by selecting a sample of the population and asking them questions. This, he asserted, was a way to take the "pulse of democracy" (455). He intended for his work to operate in favor of the republic—not to do the work of political consulting.

Pauli Murray

Poet, civil rights activist, legal scholar, and Episcopal priest Pauli Murray was born in Baltimore in 1910. She graduated from Hunter College in 1928, then went to work for the National Urban League and the Works Progress Administration (WPA). She had been denied admission to the University of North Carolina in 1938, on account of her race. Meanwhile, Murray, who identified as male, searched for a doctor who would prescribe her testosterone. She had no success. However, she insisted on challenging UNC's racism. She approached Thurgood Marshall, then a young attorney leading the NAACP's charge against discrimination. Marshall discouraged her because Murray had by then moved to New York, making her case as a nonresident weaker. Murray graduated first in her class at Howard University's law school, where she was the only woman, but was denied admission to Harvard Law School for postgraduate work, because the university barred women. She attended the University of California, Berkeley, instead, where she wrote a dissertation on "The Right to Equal Opportunity in Employment." She would encourage a reading of the 14th Amendment that fought not only Jim Crow, but also "Jane Crow," or sex discrimination.

Murray was one of the architects of the sit-in movement, which would continue into the 1960s. In 1940, she was arrested in Virginia for refusing to abide by segregated busing. Like Dr. Martin Luther King Jr., she was influenced by both Henry David Thoreau and Mahatma Gandhi, who espoused civil disobedience. Her goal, which began when she was a law student at Howard, was to dismantle Jim Crow by getting the *Plessy v. Ferguson* decision overturned. During the Second World War, Murray organized sit-ins in drugstores and eateries throughout the nation's capital.

Harry S. Truman

Harry Truman was the 33d president, best known for ending the Second World War by dropping atomic bombs on Hiroshima and Nagasaki and for making the first attempt to create national health insurance. Truman was raised in Independence, Missouri, and worked on his family farm until he went to combat in France during the First World War. He had no college degree. Truman started his political career in Missouri, where he first held a county office, then was elected to the US Senate in 1934. In 1944, Franklin Roosevelt selected Truman as his running mate because the Missouri politician was devoid of controversy. During his vice presidency, Truman had little involvement in White House business, leaving him little prepared to ascend to the presidency after President Roosevelt's death. Lepore describes him as "[m]ild-mannered and myopic [with] a common touch" (531). He expressed concern for the lives of ordinary Americans, particularly African Americans, whom he had courted since the beginning of his political career. Truman established a commission on civil rights and later desegregated the armed forces. He had some bipartisan support, particularly from then California governor Earl Warren.

Earl Warren

Earl Warren was a Republican governor of California and, later, chief justice of the Supreme Court, appointed by President Eisenhower. Warren first served as solicitor general but was promised a position on the Court. When Chief Justice Fred Vinson died in 1953, Warren was appointed chief justice—a position that he held for 16 years, "presiding over the most liberal bench in the court's history" (579). During his years as governor, Warren had proposed a compulsory health insurance funded with a payroll tax, which served as a model for the plan that Harry Truman tried to institute nationwide. As chief justice, he helped overturn segregation in public schools in 1954 with the *Brown v. Board of Education of Topeka, Kansas* decision. Warren began his career as a conservative Republican, but ended it as a liberal. Richard Nixon counted Warren among his chief enemies.

Warren was the son of a Norwegian immigrant railroad worker who was later murdered. He studied political science and law at the University of California, Berkeley. He served during the First World War and, in 1939, became California's attorney general. In that position, he supported President Roosevelt's policy of interning Japanese Americans and openly expressed racist views toward this population. In his later years, Warren expressed deep remorse for his past prejudices. In 1942, Warren ran for governor of California and won. Two years later, Warren became seriously ill with a kidney infection. Concern about the financial impact on his family led him to consider a state insurance plan. He introduced the proposal in January 1945 during his State of the State address. The California Medical Association opposed the plan and enlisted the help of an ad agency to defeat it.

Richard Nixon

Richard Milhouse Nixon was the 37th president of the United States, notorious for the Watergate scandal that led to his resignation. Paranoid, power-hungry, and known to hold grudges, particularly toward Ivy League alums, Nixon's presidential achievements (e.g., the creation of the Environmental Protection Agency) are often overlooked to focus on the shortcomings of his character.

Nixon was born in Yorba Linda, California, in 1913. He had been a sharp and ambitious child, but anxious. His family later moved to Whittier, California, "where his father ran a grocery store out of an abandoned church" (534). Nixon attended Whittier College, despite wishing that he could attend an Ivy League institution. He paid his way through college and resented his inability to afford to attend a better school. Lepore describes him as having wavy black hair in his youth, small and dark eyes, and heavy eyebrows. He was an outstanding debater, which helped him gain entry to Duke Law School. He applied to Wall Street law firms, but none would hire him. He returned home to Whittier, then served in the US Navy in the South Pacific. When he came back, he was 32-year-old Lieutenant Commander Nixon. A group of California bankers and oilmen soon recruited him to run against "five-term Democratic incumbent Jerry Voorhis for a seat in the House" in 1946 (534). During the campaign, Nixon characterized Voorhis as soft on communism and smeared his political reputation, thereby cementing his signature tactic of making false claims then feigning offense when his opponent accused Nixon of being dishonest.

Nixon later served as vice president under Dwight D. Eisenhower. Despite the Republican Party being the party of wealthy businessmen and stockholders, Nixon lived a very modest life, which included debts and little capital. He ran unsuccessfully for the presidency against John F. Kennedy in 1960, but ran again in 1968 against Hubert Humphrey and won by a landslide. He was reelected in 1972 and served until his resignation in 1974. Nixon was adept at exploiting feelings of inadequacy among the electorate, feelings he shared, which would become evident from both his paranoia and habit of recording political opponents. In his campaign against Voorhis, he exploited voters' unease with Ivy League graduates who made them feel inferior. In the 1968 election, he would use the support of the Silent Majority—that is, white working-class and white ethnic voters who felt discarded by the Democratic Party after the civil rights movement—to secure a win. In 1972, he won reelection in a landslide, becoming the first presidential candidate ever to win 49 states. His presidency ended in ignominy, however, due to the Watergate scandal. To avoid impeachment, Nixon resigned. Despite the shame around his resignation, Nixon, who had prioritized foreign over domestic policy during both of his terms, had "opened diplomatic relations with China, [...] negotiated arms limitation agreements with the Soviet Union," and ended the Vietnam War (644).

John F. Kennedy

John Fitzgerald Kennedy was the 35th president of the United States and, at 43, was the youngest ever to be elected at the time. Kennedy was known for his focus on diplomacy and anti-communism and, tragically, for being the last of four presidents assassinated, with his death in Dallas on November 22, 1963. Kennedy, like his 1960 presidential opponent, Richard Nixon, ran for a House seat in 1946. Unlike Nixon, Kennedy had been prepared for a political life from birth. Kennedy, the son of Joseph and Rose Kennedy, was born to a large, wealthy Irish Catholic family in Brookline, Massachusetts. He attended Choate and Harvard. His future running mate, Lyndon B. Johnson, referred to him as "the boy." Kennedy was a foil to Nixon—while the latter had fought hard to attend college and to climb the political ladder, Kennedy, through his father's connections, had easily been granted admission to the nation's best schools and given boosts to ascend the political ladder. The two faced off during the 1960 presidential debate, which was televised. Kennedy, who appeared cool on camera compared to an ill and sweaty Nixon, was regarded as the winner, though the race between the candidates was very tight. In the end, Kennedy prevailed in a close election.

One of the first acts of the Kennedy administration was to form the Peace Corps in March 1961. Ten years earlier, when Kennedy was contemplating a run for a Senate seat, he and his brother, Robert F. Kennedy, stopped in Vietnam during a tour of Asia and the Middle East.

Like Nixon, Kennedy was largely motivated by a wish to deter communism, and particularly the ambitions of the Soviet Union. Initially, other members of his party distrusted him due to his silence on McCarthyism. Robert "Bobby" Kennedy, who became attorney general during his brother's administration, had been a close friend and associate of Joseph McCarthy, aiding the latter in his hunts for Communists. President Kennedy's own anti-communist efforts included the Bay of Pigs disaster in Cuba—an attempt to overthrow Fidel Castro—and the nearly catastrophic

Cuban Missile Crisis. His efforts toward civil rights, both as a candidate and a president, were tentative, though he had run as a civil rights candidate to win Black votes in the North. Civil rights legislation was not carried to fruition, however, until his successor, Lyndon Johnson, became president.

Thurgood Marshall

Born Thoroughgood Marshall in Baltimore in 1908, Marshall was "the son of a steward [...] and a kindergarten teacher" (575). He began to spell his name "Thurgood" by second grade because it was simpler than his given name. He first read the Constitution when he was forced to study it as a punishment for disobedience. Marshall was enthralled by the document. His parents aspired for him to become a dentist, but Marshall "work[ed] his way through college as a dining-car waiter on the B&O Railroad" (575). Sometime thereafter, he decided to become an attorney. He got his first practice arguing with his father at the dinner table.

Barred from attending the University of Maryland on account of his race, Marshall went to Howard, despite it being 40 miles away from his home. He graduated first in his class in 1933 and, two years later, won a case against the state of Maryland, arguing that, because it provided no law school for African Americans, it defied the "separate but equal" doctrine established by *Plessy v. Ferguson*. By 1950, Marshall convinced the NAACP to abandon this argument in favor of abolishing segregation altogether.

Marshall then started the NAACP's Legal and Educational Defense Fund and served as its chief counsel. He argued hundreds of cases across the South in an effort to end Jim Crow. He started with law schools and professional schools, then worked on cases at colleges, hoping to get as far as public schools. In 1967, Marshall was appointed to the US Supreme Court, where he served until 1991.

Marshall was six foot four, had wavy black hair, which he wore slicked back, and had a thin mustache. He spoke with a slight Southern drawl. Marshall believed that the *Brown* case would put the matter of racial inequality to rest. When he realized that it would not, he continued to hope that a Supreme Court case would come into the docket that finally could. Marshall retired in 1991 due to health concerns and was succeeded by Clarence Thomas.

Martin Luther King Jr.

Born in Atlanta in 1929, Dr. Martin Luther King Jr. became the most significant civil rights activist to emerge from a period of activism (1955-1968) generally referred to as the civil rights era or the civil rights movement. His positions, particularly his stance on civil disobedience, would bring him in conflict with more militant activists like Malcolm X. After his death, his legacy would be significantly sanitized, overlooking his radicalism and his dedication to union organizing. King was the son of a minister and NAACP leader. He was influenced by evangelical Christianity, theologian Reinhold Niebuhr, and anticolonialist efforts abroad, particularly Mahatma Gandhi's commitment to nonviolence.

King, who was ordained in 1948, "had wide-set eyes, short hair, and a pencil mustache" (582). During his youth, he was lean. As he aged, his body became sturdier. Once rather quiet, his voice had become stirring and deep. He had attended a theological seminary in Pennsylvania, then completed a doctorate at Boston

University in 1955 "before becoming a pastor at the Dexter Avenue Baptist Church" in Montgomery, Alabama (583).

He, along with Rosa Parks, led the Montgomery Bus Boycott of 1955. The following year, he founded the Southern Christian Leadership Conference (SCLC). His efforts to secure the civil and economic rights of Black Americans led to the 1963 March on Washington, where King delivered his famous "I Have a Dream" speech. One year later, at age 35, he became the youngest recipient of the Nobel Peace Prize. King was murdered on April 4, 1968, while in Memphis, Tennessee, where he was working to organize sanitation workers.

Ella Baker

Ella Baker was a key civil rights activist in the 1950s and 1960s. Born in Virginia in 1903, Baker had worked for many years as an organizer with the NAACP, first as a field secretary starting in 1938, then as a director of numerous Southern branches in the 1940s. One of the projects on which she worked was equal pay for Black teachers. Baker joined the Southern Christian Leadership Conference (SCLC) in 1958 to lead "an Atlanta-based voter registration drive known as the Crusade for Citizenship" (596). She had been frustrated by Southern preachers' seeming indifference to the issue of voting rights and found Martin Luther King Jr. "too self-centered and cautious" to address the issue (596). She urged students who had been organizing sit-ins throughout the South to start their own organization instead of forming a junior chapter of the SCLC. The result was the formation of the Student Nonviolent Coordinating Committee (SNCC). Baker left the SCLC to join the new organization.

George Wallace

When George Wallace became governor of Alabama, he was only 43 and obsessed with politics. He started his career in 1935, at age 16, when he worked as a page in the state senate. He attended the University of Alabama, where he distinguished himself as both class president and an outstanding boxer. After studying law, he was an airman in the Pacific during the Second World War. Wallace ran for state congress in 1946, but he had never been particularly passionate about maintaining segregation, despite his loyalty to the South. Thus, when he served as an alternate at the 1948 Democratic convention, he refrained from leaving the floor alongside the Dixiecrats. He also endorsed Adlai Stevenson for president.

In 1958, when he ran for governor, Wallace shifted his political sympathies publicly. He posed alongside Confederate flags, but still lost the primary to John Patterson, who more strongly opposed desegregation and later became governor. In 1962, determined not to be outdone, Wallace worked with a speechwriter "who doubled as an organizer for the KKK" (608). With his help, Wallace became governor, winning 96% of the vote. During his inauguration, he famously promised "segregation now, segregation tomorrow, segregation forever" (608). He also warned educational leaders against moving forth with school desegregation efforts.

Barry Goldwater

Barry Goldwater was a longtime US senator from Arizona and the Republican presidential nominee in 1964. He was a far-right Republican who, in 1960, had published *The Conscience of a Conservative*, which became a bestseller. Goldwater, at the time, had been a fringe conservative. He advocated "for the abolition of the graduated income tax" and recommended dismantling much of the federal government—policies that would now align with certain members of the contemporary Libertarian Party. Goldwater also opposed school desegregation, as mandated by the Supreme Court in *Brown v. Board of Education*, in favor of states' rights. This position brought him supporters among Dixiecrats and members of the John Birch Society. Moderate Republicans, particularly New York governor Nelson Rockefeller, believed that Goldwater was part of "a lunatic fringe" that would "subvert the Republican party itself" (614). Rockefeller, who had been competing with Goldwater for the Republican presidential nomination, characterized him as a Nazi.

At the Republican National Convention, US Senator Margaret Chase Smith of Maine, who was also running for president on the Republican ticket, "refused to release her delegates to Goldwater" (615). Richard Nixon, who realized that he had no chance of winning the presidency that year, decided to throw his support behind the eventual nominee. Nixon then gave 156 speeches on Goldwater's behalf.

Goldwater tried to usurp some of President Johnson's support among evangelicals by campaigning for a constitutional amendment that would "guarantee Bible reading and prayer in public schools" (615). However, he failed to make inroads with evangelical voters and lost the election in a landslide.

Phyllis Schlafly

Phyllis Schlafly was the president of the National Federation of Republican Women and later became known for organizing the coalition of conservative white women who torpedoed the passage of the Equal Rights Amendment (ERA). She became one of the most notable women in US politics due to this effort.

Schlafly was born in Missouri in 1924 and was a devout Catholic. She had worked as a gunner during the Second World War and used her income to put herself through college. She later earned a graduate degree in political science from Radcliffe College. She was a supporter of Joseph McCarthy, and her husband served as president of the World Anti-Communist League. In 1952, Schlafly ran for Congress.

Schlafly never identified as a feminist, but she believed that women should have been helping to lead the Republican Party. Three months after a rival within the National Federation of Republican Women kept her from assuming the presidency, she began writing a monthly newsletter, in which she began her "crusade for law and morality" (617). Before her death in 2016, Schlafly showed public support for Donald Trump's presidential campaign.

Ronald Reagan

Ronald Reagan was the 40th president of the United States and, after the decline of Barry Goldwater's political career and Reagan's election as California's governor, he became a conservative standard bearer and leader within the Republican Party. As president, he was nicknamed "the Great Communicator," setting both the political and cultural tone of the 1980s, while leaving behind a policy agenda that impacted views on government for decades after he left office.

Reagan was raised in Illinois and was the son of a shoe salesman. His family survived the Great Depression because of Franklin Roosevelt's New Deal policies, making young Reagan a devoted Democrat. He regularly listened to Roosevelt's fireside chats and memorized the president's speeches. Reagan graduated from Eureka College in Illinois and then worked as a radio broadcaster and sports announcer. He began acting in films in 1937. He married fellow actor Jane Wyman several years later. After their divorce, he married fellow actor Nancy Davis in 1952, with whom he later appeared in a war-themed film. During World War II, he produced films for the Office of War Information. In Hollywood, he developed a reputation for being reliable and affable, leading to his being elected president of the Screen Actors Guild (SAG). As president of SAG, Reagan became an anti-communist activist. He registered as a Republican in 1962, though he had begun to support conservative candidates in the previous decade. Two years later, he supported Goldwater's presidential run.

Stokely Carmichael

Stokely Carmichael, who later renamed himself Kwame Ture, was the head of the Student Nonviolent Coordinating Committee (SNCC), credited with both coining and helping to lead the Black Power movement. Having started his career in political activism as a Freedom Rider in 1961, Carmichael later gave up on party politics after witnessing white Democratic Party leaders' exclusion of the Mississippi Freedom Democratic Party from the nominating convention in 1964. Carmichael graduated from Howard University in the same year with a degree in philosophy. For his work in registering voters in Mississippi, he was nominated for a Senior Class Humanity Award. His activism led to his getting arrested six times. The FBI started a file on Carmichael in 1964.

While the SCLC still favored working with white liberals, Carmichael helped take SNCC in a direction that "favored black consciousness and black power" (621). He borrowed the term "black" from Malcolm X and famously called for "black power" during a speech in 1966 in response to police brutality. He encouraged forms of protest that were adopted by the Black Lives Matter movement nearly half a century later and criticized the regulation of free speech, particularly where Black people were concerned.

Hillary Rodham Clinton

Hillary Rodham Clinton is a former US senator from New York, former secretary of state, and the first woman to obtain a major party's nomination for president. She entered political discourse as an object of animus for political conservatives, particularly former Nixon speechwriter Pat Buchanan, who believed that Bill Clinton's administration would usher in a liberal agenda, which Buchanan characterized as "radical feminism," that would undermine traditional America. Clinton, as Lepore notes, remained a target of the political right throughout her years as First Lady, during her careers as senator and secretary of state, and during her two failed presidential bids.

Clinton was born in Chicago in 1947 and was raised to be a Republican. She canvassed for Nixon when she was 13 and was a "Goldwater Girl" at 17. She attended Wellesley College, where she was elected president of the Young Republicans. In 1968, she worked as an intern on Capitol Hill. Her antiwar sympathies and her feminism drove her away from an increasingly conservative GOP. The following year, she became the first student at Wellesley selected to deliver a commencement address, which was featured in *Life* magazine. In 1970, she spoke before the League of Women Voters on its 50th anniversary. In 1971, while she was a student at Yale Law School, she met fellow student Bill Clinton. After graduating from Yale, she moved to Washington, DC. During Nixon's impeachment inquiry, she worked as a staff attorney for the House Judiciary Committee. She married Clinton soon thereafter but kept her name. Only when her husband began to run for political office did she call herself Hillary Rodham Clinton.

During her years as First Lady, she served more as a colleague to her husband, to the consternation of many conservatives. She led the president's health care initiative, heading the Task Force on National Health Care Reform. He referred to her as "his Bobby Kennedy" (698). Clinton, as First Lady, was unprecedented. She was the first working woman in the White House. Though she was not the first feminist in her role, she was unabashed about her feminist views. She also had more senior staff working for her than did Vice President Al Gore.

Bill Clinton

William Jefferson Clinton was the 42nd president of the United States and the spouse of former senator, secretary of state, and two-time presidential candidate Hillary Rodham Clinton. Clinton was relatively young, only 46, when he entered the White House. Born in Hope, Arkansas, in 1946, he had grown up poor and was raised by a single mother. He dodged the Vietnam War draft, earned a degree in international affairs from Georgetown University, got a Rhodes Scholarship, and enrolled at Yale Law School, where he met Hillary Rodham.

In 1978, Clinton was elected governor of Arkansas. With his humble Southern background and affable charm, he appealed to the Democratic Party's old guard while its new guard, particularly African Americans, responded to his Ivy League education and his progressive record on civil rights.

In 1992, Clinton made his bid for the presidency—an ambition that was nearly undone by news of his extramarital affairs, as well as accusations of sexual harassment. Though Clinton had spoken openly about other aspects of his private life to the media—from his past usage of marijuana to his underwear preferences—he asked the media to eschew salaciousness by avoiding further conversations about alleged affairs. Clinton eventually won the 1992 election "with the lowest popular—43 percent—since Woodrow Wilson" (697). Al Gore, a former representative and senator from Tennessee, and a scion of a well-heeled political family, served as vice president for both of Clinton's terms. Like Truman, Clinton prioritized health care reform; also like his predecessor, he failed in this effort. After the 1994 midterm elections, Clinton lost both houses of Congress.

His enduring legacy, as a liberal, was when he appointed Ruth Bader Ginsburg to the Supreme Court in 1993. On other matters, particularly economic ones, he had moved further to the right. Lepore blames this political shift on Clinton's embarrassment after losing on health care reform, as well as what she characterizes as his perpetual need to seek others' approval and be liked. Clinton ratified the North American Free Trade Agreement (NAFTA), despite opposition from labor unions. In 1994, he continued the war against crime and, particularly drugs, that had been waged for nearly 30 years. He signed a crime bill that extended "mandatory sentencing and instituted a 100:1 ratio between sentences for possession of crack and of cocaine," a policy that disproportionately impacted poor, nonwhite groups and sent more African Americans, in particular, to prison (699). Perhaps most damagingly, he pursued welfare reform, siding with conservatives who claimed that it trapped people in poverty and encouraged dependence on government. The Clinton administration, thus, abolished the Aid for Families with Dependent Children and left welfare allotments up to states. Clinton did, however, veto a Republican version of the bill that would have eliminated Medicaid.

In 1996, during his second term, Clinton signed the Telecommunications Act, which "deregulated the communications industry" and allowed for the restoration of media monopolies (732). Three years later, he repealed parts of the Glass-Steagall Act, which had been passed during FDR's administration in 1933. He thereby ended "a ban on combinations between commercial and investment banks" (700). Clinton's presidency would end in ignominy over his impeachment due to the revelation of yet another affair—this time, with White House intern Monica Lewinsky. This made him the second president after Andrew Johnson to be impeached.

Barack Obama

Barack Hussein Obama II was the 44th president of the United States, the first Black president, and a former US senator from Illinois. Obama was born in Honolulu, Hawaii, in 1961, to Stanley Ann Dunham, a white woman from Kansas, and Barack Hussein Obama, a Black Kenyan. During his 2008 campaign for the presidency, he touted the slogan "Hope and Change," adopted from the 1972 United Farm Workers campaign slogan "Sí, se puede." Obama came from a multiracial and multicultural family, all of whom were "scattered across three continents" (725). Many believed that his presidency would usher in a "post-racial America" that would finally overcome its brutal legacy of racial oppression.

Lepore describes him as a man who "spoke like a preacher and sometimes [like] a professor, but he always spoke with a studied equanimity and a determined forbearance" (750). She compares his oratory talents to those of Martin Luther King Jr. and Franklin Delano Roosevelt. This was partly aided by his working with a Shakespearean speech coach, as William Jennings Bryan had. He was young and glamorous, easily becoming the favored candidate of young Democratic voters and even generating appeal among some moderate Republicans and conservative voters in Appalachia. During a time of economic disaster, he invoked the optimism of Reagan's "morning in America" and the political commitments of FDR's New Deal. Obama defeated his Republican opponent in 2008, John McCain, a respected war hero and senator from Arizona, by 9 million votes.

Obama was also a writer who had penned his first memoir, *Dreams from My Father: A Story of Race and Inheritance*, when he was 33. Obama attended Occidental College before transferring to Columbia University, then enrolled at Harvard Law School. Before attending Harvard, he had worked as a community organizer on the South Side of Chicago, where he would later reside, teaching constitutional law at the University of Chicago Law School. He entered politics with the ambition of "reconciling seemingly irreconcilable differences," a position he had developed while studying at Harvard. When he ran for the state senate in Illinois in 1996, he advocated for a social position of moral responsibility—that is, looking out for society as we would our own families. In 2004, he was elected to the US Senate, its only Black member.

Obama was the first scholar since Woodrow Wilson to serve as president. Obama's spouse, Chicago native Michelle Obama (née Robinson), had also trained to be an attorney, studying first at Princeton University, then Harvard Law School. Like Hillary Clinton, Obama's opponent for the party nomination in 2008, Michelle Obama took on a more visible, less traditional role as First Lady, though, unlike Clinton, she never became overtly involved in policy work. Obama's signature achievement during his presidency was instituting the Affordable Care Act, dubbed "Obamacare," which has been maintained, despite bitter

Republican opposition. The idea for the plan, ironically, came out of the conservative Heritage Foundation and was modeled on a state health care plan instituted by Republican Massachusetts governor Mitt Romney, Obama's opponent in the 2012 presidential race. His other key acts were hunting down and killing Osama bin Laden, the orchestrator of the September 11 attacks, and fulfilling his promise to end the war in Iraq.

Themes

Truth and Historiography

Though matters of truth and the proper reading of history may feel like recent concerns, issues regarding textual authority, the origins of the United States, and the manipulation of historical records to form creation myths have persisted since the country's nascence. Arguably, the concern about truth in historiography, or our telling of history based on records, starts with the Dominican friar Bartolomé de las Casas and his transcription of Christopher Columbus's *Diario*. The diary had been copied in the 1530s, then disappeared twice in the 18th and 19th centuries. Lepore reminds readers that "[h]istory is the study of what remains, what's left behind" (4). It is a story subject to perpetual revision as its narrators learn more and adjust their perspectives to contemporary cultural and social mores. This consideration of historiography and truth could likely also apply to Walter Raleigh's history of the world, written in prison, Edward Coke's revision of English common law for colonial administration, and James Madison's record of the Philadelphia Convention. Though concrete facts—dates, names, and actual events—are key to the retelling of history, it is not entirely objective, as the perspective of either the witness or the narrator infiltrates the text.

Since the rise of social media in the 2000s, new sources of news, opinion, and even history have emerged, shared through Facebook memes, unverified tweets, and YouTube videos. The nation's political stratification, which began in the late 1960s and widened more deeply in succeeding decades, influenced what people would accept as truth, reiterating a concern Walter Lippmann had once expressed about how people would decide on what was true—whether they would base their views on reason or on what they wished to believe. As the culture wars came to be fought mostly online, it seemed as though the latter tendency would prevail.

The debate over US history is pronounced and, arguably, most divisive when the public engages in discourse regarding the Founding Fathers' true intentions when writing the Constitution and when discussing the origins of the Civil War. Perspectives tend to fall along political lines. Conservatives have put forth the idea of originalism, arguing for a strict interpretation of the Constitution that does not consider rights not already granted in the document, while liberals tend to advocate a loose interpretation, seeing the Constitution as a malleable document that must be interpreted in ways that are relevant and applicable to our times. Despite ample evidence that the Civil War was fought over slavery, some, particularly from the South, continue to believe that the war erupted over a states' rights argument and that Confederate generals have an honorable a place in American history, just as any war hero. Reassessments of this history, fostered by the rise of the Black Lives Matter movement and the march of white supremacists in Charlottesville, Virginia, in 2017, have aided in delegitimizing this view, which is rooted in a mythologization of antebellum history that became particularly pronounced in the 1910s and has persisted.

The title of this book, which reappropriates a line from the Declaration of Independence, deals with the matter of truth when retelling history and interpreting the documents that give us some insight into the origins of the United States. However,

Lepore seems to advocate using these documents as guides, rather than treating them as sacred texts.

The Rights and Makings of a Free People

The great irony and sin of the United States is its founding as a democracy that was economically dependent on the oppression and enslavement of people of African descent. The English colonists' rule over enslaved people coincided with their own struggle against the English king's authority. In the text, Lepore wonders when some people have the right to rule and rebel, who gets to do so, and why others' similar fight against tyranny is resisted by those in power.

Concerns about power and freedom began, not in the American colonies, but in early 17th century England when the British jurist Edward Coke revived the Magna Carta to challenge the Stuart monarchy's claims of royal privilege. Coke "insisted that the law was above the king" (41). The law, after all, would insist on truth, establishing rights to trial by a jury instead of trial by ordeal, which had earlier prevailed in Europe. African Americans, however, would not enjoy these rights, neither during the colonial era nor after the nation's establishment. According to the Enlightenment thinker John Locke, whose ideas about property and government influenced the founders, Africans could be enslaved because they supposedly existed in a state of nature. Similarly, indigenous peoples could have their land seized because they had no sense of private property. Thus, ideas of freedom and citizenship came to depend on one's ability to assimilate to Western standards of worship and habitation. While efforts were made in the 19th century to assimilate some indigenous peoples according to these standards, African Americans and certain other peoples of color, particularly the Chinese, were regarded as unassimilable—a standard rooted in notions of race. When white colonists fought against the British Empire's standard of taxation without representation, they argued that this method of levying taxes amounted to slavery. John Adams likened colonists to the "negro," keenly aware that to be Black meant to be unfree.

Questions about freedom—that is, who would enjoy the rights of citizenship and who would not—lingered as the nation expanded. When Mexican territory was annexed after the Mexican-American War, politicians wondered if Mexicans, whom they did not exactly consider white people, would be admitted as a free people. When waves of Chinese people immigrated to the Pacific West after the Gold Rush, the public and its leadership wondered if they would be classified as "white" or as "colored." Meanwhile, Black people, who had existed in the United States since its nascence, struggled for citizenship rights, long after the 14th Amendment was added to the Constitution to enshrine those rights, and longer still after the passage of the Civil Rights Act of 1964, which outlawed discrimination in public accommodations, and the Voting Rights Act of 1965, which was intended to ensure that Southern states would not attempt to prevent African Americans from exercising their right to vote.

American history, despite its ideals and its promotion of democracy abroad, has long rested on the idea that the freedom of one group, namely white people, relied on the oppression of others, namely those who were not white. Additionally, due to the history of slavery, the stigmatization of both the Chinese and Japanese, the marginalization of Mexicans, and the recent vilification of Arab and South Asian Americans, the default face of citizenship, too, has been white.

Federal Rights Versus States' Rights

Since its founding, the United States has been splintered between those who wanted a government with a strong central power, the Federalists, and those who wanted a government that remained closer to the ideal envisioned within the Articles of Confederation, in which the states remained largely autonomous—the Anti-Federalists. After the constitutional convention in 1787 and, particularly, after George Washington ended his presidency, the two parties who dominated political discourse were the Federalists, led by the second president, John Adams, and the Democratic-Republicans, led by the third president, Thomas Jefferson. As Lepore notes, the two-party system is endemic to the nation's founding, part of a persisting debate over the limits of federal power, which started with a contention, first raised by constitutional convention delegate George Mason, over the absence of a bill of rights in the Constitution.

Concerns about the extent of federal power would influence decisions ranging from the establishment of a national bank to, most notably, the rights of states to maintain slavery without interference. The nullification crisis of the 1830s started as an argument over a tariff but, as Lepore notes, was truly "about the limits of states' rights and the question of slavery" (217). It also augured the civil war that was to come. The debate that ensued between President Andrew Jackson and Senator John C. Calhoun led the former to conclude that US sovereignty preceded that of the states, while the South Carolina senator and leader of the proslavery movement insisted that slavery was essential to a republican government (218).

Over a century later, the argument for states' rights would be used again to justify the oppression of African Americans. Most Southern states would use states' rights and the 10th Amendment to defy federal orders to desegregate public schools in both 1954 and 1955. In more recent years, as the nation's political divisions have widened, the federal government has become an object of resentment among conservatives who, since the Reagan era, have insisted that government cannot solve social ills but is the likely cause of them. This position would be used to justify the repeal of a series of social welfare programs, which would further impoverish mostly poor people of color. Throughout the 20th century, as the power of the executive branch expanded, the two major parties would change their opinions about the limitations of executive power, depending on the party affiliation of the person who held presidential office.

While arguments over the extent of federal power do have roots in the nation's founding, and even in 17th-century debates in England regarding the privileges of the Crown, they have primarily been concerned with moral arguments about slavery and rights to citizenship, particularly for African Americans.

Index of Terms

Alien and Sedition Acts

Passed by Congress in 1798, the acts granted the president "the power to imprison noncitizens he deemed dangerous and to punish printers who opposed his administration" (158). As a result, 25 people were arrested for sedition, 15 were indicted, and 10 were convicted. Of those 10, seven were Democratic-Republican printers who supported Thomas Jefferson. The acts were a means for John Adams, who was president at the time, to criminalize his opposition. Jefferson and James Madison believed that the Alien and Sedition Acts violated the Constitution, seeing them as examples of presidential overreach and Congress's failure to uphold the principles within the founding document.

Another sedition act was passed by Congress in 1918 to suppress antiwar sentiment. While few people were arrested under the first Sedition Act, over 2,000 Americans were arrested under the Sedition Act of 1918, and the Justice Department convicted half of them.

American Colonization Society

The American Colonization Society was founded during a meeting at the Davis Hotel in Washington, DC. Its purpose was to create a colony in Africa to "rid our country of a useless and pernicious, if not dangerous portion of its population," as the meeting's leader, Kentucky congressman and Speaker of the House Henry Clay, defined the increasing number of free Black people who lived in the United States (176). Bushrod

Washington, George Washington's nephew and a Supreme Court justice, was president of the organization, while Andrew Jackson served as its vice president. Colonization was regarded as the only solution to dealing with emancipated Black people, as the organizers of this society believed it was impossible for the descendants of Africans to live among white people as equals. African American abolitionist David Walker called the venture a trick, insisting that Black people had as much right to remain in the United States as white people did. While some enslaved Black people were repatriated to the West African country of Liberia, ultimately only around 3,000 African Americans departed for the colony.

Articles of Confederation

The Articles of Confederation were a precursor to the American Constitution. The Articles had been hastily drafted by the Continental Congress "for the purpose of waging war against Britain," though they had proven inadequate in maintaining armed forces (114). They were nothing more than "a treaty of alliance among sovereign states" (119). The Articles were drafted in 1777 but were not ratified until 1781, due to the states' "competing claims to western land" (114). Efforts to revise the Articles of Confederation had proven to be useless, resulting in a nation with 13 different currencies and navies.

A meeting was organized on September 11, 1786, in Annapolis, Maryland, to revise the Articles. The special convention included James Madison who, to prepare, read a great deal of political history. Delegates from five of the 13 states showed up for the convention at George Mann's tavern. Twelve men from five states agreed to gather in Philadelphia the following year to devise necessary provisions "necessary to render the constitution of the Federal Government" (117).

Bill of Rights

The Bill of Rights are ten amendments added to the Constitution to satisfy Anti-Federalists, particularly George Mason, who had initially refused to ratify the document if it did not include such an enumeration of rights. James Madison drafted the 12 amendments, 10 of which were approved by three-quarters of the states on December 15, 1791. The Bill of Rights includes amendments that remain some of the most contentious, including the First Amendment, which grants freedoms of speech and religion, and the 2nd Amendment, which has been interpreted to grant citizens the rights to own and carry firearms.

Brown v. Board of Education of Topeka, Kansas (1954, 1955)

Initiated by Thurgood Marshall, *Brown v. Board of Education* struck down *Plessy v. Ferguson* (1896), declaring its doctrine of "separate but equal" unconstitutional. Marshall began building the case in 1951, as part of his effort to eliminate Jim Crow laws by targeting schools. A third-grader named Linda Brown lived in Topeka, Kansas. Her father, Oliver, wanted her to attend a school several blocks away from their home, but it was a white school that she was forbidden to attend. Instead, the nearest Black school was a long walk and a bus ride away. Brown joined the civil suit against the Topeka Board of Education filed by the NAACP's Legal Defense Fund.

The first oral arguments took place in December 1952. At first, it seemed as though the court would rule in favor of segregation. Chief Justice Fred Vinson, a native of Kentucky, believed that Congress should be responsible for desegregating schools. Then, on September 8, 1953, Vinson died and Earl Warren took his place on the Court. Warren agreed with Marshall's premise that the "separate but equal" doctrine rested on the notion that Black people were inherently inferior to white people. Warren used Marshall as an example of how that premise could not be true. Warren's vote, added to the four justices who were already in favor of overturning *Plessy*, meant that Warren's argument against segregation prevailed. Future chief justice William Rehnquist, then a clerk, believed that *Plessy* had been right.

The court handed down its decision on May 17, 1954. Some African Americans, particularly educators, were skeptical of the ruling's benefit, believing that Black teachers would lose their jobs and that school desegregation would distract from goals they believed were more pressing. White people, especially in the South, strongly resisted and called for Earl Warren's impeachment. In 1955, the Court issued a second opinion, "urg[ing] schools to desegregate with 'all deliberate speed'" (581). Most did not follow the Court's ruling. By 1955, in eight Southern states, not one Black child attended school with a white child. The fight to end Jim Crow, which the case symbolized, put Black children on the front lines of that battle. The fight next took place in other spaces of public accommodation. After the *Brown* decision, reporters began to take greater notice of the clashes between civil rights activists and segregationists. President Eisenhower never publicly endorsed the Court's decision, and he never asked Congress for a more robust civil rights bill.

Chinese Exclusion Act

The Chinese Exclusion Act of 1882 was the first immigration law ever passed by Congress. The legislation "barred immigrants from China from entering the United States" and declared that the 14th Amendment "did not apply to people of Chinese ancestry" (335). Additionally, it declared that Chinese people already residing in the United States "were permanent aliens who could never become citizens" (335). The Chinese Exclusion Act further solidified the notion that race determined citizenship, in addition to establishing the prejudice of assuming that Asian Americans are non-natives. The Chinese Exclusion Act was extended in 1924 with the passage of the Asian Exclusion Act.

Compromise of 1850

The Compromise of 1850 was an agreement brokered by Henry Clay, "the Great Compromiser" who had engineered the Missouri Compromise 30 years earlier, and Illinois senator Stephen Douglas. The agreement was brokered as a result of California's entry into the union in September 1850. To avoid disturbing the delicate balance between free states and slave states, California was admitted as a free state; the slave trade was to be abolished in the nation's capital; and Texas would give New Mexico a piece of land over which they had disputed in exchange for $10 million. To appease proslavery advocates, the territories of Arizona, Nevada, New Mexico, and Utah were to decide for themselves if they wanted slavery when they applied for statehood. Otherwise, the territories were organized with no mention of slavery.

The most key and notorious piece of legislation within the compromise was the Fugitive Slave Act, which "required citizens to turn in runaway slaves and denied fugitives the right to a jury trial" (261). The law initiated what former slave and autobiographer Harriet Jacobs called "a reign of terror to the colored population," as slave catchers and bounty hunters worked to track down, capture, and return runaway slaves in exchange for lucrative rewards (261). Runaways who escaped to the North could still be tracked down, arrested, and taken back to the South. The law also encouraged the capture and trade of free Black people who were then sold to the South. One well-known example is that of Solomon Northrup.

Connecticut Compromise

The Connecticut Compromise, adopted by the Constitutional Convention of 1787 on July 17, "establish[ed] equal representation in the Senate, with two senators for each state" and, in the House of Representatives, apportioned "one representative for every 40,000 people" (124). The latter number was changed to 30,000. Each slave was counted as three-fifths of a person, according to the ratio, later known as the Three-Fifths Compromise, that Madison had created in 1783. A federal census would be taken every decade to count state populations. The result was that slave states had far greater representation in Congress than free states.

Dawes Act

Initiated by Massachusetts senator Henry Laurens Dawes in 1887, the Dawes Act provided the federal government with "the authority to divide Indian lands into allotments and guaranteed US citizenship to Indians who agreed to live on those allotments and renounce tribal membership" (337). The legislation, as Senator Dawes explained, was designed to force Indigenous Americans to "choose between 'extermination or civilization,'" while offering white Americans the opportunity to "wipe out the disgrace of our past treatment" and "lift Indians up 'into citizenship and manhood'" (337). The Dawes Act not only patronized indigenous peoples, it was also the first step in termination—or, the federal government's attempt to eliminate tribes and bands. Finally, it was yet another scheme to seize hold of tribal lands. The government reserved the right to seize what it called "residual" lands, or those parcels of land that were not reserved for allotment.

Dred Scott v. Sandford (1857) was a seminal Supreme Court
case for which Chief Justice Roger Taney wrote the court's 7-2
majority's opinion. The plaintiff, Dred Scott, had been born into
slavery. After his owner took him to a free state (Wisconsin),
Scott sued for his freedom. Before filing the suit, Scott had been
living with his owner, army surgeon Dr. John Emerson, on an
army post in Illinois—another free state—for several years. After
his owner died, Scott offered to purchase his and his wife's
freedom. After Emerson's widow refused, Scott decided to sue
for his liberty. Publicly, James Buchanan, who had recently been
sworn in as president by Chief Justice Taney, claimed that he
was content to leave both this decision and the broader question
of extending slavery in the West to the court. Privately,
Buchanan had tried to postpone the ruling and attempted to get
at least one justice to join the court's proslavery majority.

The Dred Scott decision was the second instance in the
Supreme Court's history in which the judicial branch had
overturned federal legislation. The first was *Marbury v. Madison*.
Writing for the majority, Taney asserted that the Missouri
Compromise was unconstitutional. He also claimed that
Congress had no power to circumscribe slavery in any state
"because the men who wrote the Constitution considered people
of African descent 'beings of an inferior order [with] no rights
which the white man was bound to respect'" (268). The court
also used the case to consider the question of Black citizenship,
ultimately deciding that those who were descended from slaves
could never become "entitled to all the rights, and privileges, and
immunities, guaranteed by [the Constitution]" (313). Five of the
justices on the Supreme Court at the time were slaveholders,

while two others were favorable to the proslavery faction and had likely been appointed for this reason.

Both Abraham Lincoln and Frederick Douglass gave speeches in which they condemned the decision, while slave owners gleefully declared that the Dred Scott decision "had settled the question of slavery for good" (270). Dred Scott died only months after the decision was handed down. He was 58. He and his wife, Harriet, had been formally freed on May 26, 1857, independent of the Court's ruling against them. He had found employment as a porter at Barnum's Hotel in St. Louis, despite having tuberculosis, while his wife worked as a laundress. Scott was buried in St. Louis. Harriet Robinson Scott, who died in St. Louis on June 17, 1876, lived long enough to witness both the Civil War and passage of the 13th Amendment, which abolished slavery.

Electoral College

Proposed by constitutional convention delegate James Wilson, the Electoral College was to be elected by the people to elect the president of the United States. To overcome the problem of the overrepresentation of enslaved people in Southern states, the delegates decided that the number of delegates sent to the Electoral College would be determined not by a state's overall population, but by its number of representatives in the House. There was one member of Congress for every 40,000 people in a state, with those enslaved counting as three-fifths of one person. The federal government had left it to the states to choose their delegates. Originally, delegates were to use their own judgment when deciding on how to cast votes in the Electoral College.

Lepore describes the Electoral College as a concession to slaveholders. To determine the size of a state's representation in the Electoral College, a census was required. Article I, Section 2 of the Constitution calls for a census to be taken every 10 years. All free people were counted, but not unassimilated indigenous peoples, even if they lived within American territory. The first federal census was taken in 1790 and "counted 3.9 million people, including 700,000 slaves" (157).

Equal Rights Amendment (ERA)

The Equal Rights Amendment (ERA) is a proposed amendment to the Constitution that guarantees equal legal rights to all citizens, regardless of sex or gender. The amendment was first drafted in 1923 by suffragists. It was further amended over the years, approved by Congress, and sent to the states for ratification in 1972. The amendment was initially very popular among both Democrats and Republicans. Within one year, 30 out of 38 states moved to ratify the amendment. This momentum slowed down as white conservative women activists, led by Phyllis Schlafly, used an essentialist argument that had emerged during the Progressive Era to demonstrate that the amendment would reduce special protections for women and undermine the traditional family. By 1977, only 35 states had ratified the amendment, and five had rescinded their earlier support. By 1982, after the extended deadline for ratification had expired, the public accepted the defeat of the ERA. Since 2018, there has been a revival of interest in ratifying the amendment.

Eugenics

Born out of Herbert Spencer's social Darwinist ideas, eugenics was a field of study defined by zoologist Charles Davenport, who had coined the term, as "the science of human improvement by

270

better breeding" (392). Davenport also founded the American Breeders' Association, a committee chaired by Stanford University president and biologist David Jordan. The association's purpose was to "investigate and report on heredity in the human race" and to demonstrate "the value of superior blood and the menace to society of the inferior" (392). The result of such studies was sterilization laws. The first was passed in Indiana in 1907. Two-thirds of all states followed suit. Even after eugenics fell out of favor by the Second World War, numerous states continued to perform some version of sterilization, typically on women of color, either through coercion or targeted birth control campaigns.

Scientific racism received further legitimacy when Madison Grant, president of New York's Museum of Natural History, published *The Passing of the Great Race; Or, the Racial Basis of European History* (1916), in which he dissected Europeans according to their geographical origins and phenotypes. He called Northern Europeans the "Nordic race" and characterized them as having blond hair and blue eyes. He warned that they were being overwhelmed by southern Europeans, whom he termed the "Alpine race," which was characterized by their dark eyes and dark hair. Grant warned that democracy could not survive with "two races of unequal value liv[ing] side by side" (392). The American Eugenics Society, which was founded in 1922, would play a role in ensuring that recent Mexican immigrants would not attain citizenship.

Filibuster

Filibusters were originally Southern vigilantes, as Lepore describes them, or Americans who incited insurrections in Latin America in the 1850s "to extend a market for slaves" (281). From the Spanish word *filibustero* ("freebooting"), the term had originally been used to describe 16th-century piratical persons or ships. Americans who went south looking to expand slavery into Latin America "outfitted ships with arms and ammunition and attempted to conquer Cuba, Nicaragua, Guatemala, El Salvador, Mexico, and Brazil" (281). Future secessionist William Lowndes Yancey argued that, if it was legal to buy slaves in Virginia and transport them elsewhere, why was it not equally permissible to buy them in other countries and import them to the South?

The filibuster now refers to a rhetorical device used in the Senate to delay and, ultimately, block the passage of legislation. During the antebellum years, it was a tool of Southern senators to impede any antislavery legislation. During the civil rights era, it was a tool of Southern senators used to uphold legal segregation. Some contemporary filibusters are also used to block legislation on issues concerning race, such as voting rights and police reform.

Fourteen Points

Woodrow Wilson's Fourteen Points, which helped to bring peace after the First World War, was drafted from a report written by Walter Lippmann called "The War Aims and Peace Terms It Suggests." Wilson submitted his Fourteen Points to a joint session of Congress on January 8, 1918. The policy's main proposals were "free trade, freedom of the seas, arms reduction, the self-determination of colonized peoples, and a League of Nations" (396).

The French and Indian War

The French and Indian War is the name that North American colonists gave to their arena of the Seven Years' War (1756-1763), which "stretched from Bengal to Barbados" and involved

"Austria, Portugal, Prussia, Spain, and Russia, and engaged armies and navies in the Atlantic and the Pacific," as well as those in the Mediterranean and Caribbean seas. The war was also instrumental in encouraging union among the British North American colonies.

During the earlier battles, the colonists had done their own fighting and raised their own provincial armies and militias. Then, in 1755, Britain sent its own regiments to North America, led by General Edward Braddock. Benjamin Franklin believed that the Crown's decision was an "attempt to keep the colonies weak" (77). Braddock and his troops pillaged, instilling fear among the colonists. Braddock's troops were later defeated, and Braddock himself was shot. Washington carried the dying general off the battlefield.

The French and Indian War was the most expensive in history and revealed the schism between British and American troops. The colonists regarded the British as "lewd, profane, and tyrannical," while the British regarded "the colonists [as] inexpert, undisciplined, and unruly" (78). To the British, rank was everything, and their officers were wealthy, upper-class gentlemen, while enlisted men were drawn from the poor. In the colonial forces, on the other hand, there were hardly such distinctions. In Massachusetts, for example, one in three men served in the war, "whether they were penniless clerks or rich merchants" (78).

In 1759, the British and American forces defeated the French in Quebec. This led the Iroquois to abandon their previous position of neutrality to side with the British, which shifted the course of the war. In 1763, when peace was reached with the Treaty of Paris, the map of North America was redrawn. France gave all of

Canada and New France east of the Mississippi River to Great Britain, while all of its land west of the Mississippi—a territory called Louisiana—went to Spain. Spain, meanwhile, gave Cuba and half of Florida to Britain. The war also left Britain nearly bankrupt. It also "led to a contraction of debt, followed by a crippling depression" (81).

The Great Migration

The Great Migration was a movement of African Americans from the South to the North and West. Prior to the migration, 90% of all Black people in the US lived in the South. Five hundred thousand African Americans left the region between 1915 and 1918 for Detroit, New York, Chicago, Los Angeles, Philadelphia, and other cities. Between 1920 and 1930, another 1.3 million left the South. By the beginning of World War II, nearly half of all Black people in the US lived outside of the South.

Griswold v. Connecticut

In *Griswold v. Connecticut*, a 1965 landmark case on reproductive rights, the Supreme Court "struck down state bans on contraception" (649). Estelle Griswold, who led a Planned Parenthood clinic in Connecticut, was arrested for providing contraceptives—ironically, just as Margaret Sanger had been 50 years earlier. As it later did in *Roe v. Wade*, the Supreme Court based its ruling on a constitutional argument about privacy, not equality. In 1972, the court extended the precedent of privacy established in *Griswold* from married couples to the unmarried.

Homestead Act

The Homestead Act of 1862 made available "up to 160 acres of 'unappropriated public lands'" to individuals and heads of household who would agree to farm them for five years in exchange for a small fee (317). In October 1864, the National Convention of Colored Men called for legislative reforms that would allow all Black men—not women—to settle on lands granted to citizens by the Homestead Act.

House Un-American Activities Committee (HUAC)

Formed in May 1938 by 37-year-old conservative Texas Democrat Martin Dies Jr., the House Un-American Activities Committee (HUAC) was organized to investigate and root out "suspected communists and communist organizations" (442). Dies's work continued the campaign waged by Federal Bureau of Investigation (FBI) director J. Edgar Hoover, who had been surveilling Black writers and artists for many years. During Congressional hearings, Dies tried to convince the public that the writers and artists employed by the WPA had embedded Communist messages in the poems, plays, documentary photographs, and folklore collections on which they had worked. HUAC was later led by Republican Wisconsin senator Joseph McCarthy whose "witch hunts," or rabid investigations into suspected communists, particularly in Hollywood, led to "blacklisting," or the destruction of careers.

The Immigration Act

The 1924 Immigration Act had two parts—the Asian Exclusion Act, an extension of the Chinese Exclusion Act of 1882, and the National Origins Act. The Immigration Act instituted a quota system that was to end immigration from Asia and limit it from Eastern and Southern Europe. It also hardened immigration along racial lines, codifying the idea of a "white race." Those who were deemed "white" came from European countries regarded as nations. Its citizens were believed to be more assimilable than those who came from Asian countries, who were classified as "races." The Immigration Act did not restrict immigration from Mexico, however.

John Birch Society

The John Birch Society, whose members were nicknamed "Birchers," was formed in 1958 and defines itself as a right-wing political advocacy group. Its "goals included impeaching [Supreme Court Chief Justice] Earl Warren and withdrawing the United States from the United Nations" (614). Its leader, Robert Welch, had suggested that President Eisenhower might have been a communist agent. All of them especially loathed President Kennedy. Birchers also believed that the launch of Sputnik was a hoax.

Kansas-Nebraska Act

The Kansas-Nebraska Act started as a bill designed to organize Permanent Indian Territory into what became the states of Kansas and Nebraska. The law, which was passed in 1854, allowed for the citizens of the new states to decide by popular sovereignty if they wanted slavery. The act also effectively repealed the Missouri Compromise, which would have prohibited slavery in Kansas. Nebraska was far north, making it inevitable that it would enter the Union as a free state. Kansas, however, became a battleground between proslavery activists and Free-Soilers. Both factions struggled for control over the territory, resulting in a small civil war nicknamed "Bleeding Kansas" by newspaper publisher Horace Greeley. In 1854, the Republican Party was founded by citizens who had been determined to defeat the bill in Congress. Though Kansas had applied for admission to the Union in 1859, its progress was stalled by proslavery forces in the state who did not want Kansas to enter the Union as a free state. Kansas finally entered the Union in

1861 as a free state, after the Confederate states, which comprised much of the South, seceded.

Lochner v. New York

Lochner v. New York (1905) was a Supreme Court decision that both intensified the debate around judicial review and worked to undo some Progressive labor reforms. In a 5-4 decision, the Supreme Court used the 14th Amendment to uphold the notion of "liberty of contract," or a business owner's freedom to forge agreements with employees. This notion led the court to void a New York state law stating that bakers "could work no longer than ten hours a day, six days a week" (377). In a dissenting opinion, Justice Oliver Wendell Holmes accused the court of applying social Darwinism to the Constitution, as the majority believed that the more advantaged side in a dispute had the right to win.

Louisiana Purchase

The Louisiana Purchase (1803) was Thomas Jefferson's purchase of Louisiana Territory, an expanse of land "nearly a million square miles west of the Mississippi," from Napoleon Bonaparte. The land had been claimed by the Spanish since 1763 and "inhabited by Spaniards, Creoles, Africans, and Indians generally loyal to Great Britain" (169). Napoleon had secretly purchased the territory in 1800, one year after he took control of France. The Louisiana Territory was to be part of Napoleon's New World empire, with Haiti, which had declared its independence in 1803. However, with Haiti, which was going to be the crown jewel of his empire, out of his hands, Napoleon saw little reason to hold on to the swath of land bordering the United States. Also, at war with Great Britain, he needed revenue.

President Jefferson and James Madison arranged for fellow Virginian James Monroe to go to Paris and offer Napoleon $2 million for New Orleans and Florida, though he was authorized to offer as much as $10 million. Napoleon unexpectedly offered to sell all of the Louisiana Territory for $15 million. Monroe seized the chance and agreed. As a result of the purchase, the size of the United States doubled.

Manifest Destiny

Manifest Destiny was the notion that the United States was destined to cover the North American continent from east to west. Historian and politician George Bancroft, who played a key role in the nation's origin story, was a believer in Manifest Destiny. The nation's devotion to westward expansion contributed to its policies of removing Indigenous Americans, as well as its development of the Trans-Pacific Railroad.

Marbury v. Madison

Marbury v. Madison (1803) was a lawsuit filed by Federalist Party leader William Marbury against Thomas Jefferson's secretary of state, James Madison. The seminal case created the precedent for judicial review. Chief Justice John Marshall granted the Supreme Court the power to decide if laws passed by Congress (the legislative branch) are constitutional. The Constitution had not previously granted the Court this power.

Missouri Compromise

The Missouri Compromise (1820) was an agreement in Congress, brokered by Kentucky congressman and Speaker of the House Henry Clay, to admit Missouri to the Union as a slave state, while Maine, which had petitioned for admission, would be admitted as a free state. As a result of organizing the deal, Clay earned the nickname "the Great Compromiser." Additionally, a line was formed above the border of Missouri. All territories "above that line would enter the Union as free states, and any states below that line would enter as slave states" (179).

Monroe Doctrine

The Monroe Doctrine (1823), named after the fifth US president, James Monroe, "establish[ed] the principle that the United States would keep out of wars in Europe," but would deem any attempt by European powers to colonize parts of the Americas "as acts of aggression" (180). Drafted by John Quincy Adams, Monroe's secretary of state and successor as president, the Monroe Doctrine was an assertion of both American power and sovereignty.

Muckraking

Muckraking was a kind of investigative journalism that first developed at *McClure's* magazine in 1902 when its publisher, the Irish immigrant Samuel Sidney McClure hired three of his best writers "to expose corruption and lawlessness" in unions, corporations, and big-city politics (371). Theodore Roosevelt coined the term. Quoting from *Pilgrim's Progress*, Roosevelt cursed "the Man with the Muck-rake" who focused "only on that which is vile and debasing" (371).

Muller v. Oregon

A laundryman named Curt Muller challenged an Oregon 10-hour work day law in the Supreme Court. The Court upheld the Oregon law. The precedent established by the case solidified the constitutionality of labor laws for women, legitimized sex discrimination in employment, and allowed social science research to be used in court decisions. The latter would be integral in the *Brown v. Board of Education* case. *Muller v. Oregon* also reaffirmed the notion that women, as a presumably weaker sex, needed special protections, making them dependent on the state.

National Origins Act

The National Origins Act, which was part of the Immigration Act of 1924, "restricted the annual number of European immigrants to 150,000" and placed a limit on the number of new arrivals that was "proportional to their representation in the existing population" (407). The purpose of the law, and similar quota systems, was to discontinue immigration from Asia and to limit the admission of immigrants from Southern and Eastern Europe.

National Security Act

The National Security Act of 1947 was a post–World War II law that established the National Security Agency (NSA) and the Central Intelligence Agency (CIA). It changed the War Department into the Department of Defense, which was housed in the newly constructed Pentagon. Finally, the act created the position of chairman of the Joint Chiefs of Staff.

New Deal

Franklin Delano Roosevelt first announced his "new deal" as a political slogan when he accepted his party's nomination at the Democratic National Convention in Chicago in 1932. Roosevelt likened the New Deal to Christian ethics and delivered stump speeches all over the nation to promote it. His speeches were "the first presidential campaign speeches recorded on film and screened in movie theaters as newsreels" (430). Roosevelt's New Deal legislation reform, which came in two parts, helped to pull the United States out of the Great Depression, while also creating social and economic safety net programs, particularly Social Security and the Federal Deposit Insurance Corporation (FDIC), which still exist today. Banking reforms included the Emergency Banking Act, in which banks had to prove that they were solvent to become established, and the Glass-Steagall Act, which led to the creation of the FDIC and the Securities and Exchange Commission (SEC). The Public Works Administration created tens of thousands of infrastructure projects, including cultural and arts institutions, such as the Federal Writers' Project and the Federal Theater Project. The Federal Writers' Project "produced some eight hundred books" (441).

The Agricultural Adjustment project addressed crises among agrarian workers. As governor of New York, Roosevelt had seen over 3,000 farms become abandoned. The Agricultural Adjustment Act, the Farm Security Administration, and other agrarian initiatives "extended a better and fairer distribution of resources like land, power, and water to a national scale" (437).

Congress also passed the National Labor Relations Act in 1935 to "[grant] workers the right to organize, and established the Works Project Administration, to hire millions of people" who built key infrastructure, such as "roads and schools and hospitals," in addition to employing "artists and writers" (438). Later that year, Congress passed the Social Security Act, which "established pensions, federal government assistance for fatherless families, and unemployment relief" (438).

Despite being a relief program, the New Deal did not evenly distribute resources to all groups. African Americans were excluded from certain programs, despite suffering poverty at higher rates than white people. To ensure the compliance of Southern Democrats with his legislation, President Roosevelt permitted discriminatory practices within New Deal programs. By 1938, New Deal reforms resulted in "the top [one] percent of American families earn[ing] only 16 percent of all income," a rate that alarmed conservatives (442).

North Atlantic Treaty Organization (NATO)

NATO is a military alliance that the US signed with Western Europe after the Second World War in the interest of forming "a united front against the USSR and any further Soviet aggression" (539).

Northwest Ordinance

The Northwest Ordinance was a deal brokered at the Constitutional Convention of 1787 in which the delegates decided that "any new states entering the Union formed north of the Ohio River" would not have slavery, while those south of the river would be slaveholding states (124). The measure was passed on July 13.

Nullification

Nullification was a state's presumed right to nullify, or to invalidate and override, a federal law. The crisis over nullification set the stage for the South's secession from the Union. The most vocal proponent of the legislative tactic was the South Carolina congressman, former secretary of war, and former vice president John C. Calhoun, who sought to "nullify" a tariff that Congress had established. The tariff worried Southerners "who argued that it put the interest of northern manufacturers above southern agriculturalists" (217). Its opponents supported, instead, what they called "free trade." In protest of the tariff, Calhoun wrote a treatise on behalf of his state's legislature in which he developed a theory of constitutional interpretation, arguing that states could declare federal laws null and void. If a state declared a federal law unconstitutional, the Constitution would need to be amended. If the proposed amendment were not to be ratified, the objecting state retained the right to secede from the Union. The states, Calhoun insisted, were sovereign before the Constitution was written, and they were to remain sovereign.

Nullification was an anti-majoritarian policy—that is, if states could secede from the Union for objecting to a law, then the majority could not rule. The nullification crisis that ensued was not really about the tariff, but about states' rights, which also pressed the question of slavery. South Carolina, which by then had the largest number of enslaved people in the nation, was trying to reject the federal government's power to pass laws that were contrary to its interests, particularly its interests in slaveholding. The nullification crisis also hardened the line between sectionalists and nationalists.

Originalism

Originalism is a conservative constitutional argument rooted in the idea that the Constitution should be strictly interpreted according to the Founders' original intentions for government. The legal argument developed in the late 1970s as part of a campaign to expand access to firearms, using the 2nd Amendment as justification. Ironically, those who touted originalism in this context negated the "well-regulated militia" clause that is key to the 2nd Amendment.

Patriot Act

In response to the new war on terror, President George W. Bush signed the Patriot Act on October 26, 2001, which "grant[ed] the federal government new powers to conduct surveillance and collect intelligence to prevent and investigate terrorist acts" (744). Critics of the law, which quickly passed both houses of Congress shortly after the September 11 attacks, "cit[ed] violations of civil liberties, especially as established under the Fourth Amendment, and civil rights, especially the due process provision of the Fourteenth Amendment" (744).

Plessy v. Ferguson

The landmark Supreme Court case *Plessy v. Ferguson* (1896) legitimized Jim Crow laws through the court's determination of "separate but equal." Homer Plessy, "a shoemaker from New Orleans who looked white but who, under Louisiana's race laws was technically black," had been arrested for violating an 1890 Jim Crow law that enforced separate railcars for Black and white residents (358). Plessy had intentionally gotten arrested so that he could challenge the state's law. A lower court, presided over by Judge John Ferguson, had ruled against Plessy, leading the plaintiff to appeal to the Supreme Court.

In a 7-1 decision, the Supreme Court upheld the Louisiana court's ruling. The court decided that Jim Crow laws did not violate the Constitution because "separate accommodations were not necessarily unequal accommodations" (359). Justice John Marshall Harlan, the sole dissenter in the case, disagreed with "the establishment of separate classes of citizens" and insisted that the Constitution was "color-blind" (359). He pointed out both the absurdities of Jim Crow laws and the 1882 Chinese Exclusion Act. While Chinese people could not become American citizens, they were free to ride in passenger coaches with white citizens. Conversely, African Americans, who were citizens, could be arrested and declared criminals if they were to ride in coaches alongside white people. Harlan found it ridiculous that a set of laws could grant more rights to noncitizens than to citizens. Harlan also rightfully predicted that the ruling would prove to be as harmful as the Dred Scott decision. Until 1954, Black people had no recourse to fight segregation. Forms of de facto segregation spread to the North and the West.

Populism

Populism is the notion that "the best government is that most closely directed by a popular majority" (181). American populism developed alongside Andrew Jackson's rise to political power. Lepore notes that, while populism is intended to be about the people, it is truly an argument about the significance of numbers. As the electorate grew, some Americans expressed concern about both the kinds of men who could vote and who could be elected to office.

Second Great Awakening

The Second Great Awakening was a period of evangelical fervor that occurred in the early 19th century. The movement reached its height in the 1820s and 1830s, particularly in factory towns. Its proponents believed that they could eliminate sin from the world, in preparation for the Second Coming of Christ, whom some believed would arrive as early as within three months. They did not expect the Savior's return to Bethlehem or Jerusalem, but to industrial American cities, such as Detroit or Cincinnati. The movement emphasized spiritual equality, which strengthened antislavery protests and paved the way for the early women's suffrage movement. Evangelicals also "recast the nation's origins as avowedly Christian" (200).

Social Gospel Movement

The name of the movement dates back to 1886, when a Congregationalist minister named Henry George referred in his book *Progress and Poverty* to "a social gospel" (365). Academic theologians led the Social Gospel movement. They accepted Darwin's theory of evolution, seeing it as consistent with the purposeful universe that is depicted in the Bible. Conversely, they rejected the social Darwinism promoted by Herbert Spencer, the English natural scientist who introduced the phrase "survival of the fittest." Proponents of the Social Gospel busied themselves with the problems wrought by industrialism, particularly poverty and child labor.

Three-Fifths Compromise

The Constitution's three-fifths clause was an addition to the Constitution devised by James Madison in 1783. Based on a federal census conducted every decade starting in 1790, the arrangement provided slave states with more representation in Congress than free states. Virginia, for example, had three extra seats in the House and, thus, six more electors in the Electoral College. In 1804, after the nation acquired the Louisiana Territory, Connecticut and Massachusetts "called for the abolition of the three-fifths clause" (172). At the Hartford Convention in 1814, delegates from five New England states threatened secession over what they deemed an uneven distribution of power due to the South's unofficial slave representation. The call to eradicate the clause was abandoned after General Andre Jackson's victory at the Battle of New Orleans during the War of 1812. With the passage of the 13th Amendment, the three-fifths compromise became obsolete.

Treaty of Paris

Signed on September 3, 1783, the Treaty of Paris ended the Revolutionary War, resulting in Great Britain's recognition of the United States' independence and sovereignty. In exchange, indebted Americans agreed to pay their British creditors. When the states defaulted on their debts, the British threatened to default on their commitment to surrender their northwestern fronts in Oswego, Niagara, and Detroit to the United States. The treaty also changed the composition of the British Empire and reduced the number of enslaved Africans in the empire by half. The American negotiators of the peace were Benjamin Franklin, John Adams, and John Jay.

Wilmot Proviso

Named after the 32-year-old Pennsylvania congressman David Wilmot, the Wilmot Proviso (1846) was an agreement to add a stipulation to any future treaty that would end the war with Mexico. The stipulation asserted that slavery and involuntary servitude would ever exist in any of the lands acquired from the Mexican-American War.

Women's Christian Temperance Union (WCTU)

The Women's Christian Temperance Union (WCTU) was "a federation of women's clubs formed in Cleveland in 1874" (339). They had developed out of the Woman's Crusade—an anti-saloon campaign formed by women who were concerned about the neglect and domestic violence that often resulted from alcohol abuse. To have some agency against these abuses, members of the WCTU insisted that women needed the right to vote. The WCTU's activism reshaped party politics, leading suffragists, such as WCTU leader Frances Willard, to leave the Republican Party and found the Home Protection Party, which merged with the Prohibition Party in 1882.

Works Progress Administration (WPA)

The Works Progress Administration (WPA) was a work program created under the New Deal in 1935. The WPA also included the Federal Writers Project and the Federal Theatre Project, which also involved the Radio Division. More than 7,000 writers were employed under the Federal Writers Project, including Zora Neale Hurston, Richard Wright, Ralph Ellison, Sterling A. Brown, and John Cheever. As part of the Federal Writers Project, slave narratives were recorded from 1936 to 1938, providing a public record of those who lived during the antebellum period and survived to the 1930s. Excerpts from over 2,000 interviews with formerly enslaved people were collected in *These Are Our Lives*.

Important Quotes

1. "As summer faded to fall, the free people of the United States, finding the Constitution folded into their newspapers and almanacs, were asked to decide whether or not to ratify it, even as they went about baling hay, milling corn, tanning leather, singing hymns, and letting out the seams on last year's winter coats, for mothers and fathers grown fatter, and letting down the hems, for children grown taller."
(Introduction, Page XII)

Lepore illustrates what mundane colonial life must have looked like. She is careful to denote "free people," helping the reader to realize that life would have looked different for white indentured servants and, particularly, for enslaved Africans. She describes people who are industrious, agrarian, and simple—people who may not have understood the seriousness of the task they were being asked to perform by the more learned delegates, but who were entrusted with the responsibility of determining the fate of their new nation.

2. "Its infancy is preserved, like baby teeth kept in a glass jar, in the four parchment sheets of the Constitution, in the pages of almanacs that chart the weather of a long-ago climate, and in hundreds of newspapers, where essays for and against the new system of government appeared alongside the shipping news, auction notices, and advertisements for the return of people who never were their own masters—women and children, slaves and servants—and who had run away, hoping to ordain and establish, for themselves and their posterity, the blessings of liberty."

(Introduction, Page XII)

Lepore describes how the United States' nascence is preserved in documents. She analogizes these documents to a parent's retention of baby teeth to show how these artifacts work to show the transition from one stage to another—British colonies to independent nation. She contrasts the colonialists' pursuit of independent government with their simultaneous embrace of slavery.

3. "Americans are descended from conquerors and from the conquered, from the people held as slaves and from the people who held them, from the Union and from the Confederacy, from Protestants and from Jews, from Muslims and from Catholics, and from immigrants and from people who have fought to end immigration."
(Introduction, Page XV)

Lepore illustrates the motley and contrasting elements that make up the American populace. This passage also demonstrates how wondrous it is that the United States has survived as a democracy, despite the coexistence of historically antagonistic groups within its borders.

4. "In the brutal, bloody century between Columbus's voyage and John White's, an idea was born, out of fantasy, out of violence, the idea that there exists in the world a people who live in an actual Garden of Eden, a state of nature, before the giving of laws, before the forming of government. This imagined history of America became an English book of genesis, their new truth."
(Part 1, Chapter 1, Page 30)

Lepore describes the origin of the idea of a "new world" in what would become the United States. The idea, as Lepore is careful to illustrate, was born both out of the stories European colonists told themselves and the nation that they forcefully constructed to suit their needs. They invented the idea of a land that was pristine, innocent, and unformed, despite the prevalence of civilizations among the tribes who had long occupied North America.

5. "Twenty Englishmen were elected to the House of Burgesses. Twenty Africans were condemned to the house of bondage. Another chapter opened in the American book of genesis: liberty and slavery became the American Abel and Cain."
(Part 1, Chapter 1, Page 38)

Lepore illustrates the division at the root of the nation's founding. At Jamestown, where the first enslaved Africans landed, the United States initiated both the institution of slavery and its earliest notions of who would be enslaved and who would be free, who would receive equal protections under the law and who would not. Both Black and white people would be integral to the nation's founding, but the racist ideology born out of slavery would reduce Black Americans to a permanent second class.

6. "The only way to justify this contradiction, the only way to explain how one kind of people are born free while another kind of people are not, would be to sow a new seed, an ideology of race. It would take a long time to grow, and longer to wither."
(Part 1, Chapter 2, Page 54)

Lepore describes how those who institutionalized slavery created the demarcation between "black and white" to define who would be enslaved and who would be free. Arguably, this is how the

notion of race was born or, at least, codified within economic
terms. The ideology, as Lepore notes, would not develop into a
"science" for another two centuries.

7. "The Constitution drafted in Philadelphia acted as a check on
the Revolution, a halt to its radicalism; if the Revolution had tilted
the balance between government and liberty toward liberty, the
Constitution shifted toward government."
(Part 1, Chapter 4, Page 121)

Lepore explains how the Constitution provided the nascent
nation with structure, something that other countries in a state of
revolution in the late 18th century—France and Haiti, for
example—lacked, which led to periods of tumult and despotism.

8. "With the ratification of the Bill of Rights, new disputes
emerged. Much of American political history is a disagreement
between those who favor a strong federal government and those
who favor the states."
(Part 1, Chapter 4, Page 138)

Disputes over the ratification of the Constitution resulted from the
absence of a bill of rights. This dispute, Lepore tells us, set the
precedent for today's two-party system, as the debate created
Federalists, those who sought to ratify the Constitution, and Anti-
Federalists, which later transformed into the Democratic-
Republican Party. With the inclusion of the Bill of Rights—that is,
10 of the 12 amendments drafted by James Madison—the
dispute did not end, but merely transformed into one between
those who favored a strong central government and those who
favored states' rights. This argument lingers to date.

9. "The newspaper would hold the Republic together; the telegraph would hold the Republic together; the radio would hold the Republic together; the Internet would hold the Republic together. Each time, this assertion would be both right and terribly wrong."
(Part 1, Chapter 4, Page 145)

Using repetition, Lepore describes the nation's misguided tradition of believing that technology would serve to maintain the Union. Though each form of technology expanded the populace's access to information, none succeeded in forming any commonality around what people knew. All forms would become tools of those who would seek to manipulate public opinion for selfish gains.

10. "The first factories in the Western world weren't in buildings housing machines powered by steam: they were out of doors, in the sugarcane fields of the West Indies, in the rice fields of the Carolinas, and in the tobacco fields of Virginia."
(Part 2, Chapter 5, Page 169)

Lepore uses the metaphor of industrial machinery to illustrate how human beings were enslaved and mechanized to plant and harvest lucrative cash crops. The profits from those crops funded the Industrial Revolution, which also relied on enslaved Black people to harvest the cotton that supplied textile mills.

11. "A picture of progress as the stages from 'barbarism' to 'civilization'—stages that could be traced on a map of the American continent—competed with a picture of progress as an unending chain of machines."
(Part 2, Chapter 6, Page 192)

Lepore illustrates for the reader how the notion of American progress, which would become an especially significant theme during the Progressive Era, was often hierarchical. Not only was progress contextualized by industrial innovation, but also by the belief that some groups, particularly people of African descent, were best suited to a subordinate position in the social order due to being regarded as less civilized and intelligent than those of European descent.

12. "Slavery wasn't an aberration in an industrializing economy; slavery was its engine."
(Part 2, Chapter 6, Page 202)

Lepore once again connects slave labor to the Industrial Revolution, underscoring how much the textile mills of New England and Great Britain depended on cotton production in the American South. She compares the power of machines— measured in horsepower—to the slaves' "hand power," reiterating an earlier point about the ways in which African Americans were commodified and mechanized.

13. "It would become politically expedient, after the war, for ex-Confederates to insist that the Confederacy was founded on states' rights. But the Confederacy was founded on white supremacy."
(Part 2, Chapter 8, Page 290)

Using a speech from Alexander Stephens, vice president of the Confederate States of America, Lepore undermines the myth that the South's primary interest in going to war was states' rights. This myth has been perpetuated to veil the South's racist history and its economic dependence on slavery. The pursuit of states' rights as the justification for war is an untruth that has been reiterated in Southern classrooms and validated in history textbooks.

14. "The seventeenth-century battle for freedom of expression had been fought by writers like John Milton, opposing the suppression of religious dissent; the eighteenth-century struggle for the freedom of the press had been fought by printers like Benjamin Franklin and John Peter Zenger, opposing the suppression of criticism of the government; and the nineteenth century's fight for free speech had been waged by abolitionists opposing southern slave owners, who had been unwilling to subject slavery to debate."
(Part 2, Chapter 8, Page 291)

Lepore ties the fight for free speech to the effort to limit institutional power. People in every modern century, as she notes, have contended with religious, political, and economic powers who resisted dissent by trying to limit or eradicate free speech. This tradition of legitimized suppression, which the South tried to reinstitute, explained why the founders included the right of free speech in the First Amendment. This detail also reiterates Lepore's point about the Confederacy being antagonistic to the democratic values that the Union tried to uphold.

15. "The American Odyssey had barely begun. From cabins and fields they left. Freed men and women didn't always head north. They often went south or west, traveling hundreds of miles by foot, on horseback, by stage, and by train, searching. They were husbands in search of wives, wives in search of husbands, mothers and fathers looking for their children, children for their parents, chasing word and rumors about where their loved ones had been sold, sale after sale, across the country. Some of their

wanderings lasted for years. They sought their own union, a union of their beloved."
(Part 2, Chapter 8, Page 299)

Lepore recounts the exodus of enslaved Black Americans from Southern plantations after the Emancipation Proclamation, likening it to Homer's Odyssey, *as a journey of both necessity and self-discovery. She also likens the journey to the Civil War's purpose of reuniting the Union. The condition of the enslaved people was the cause of secession, and the centuries of violence they endured were visited upon many of those who either sought to keep them in bondage or who expressed indifference to their condition. While the Civil War was a means of healing politically through violent methods, the journey of the newly freed to find their lost ones, however in vain, was a journey of love and an expression of hope for future of peace.*

16. "Populism entered American politics at the end of the nineteenth century, and it never left. It pitted 'the people,' meaning everyone but the rich, against corporations, which fought back in the courts by defining themselves as 'persons'; and it pitted 'the people,' meaning white people, against nonwhite people who were fighting for citizenship and whose ability to fight back in the courts was far more limited, since those fights require well-paid lawyers."
(Part 3, Chapter 9, Page 347)

Lepore illustrates how populism—a movement whose ideology was meant to promote inclusion—ironically led to more divisive politics. The wealthy, threatened by the power of numbers, found political loopholes to protect their power. More dismayingly, white people used populism to frame themselves as the true American

people, which led to a century of support for discriminatory
policies against nonwhite people.

17. "If the railroad served as the symbol of progress in the
nineteenth century, the automobile served as its symbol in the
twentieth, a consumer commodity that celebrated individualism
and choice."
(Part 3, Chapter 10, Page 383)

Lepore depicts the shift in transportation, which helped
characterize the 20th century as an era of individualist
consumerism. The railroad was essential to this progress, as it
contributed to the nation's westward expansion which led,
indirectly, to the development of the interstate highway system.

18. "The immigration restriction regime begun in 1924 hardened
racial lines, institutionalized new forms of race-based
discrimination, codified the fiction of a 'white race,' and
introduced a new legal category into American life: the 'illegal
alien.'"
(Part 3, Chapter 10, Page 408)

Lepore describes the long-term consequences of the Asian
Exclusion Act and the National Origins Act, both of which were
passed as parts of the Immigration Act of 1924. The white race,
which would bring together what were regarded as "assimilable"
Europeans and white Americans, would be positioned against
those who were deemed nonwhite, or "colored." Additionally the
term "illegal alien," which still exists in our political lexicon, would
work to dehumanize and distance noncitizens, particularly those
of color, from the main populace.

19. "With enough money, and with the tools of mass communication, deployed efficiently, the propagandist can turn a political majority into a truth."
(Part 3, Chapter 10, Page 419)

Lepore follows Walter Lippmann's ominous train of thought to describe how both mechanization and the field of public relations that Lippmann had helped invent could lead to the rise of demagoguery. If a political majority could coalesce around an idea, no matter how false or immoral, it could be elevated as truth. The framers of the Constitution, who had tried to protect the majority from factions, had not anticipated the possibility of the majority being antithetical to reason.

20. "The war Europe would have, the war the world would have, would be the first war waged in the age of radio, a war of the air. The fighting would unleash forces of savagery and barbarism. And the broadcasting of the war would suggest how, terrifyingly, 'fake news' had become a weapon of tyrants."
(Part 3, Chapter 11, Page 468)

Lepore uses Orson Welles's notorious radio broadcast of H. G. Wells's War of the Worlds *as a metaphor for the rising atmosphere of panic over a looming evil, fostered by Nazi Germany's increasing dominance of Europe. The Nazis, led by Minister of Propaganda Joseph Goebbels, had been masters of public relations through radio, using the technology to legitimize their fascist and anti-minority politics—a fate that Walter Lippmann had predicted and feared.*

21. "The Second World War would bring the United States out of depression, end American isolationism, and forge a renewed spirit of civic nationalism. It would also call attention to the

nation's unfinished reckoning with race, reshape liberalism, and form the foundation for a conservative movement animated by opposition to state power."
(Part 3, Chapter 12, Page 473)

Lepore outlines the ways in which the United States' entry into World War II transformed the nation domestically and internationally. The war also led to President Roosevelt's expanded executive powers, which worried conservatives who disliked both his New Deal policies and his dominance over other branches of government.

22. "The parties began to drift apart, like continents, loosed. The Republican Party, influenced by conservative suburban housewives, began to move to the right. The Democratic Party, stirred by the moral and political urgency of the struggle for civil rights, began moving to the left. The pace of that drift would be determined by civil rights, the Cold War, television, and the speed of computation."
(Part 4, Chapter 13, Page 573)

Lepore describes how Democrats and Republicans became more markedly distinct at the dawn of the 1950s. While both foreign and domestic policies widened the chasm between the parties, technology, particularly the propagandistic power of television, also influenced their respective party platforms.

23. "Equality was never going to be a matter of a single case, or even of a long march, but, instead, of an abiding political hope."
(Part 4, Chapter 13, Page 587)

Lepore refers to the lingering hope of former NAACP attorney and Supreme Court Justice Thurgood Marshall that Brown v.

Board of Education, *or some other Supreme Court case, would finally end segregation and racial inequality in the US. Lepore points out that neither a Supreme Court decision, nor the courageous efforts of the civil rights movement were enough to eradicate the nation's deeply entrenched racism. True justice and political equality remain the nation's hope. The US has faced significant advances in this direction as well as setbacks.*

24. "And what of the American past? Was the schoolbook version of American history a lie? The civil rights movement and the war in Vietnam called attention to aspects of American history that had been left out of American history textbooks from the very start."
(Part 4, Chapter 14, Page 634)

Lepore describes the ways in which the Vietnam War bred cynicism among American youth and how the civil rights movement and the rights movements of other marginalized groups led to a reassessment of historiography. She uses rhetorical questions to express the questions that these groups were asking themselves and their elders at the time. The mid-20th century resulted in a reckoning with both the nation's past and the truths that it buried beneath mythologies.

25. "Both reproductive rights and gun rights arguments rest on weak constitutional foundations; their very shakiness is what makes them so useful for partisan purposes: gains seem always in danger of being lost."
(Part 4, Chapter 15, Page 676)

Lepore reflects on how the Left's focus on reproductive rights, particularly access to abortion, and the Right's focus on gun rights—two issues that concern public health and personal liberties—have helped with voter turnout, while both are rooted in relatively poor constitutional arguments. Elsewhere in the book, Lepore cites legal scholars, particularly Ruth Bader Ginsburg, who have noted that Roe v. Wade *should have been rooted in a 14th Amendment argument based on equal protection instead of right to privacy, while the 2nd Amendment became the tool of conservative originalists.*

Essay Topics

1. Do you think that Lepore succeeds in presenting a cohesive chronicle of American history within a single volume? Why or why not? Compare Lepore's experiment to that of other historians, particularly those who have written histories as civics books. How does Lepore's volume expand upon those other works? What does she overlook?

2. Since the emergence of Nikole Hannah-Jones's 1619 Project, there has been recurring debate on the presentation of American history, with conservatives arguing that history ought to be regarded as a collection of fixed artifacts, while liberals argue that primary historical sources are materials through which we should continually re-examine our understanding of historical events. Which position do you think Lepore takes? Support your answer with examples from the text.

3. Consider the intellectual debate that simmered between John Adams and Thomas Jefferson for much of their lives. Can you think of examples of other political figures, particularly in the present day, who have similar ideological debates in public?

4. What is your assessment of Jacksonian Democracy? Was this expansion of the electorate a good thing for the nation's development? Why or why not? What evidence of the populist legacy do you recognize in contemporary politics?

5. The adjective "progressive" has re-entered the political lexicon, embraced by those on the far left who seek to distance themselves from the mainstream Democratic Party, as well as

from the taint that conservatives have imposed on the term "liberal." How do contemporary progressives (e.g., Bernie Sanders, Elizabeth Warren, Alexandra Ocasio-Cortez) compare to their forebears from the Progressive Era? How have their political positions evolved? What comparable mistakes have they made?

6. Lepore traces the schism in women's politics—that is, the division between those who sought social equality (e.g., the Women's League for Equal Opportunity, the Equal Rights Association) and protectors of traditional gender roles (e.g., the League of Women Voters). This schism became particularly apparent, as Lepore notes, when the Equal Rights Amendment neared ratification in the late 1970s. During this decade, social equalizers (e.g., Bella Abzug) and protectionists (e.g., Phyllis Schlafly) once again argued over women's proper roles. Does this schism in American gender politics still exist? If so, which figures in politics and media illustrate its prevalence?

7. How did Franklin Delano Roosevelt's approach to civil rights reform differ from Lyndon Baines Johnson's? What advances and concessions did both presidents make when passing their respective reforms? How did their approaches to reform set the nation's tone for conversations about social and political equality, both during their terms and today?

8. Two-time presidential candidate and former US ambassador to the United Nations Adlai Stevenson asserted that television was an instrument of artifice, using the television in his own home to demonstrate to voters how the technology could be used to manipulate them. How did Stevenson's opinions about television coincide with Walter Lippmann's ideas about public opinion and publicity? Was television a uniquely dangerous

instrument, or have previous technologies (e.g., newspaper printing, radio) offered similar opportunities to manipulate public opinion? Explain.

9. When he was a clerk at the Supreme Court, future Supreme Court Chief Justice William Rehnquist believed that Plessy v. Ferguson (1896) had been legally correct, despite being a humanitarian failure. Do you agree with Rehnquist? Why or why not? Is it possible, considering the origins and goals of the Constitution (i.e., a document that would support and protect citizens' natural rights), for it to support Supreme Court decisions that are inhumane? Why or why not?

10. Consider Richard Nixon's presidential campaign tactics in both 1968 and 1972. How has the legacy that he built with the Silent Majority been repeated in subsequent Republican presidential campaigns? How have the grievances and concerns of the Silent Majority been channeled into other aspects of American life (e.g., media outlets)?

Further Reading & Resources

Further Reading: Literature

Black Thunder: Gabriel's Revolt: Virginia, 1800 by Arna Bontemps (1936)

Babbitt by Sinclair Lewis (1922)

- *Babbitt* on SuperSummary

A Tree Grows in Brooklyn by Betty Smith (1943)

- *A Tree Grows in Brooklyn* on SuperSummary

Complete Poetry and Prose by Walt Whitman, ed. Justin Kaplan (1982)

Further Reading: Beyond Literature (Nonfiction)

Frederick Douglass: Prophet of Freedom by David W. Blight (2018)

- *Frederick Douglass: Prophet of Freedom* on SuperSummary

Landslide: LBJ and Ronald Reagan at the Dawn of a New America by Jonathan Darman (2015)

At the Hands of Persons Unknown: The Lynching of Black America by Philip Dray (2002)

The Souls of Black Folk by W. E. B. Du Bois (1903)

- *The Souls of Black Folk* on SuperSummary

The Worst Hard Time: The Untold Story of Those Who Survived the Great American Dust Bowl by Timothy Egan (2006)

Reconstruction, America's Unfinished Revolution, 1863-1877 by Eric Foner (1988)

- *Reconstruction, America's Unfinished Revolution, 1863-1877* on SuperSummary

The Enlightenment (Volume II): The Science of Freedom by Peter Gay (1969)

From Rebellion to Revolution: Afro-American Slave Revolts in the Making of the Modern World by Eugene Genovese (1979)

Roll, Jordan, Roll: The World the Slaves Made by Eugene Genovese (1976)

- *Roll, Jordan, Roll: The World the Slaves Made* on SuperSummary

The Hemingses of Monticello: An American Family by Annette Gordon-Reed (2008)

- *The Hemingses of Monticello: An American Family* on SuperSummary

Incidents in the Life of a Slave Girl by Harriet Jacobs (1861)

- *Incidents in the Life of a Slave Girl* on SuperSummary

The Black Jacobins: Toussaint L'Ouverture and the San Domingo Revolution by C. L. R. James (1963)

- *The Black Jacobins: Toussaint L'Ouverture and the San Domingo Revolution* on SuperSummary

Notes on the State of Virginia by Thomas Jefferson (1781, 1832)

The 1619 Project: A New Origin Story by Nikole Hannah-Jones (2021)

- *The 1619 Project: A New Origin Story* on SuperSummary

Stokely: A Life by Peniel E. Joseph (2014)

Two Treatises of Government by John Locke (1689)

The Communist Manifesto by Karl Marx and Frederick Engels (1906)

- *The Communist Manifesto* on SuperSummary

They Were Her Property: White Women as Slave Owners in the American South by Stephanie E. Jones-Rogers (2019)

- *They Were Her Property: White Women as Slave Owners in the American South* on SuperSummary

Malcolm X: A Life of Reinvention by Manning Marable (2011)

- *Malcolm X: A Life of Reinvention* on SuperSummary

The Negro's Civil War: How American Blacks Felt and Acted During the War for the Union by James M. McPherson (1993)

American Lion: Andrew Jackson in the White House by Jon Meacham (2008)

- *American Lion: Andrew Jackson in the White House* on SuperSummary

The Enlightenment and Why It Still Matters by Anthony Pagden (2013)

The Bridge: The Life and Rise of Barack Obama by David Remnick (2010)

The Other Slavery: The Uncovered Story of Indian Enslavement in America by Andrés Reséndez (2016)

- *The Other Slavery* on SuperSummary

A Different Mirror: A History of Multicultural America by Ronald Takaki (1993)

- *A Different Mirror: A History of Multicultural America* on SuperSummary

American Colonies by Alan Taylor (2001)

- *American Colonies* on SuperSummary

"**On the Duty of Civil Disobedience**" by Henry David Thoreau (1849)

- "Civil Disobedience" on SuperSummary

The Heartbeat of Wounded Knee, Native America from 1890 to the Present by David Treuer (2019)

- *The Heartbeat of Wounded Knee, Native America from 1890 to the Present* on SuperSummary

Up from Slavery: An Autobiography by Booker T. Washington (1907)

- *Up From Slavery: An Autobiography* on SuperSummary

A. Lincoln by Ronald C. White Jr. (2009)

The Warmth of Other Suns: The Epic Story of America's Great Migration by Isabel Wilkerson (2010)

- *The Warmth of Other Suns: The Epic Story of America's Great Migration* on SuperSummary

Other Relevant Media Resources

John Adams (miniseries), HBO (2008)

Adapted from historian David McCullough's Pulitzer Prize–winning book of the same name, published in 2001, the seven-episode miniseries starring Paul Giamatti starts during the Boston Massacre and ends during John Adams's retirement from public life.

Exterminate All the Brutes (documentary miniseries), HBO (2021)

The four-part miniseries directed by Raoul Peck examines the Western history of colonization, starting during the Age of Exploration, and the history of genocide, fostered by the development of scientific racism and culminating in the Holocaust and "ethnic-cleansing" programs of the 1990s.

Eyes on the Prize (documentary miniseries), PBS (1987)

The seminal 14-part documentary series documents the civil rights movement, including the 1955 Montgomery Bus Boycott, the desegregation of Little Rock High School, Freedom Summer, the passage of the Civil Rights Act and Voting Rights Act, and the rise of militant politics, including the rise of the Nation of Islam, the radicalization of the Student Nonviolent Coordinating Committee (SNCC), and the growth of the Black Panther Party.

Made in the USA
Middletown, DE
05 July 2022

68541520R00176